More Praise for *Corporations Are Not People*

"You must read this book. Clements tells how the logic of 'corporate personhood' has allowed corporations to trump the rights of people. In vivid stories he recounts the real consequences of that tortured logic."
—Fran Korten, Publisher, YES! Magazine

"Clements is our 21st-century Paul Revere, spreading the word that we must rise against the economic royalists. The billionaires are on the march, but Clements is faster and smarter, and his is the noble cause of democracy unbound."
—John Nichols, coauthor of Dollarocracy; Correspondent, The Nation; and cofounder, Free Press

"As a conservative, I support property rights and freer markets but have to question the notion that corporations deserve the same constitutional protections as 'we the people.'"
—Michael D. Ostrolenk, cofounder and National Director, Liberty Coalition

"Reclaiming our democracy from corporate domination is the great struggle of our time. The good news, as *Corporations Are Not People* shows, is that a growing movement is mobilizing to take back our democracy."
—Robert Weissman, President, Public Citizen

"Ben Cohen is a person. Jerry Greenfield is a person. Ben & Jerry's Ice Cream, Inc.? Not a person. Clements tells how corporations took over our Constitution, our democracy, and our economy that used to work for everyone. Best of all, he shows how we can get them back."
—Ben Cohen and Jerry Greenfield, founders, Ben & Jerry's Homemade Ice Cream, and cofounders, Business for Democracy

"Question for the Supreme Court: If a corporation is a person, where's its navel? *Corporations Are Not People* is more than a book—it's a democracy manual. Let's put it to work."
—Jim Hightower, bestselling author; national radio commentator; and Editor, Hightower Lowdown

"If you care about our democracy and want to know what 'we the people' can do to reclaim it, read this book. You will be inspired to stand up to demand our country back."
—John Bonifaz, cofounder ;

D0400777

"A clarion call to action in defense of democracy...Arguably the most important book on corporations ever written. Essential reading for every citizen."
—**David Korten, author of *When Corporations Rule the World***

"Clements makes a powerful case against the doctrine that corporations enjoy the same free speech protections as individual Americans and lays out in chilling detail the dangerous implications for our democracy."
—**Caroline Fredrickson, President, American Constitution Society**

"A must-read for every real person who is fed up with the reign of corporate supercitizens in American politics. Clements insightfully explains why and how 'we the people' must kill the runaway Frankenstein monster created by the Supreme Court."
—**James Nelson, Montana Supreme Court Justice (Retired)**

"Excessive corporate influence is one of the greatest threats to our democracy. This book will help citizens make real progress in freeing our political system from manipulation."
—**Congresswoman Donna F. Edwards**

"Clements's definitive work on the capture of America's political process by corporate power is clearly written and persuasive."
—**Robert A. G. Monks, author of *Citizens DisUnited*; business leader and shareholder activist; and former Chair, Maine Republican Committee**

"*Corporations Are Not People* will inform you, outrage you, and inspire you to return corporations to their proper position as tools of public policy rather than masters of it."
—**Barry Eisler, author of *The Last Assassin***

"There is no better primer to describe how we arrived where we are today and our opportunity to change the direction of our nation."
—**Peg Lautenschlager, former Attorney General of Wisconsin**

"This book gives you valuable tools."
—**David Cobb, cofounder, Move to Amend**

"A brilliant contribution to the literature on the crime of corporate personhood—and what we can do about it."
—**Thom Hartmann, bestselling author of *Unequal Protection* and host of the *Thom Hartmann Program***

Second Edition

CORPORATIONS
ARE NOT
PEOPLE

RECLAIMING DEMOCRACY
FROM BIG MONEY AND GLOBAL
CORPORATIONS

JEFFREY D. CLEMENTS

BK

Berrett–Koehler Publishers, Inc.
San Francisco
a BK Currents book

Berrett-Koehler Publishers, Inc.
235 Montgomery Street, Suite 650
San Francisco, CA 94104-2916
Tel: (415) 288-0260   Fax: (415) 362-2512   www.bkconnection.com

Ordering Information

Quantity sales. Special discounts are available on quantity purchases by corporations, associations, and others. For details, contact the "Special Sales Department" at the Berrett-Koehler address above.

Individual sales. Berrett-Koehler publications are available through most bookstores. They can also be ordered directly from Berrett-Koehler: Tel: (800) 929-2929; Fax: (802) 864-7626; www.bkconnection.com

Orders for college textbook/course adoption use. Please contact Berrett-Koehler: Tel: (800) 929-2929; Fax: (802) 864-7626.

Orders by U.S. trade bookstores and wholesalers. Please contact Ingram Publisher Services, Tel: (800) 509-4887; Fax: (800) 838-1149; E-mail: customer.service@ingram publisherservices.com; or visit www.ingrampublisherservices.com/Ordering for details about electronic ordering.

Berrett-Koehler and the BK logo are registered trademarks of Berrett-Koehler Publishers, Inc.

Printed in the United States of America

Berrett-Koehler books are printed on long-lasting acid-free paper. When it is available, we choose paper that has been manufactured by environmentally responsible processes. These may include using trees grown in sustainable forests, incorporating recycled paper, minimizing chlorine in bleaching, or recycling the energy produced at the paper mill.

Library of Congress Cataloging-in-Publication Data

Clements, Jeffrey D.
    Corporations are not people : reclaiming democracy from big money and
        global corporations / Jeff Clements. -- Second edition.
            pages cm
    Includes bibliographical references and index.
    ISBN 978-1-62656-210-3 (pbk. : alk. paper)
    1. Business and politics--United States. 2. Corporations--Political
    aspects--United States. 3. Corporations--Political activity--United
    States. I. Title.
    JK467.C55 2014
    322'.30973--dc23
                                                                        2014014390

Second Edition

19 18 17 16 15 14   10 9 8 7 6 5 4 3 2 1

Interior design and project management: Dovetail Publishing Services
Cover design: Mark van Bronkhorst

For Bob Clements

And for all of the people working to renew American democracy, for whom this book is dedicated, and to the cause of which 100 percent of author royalties are committed.

CONTENTS

Preface
to this Second Edition

Three years ago, with the original edition of *Corporations Are Not People*, I thought that the title might require some explanation. I am not sure that is still true.

When politicians from Massachusetts Democrat Elizabeth Warren to Arizona Republican John McCain join in unison to declare, "Corporations are not people!" and when a major presidential candidate has been ridiculed and rebutted for his pronouncement that "corporations are people, my friend," it may be that the phrase now has some resonance.

In these past three years, the country has shared in the catastrophe that is *Citizens United v. Federal Election Commission*. Since the Supreme Court struck down our election spending laws to vindicate, in the Court's words, the "disadvantaged class of persons" that are corporations, we have had a $10 billion election brought to us, often secretly, by a few corporations, unions, and billionaires. We have become all too familiar with Super PACs, dark money, and dysfunctional government.

As we, the people are losing our role in elections and representative government, we also are losing our voice and power in the courts: global corporations and activist judges have deployed the reasoning of *Citizens United* to create a new "corporate veto" in the courts over financial, health care, environmental, and energy laws, among others. Some corporations have even had epiphanies, and now claim First Amendment religious rights to evade the law.

This book explains how this happened in America and how we can fix it. On both scores, this edition has a great deal of new material. The danger of "corporate rights" and big money domination of our elections and government has accelerated rapidly in the past three years. You will find a lot of new information on that. At the same time, the growing response of so many Americans over the past three years is nothing short of historic. That story, and how you can help, is here, too.

Largely under the radar of a mainstream media that seems able to see only binary smack-down politics, Americans are coming together to accelerate several related engines of reform:

> *A vibrant national movement for a Twenty-Eighth Amendment to the Constitution to overturn Citizens United has moved "from pipedream to mainstream." Six hundred cities and towns, and sixteen states, have enacted amendment resolutions by overwhelming, cross-partisan majorities. More than 160 members of Congress are now cosponsoring proposals for the Twenty-Eighth Amendment, and the president of the United States and former Supreme Court Justice John Paul Stevens have expressed support;*
>
> *A revolt is breaking out among judges, law professors, lawyers, state Attorneys General, and others who are fighting back in the courts, determined to defend the Constitution's purpose of enhancing rather than defeating the possibility of republican democracy;*
>
> *From North Carolina to New York, Maine to California, and even in Washington, D.C., a vigorous demand to "get money out and voters in" is expanding, with small donor–public funding initiatives, voting rights for everyone, transparency and*

accountability reforms, and more reforms to make a democracy that works;

Reform of our corporate laws and new thinking about our economy have made more progress in the past three years than in many previous decades—one example alone being the more than twenty states that have enacted benefit corporation laws and the more than nine hundred new benefit corporations that eschew and will replace the "shareholders and CEOs above all" ideology that no longer works.

Corporations Are Not People is about why these engines of reform are so necessary and how you can help accelerate them to the scale that our country and the world urgently need.

I have been inspired by so many Americans who working to save our country. This edition is dedicated to all of them, and all author royalties will be donated to organizations helping them in their work.

Thanks to all of them, and to all of you who join this work, *Citizens United* will not stand, our Constitution will serve human beings and protect an effective democracy, and we will restore the promise of a republic governed by "We, the People."

Jeff Clements
Concord, Massachusetts
July 4, 2014

Preface
to the First Edition

Of course corporations are not people. Do we really need a book about that obvious truth? Unfortunately, we do.

After the United States Supreme Court's decision in *Citizens United v. Federal Election Commission* in 2010, the identity of corporations and their place in our government of the people is not so obvious anymore, at least not to the Supreme Court and to the armies of corporate lawyers pushing for more corporate constitutional rights. And the fact that corporations are not people does not seem to be obvious to too many cowed and trembling lawmakers at all levels of government. There are exceptions, to be sure, but in the face of wildly unbalanced corporate money and influence, too few of our elected officials stand with conviction and firmness to state the obvious about corporations in defense of the public interest.

Citizens United is the biggest and most radical (to use a word from the dissent of Justice Stevens) decision in a regular series of recent Supreme Court decisions in favor of corporations. In *Citizens United*, the Supreme Court overturned decades of precedent, reversed a century of legislative effort to keep corporate money from corrupting democracy, and upended the American ideal that we are a government of people rather than a government of corporate wealth. The decision, in many ways, symbolizes how far off track we have fallen from our ideal of the American Republic, governed by the people.

In the pages that follow, I hope to show what *Citizens United* is all about, where it came from, and what I think this triumph of corporate power means for you and for all Americans. Much of the book is about what I see as the devastating effect of unbalanced corporate power, sustained and strengthened by a deliberate, organized, and extremely well funded campaign to transform—I would say, pervert—our Bill of Rights into a charter for corporations as much and even more than for people.

I also hope to show, however, why we do not have to leave it at that depressing juncture. As I describe in Chapter Seven, thanks to the mechanism of constitutional amendment that has come through before when our democracy is on the line, we can fight back to restore government of the people and to save our country. Thousands of people have started that work already, working for the People's Rights Amendment as the Twenty-Eighth Amendment to the Constitution. I hope that you will join us; the Resources section that follows Chapter Eight offers some ways you can do that.

Many people across the country have taken up the effort to preserve our nation and world against unbalanced corporate power and have shared their ideas, time, spirit, and hard work with me. I hope that all of them will know how much they have influenced this book and how grateful I am, even if I could not list everyone here.

Bill Moyers is at the top of the list of a few who deserve special mention. Bill has been a hero and a teacher for me and for so many Americans. He tells the truth. Calmly and clearly, to be sure, but make no mistake, he tells the truth, out loud for all to hear. He never gives up on the journey of America and of humanity, and his curiosity, determination, and grace make that journey live for all of us. I cannot say how grateful and honored I am to have him write the Foreword to this book.

I am blessed to be part of the Clements family. Thank you to Marilyn Clements and this wonderful extended clan of opinionated, smart, loving, patriotic people, who work hard for the good, stand for principle, and believe in writing and in books. They put in hours helping me to make this one better.

I am deeply appreciative of so many who early on understood the danger of *Citizens United* and corporate power, who have worked so hard, and who are bringing such hope and purpose to the cause of liberty and democracy. They have picked up the constitutional amendment banner used so well by our forefathers and foremothers. These modern-day heroes do not accept that our generation is less determined or less true to the American cause of freedom and democracy than those who came before. They reject defeatism. They are standing for people's rights and against corporate rights, and they have inspired much of this book.

One of these heroes is John Bonifaz, a determined visionary and leader. On top of launching Free Speech for People, a nationwide campaign to overturn *Citizens United*, he took the time to read drafts and helped make this book better than it would have been. I thank John and all of the friends and supporters who are helping move Free Speech for People and the People's Rights Amendment forward.

Many others generously shared their time, ideas, comments, and criticisms. My colleague Gwen Stowe, associate at Free Speech for People and manager at Clements Law Office, LLC, made far more contributions to all aspects of this project than I can list. Pam Kogut, my old friend and colleague, first at the Massachusetts attorney general's office and now at Clements Law Office, LLC, provided smart edits and wise suggestions. I am lucky to work with Pam and Gwen.

I also am grateful for the terrific work of Neal Maillet and the Berrett-Kohler team and for many people who provided comments, suggestions, and correction of errors, including David Korten,

Daniel Greenwood, Rob Ellman, Shauna Shames, Kristen Mousalli, Ariel Jolicoeur, Ted Nace, Steve Cobble, and David Swanson. I know that the final product is not everything they might have thought possible, but I also know that it is better thanks to them. Thanks, too, to Thom Hartmann.

Finally, as always, my loving gratitude to Nancy, Will, Sophie, and Ben.

Jeff Clements
Concord, Massachusetts
October 2011

Foreword

Fighting Back

Bill Moyers

Rarely have so few imposed such damage on so many. When five conservative members of the Supreme Court handed for-profit corporations the right to secretly flood political campaigns with tidal waves of cash on the eve of an election, they moved America closer to outright plutocracy, where political power derived from wealth is devoted to the protection of wealth. It is now official: just as they have adorned our athletic stadiums and multiple places of public assembly with their logos, corporations can officially put their brand on the government of the United States as well as the executive, legislative, and judicial branches of the fifty states.

The decision in *Citizens United v. Federal Election Commission* giving "artificial entities" the same rights of "free speech" as living, breathing human beings will likely prove as infamous as the Dred Scott ruling of 1857 that opened the unsettled territories of the United States to slavery whether future inhabitants wanted it or not. It took a civil war and another hundred years of enforced segregation and deprivation before the effects of that ruling were finally exorcised from our laws. God spare us civil strife over the pernicious consequences of *Citizens United*, but unless citizens stand their ground, America will divide even more swiftly into winners and losers with little pity for the latter. *Citizens United* is but the latest battle in the class war waged for thirty years from the top down by the corporate and political right. Instead of creating a fair and level playing field for all, government would become the agent of the powerful and privileged. Public institutions, laws, and regulations, as well as the ideas, norms, and beliefs that aimed to protect the common good and helped create America's iconic middle class, would become increasingly vulnerable. The Nobel Laureate economist Robert Solow succinctly summed up the results: "The redistribution of wealth in favor of the wealthy and of power in favor of the powerful." In the wake of *Citizens United*, popular resistance is all that can prevent the richest economic interests in the country from buying the democratic process lock, stock, and barrel.

America has a long record of conflict with corporations. Wealth acquired under capitalism is in and of itself no enemy to democracy, but wealth armed with political power—power to choke off opportunities for others to rise, power to subvert public purposes and deny public needs—is a proven danger to the "general welfare" proclaimed in the Preamble to the Constitution as one of the justifications for America's existence.

In its founding era, Alexander Hamilton created a financial system for our infant republic that mixed subsidies, tariffs, and a central bank to establish a viable economy and sound public credit. James Madison and Thomas Jefferson warned Americans to beware of the political ambitions of that system's managerial class. Madison feared that the "spirit of speculation" would lead to "a government operating by corrupt influence, substituting the motive of private interest in place of public duty." Jefferson hoped that "we shall crush in its birth the aristocracy of our monied corporations which dare already to challenge our government to a trial of strength and [to] bid defiance to the laws of our country." Radical ideas? Class warfare? The voters didn't think so. In 1800, they made Jefferson the third president and then reelected him, and in 1808 they put Madison in the White House for the next eight years.

Andrew Jackson, the overwhelming people's choice of 1828, vetoed the rechartering of the Second Bank of the United States in the summer of 1832. Twenty percent of its stock was government owned; the rest was held by private investors, some of them foreigners and all of them wealthy. Jackson argued that the bank's official connections and size gave it unfair advantages over local competition. In his veto message, he said: "[This act] seems to be predicated on the erroneous idea that the present stockholders have a prescriptive right not only to the favor but to the bounty of Government. . . . It is to be regretted that the rich and powerful too often bend the acts of government to their selfish purposes." Four months later, Jackson was easily reelected in a decisive victory over plutocracy.

The predators roared back in the Gilded Age that followed the Civil War. Corruption born of the lust for money produced what one historian described as "the morals of a gashouse gang." Judges, state legislators, the parties that selected them, and the editors who supported them were purchased as easily as ale at the local pub. Lobbyists roamed the halls of Congress proffering gifts of cash, railroad passes, and fancy entertainments. The US Senate became a "millionaires' club." With government on the auction block, the notion of the "general welfare" wound up on the trash heap; grotesque inequality and poverty festered under the gilding. Sound familiar?

Then came a judicial earthquake. In 1886, a conservative Supreme Court conferred the divine gift of life on the Southern Pacific Railroad and by extension on all other corporations. The railroad was declared to be a "person," protected by the recently enacted Fourteenth Amendment, which said that no person should be deprived of "life, liberty or property without due process of law." Never mind that the amendment was enacted to protect the rights of freed slaves who were now US citizens. Never mind that a corporation possessed neither a body to be kicked nor a soul to be damned (or saved!). The Court decided that it had the same rights of "personhood" as a walking, talking citizen and was entitled to enjoy every liberty protected by the Constitution that flesh-and-blood individuals could claim, even though it did not share their disadvantage of being mortal. It could move where it chose, buy any kind of property it chose, and select its directors and stockholders from anywhere it chose. Welcome to unregulated multinational conglomerates, although unforeseen at the time. Welcome to tax shelters, at home and offshore, and to subsidies galore, paid for by the taxes of unsuspecting working people. Corporations were endowed with the rights of "personhood" but exempted from the responsibilities of citizenship.

That's the doctrine picked up and dusted off by the John Roberts Court in its ruling on *Citizens United*. Ignoring a century of modifying precedent, the Court gave our corporate sovereigns a "sky's the limit" right to pour money into political campaigns for the purpose of influencing the outcome. And to do so without public disclosure. We might as well say farewell to the very idea of fair play. Farewell, too, to representative government "of, by, and for the people."

Unless.

Unless "We, the People"—flesh-and-blood humans, outraged at the selling off of our government—fight back.

It's been done before. As my friend and longtime colleague, the historian Bernard Weisberger, wrote recently, the Supreme Court remained a procorporate conservative fortress for the next fifty years after the Southern Pacific decision. Decade after decade it struck down laws aimed to share power with the citizenry and to promote the "general welfare." In 1895, it declared unconstitutional a measure providing for an income tax and gutted the Sherman Antitrust Act by finding a loophole for a sugar trust. In 1905, it killed a New York state law limiting working hours. In 1917, it did likewise to a prohibition against child labor. In 1923, it wiped out another law that set minimum wages for women. In 1935 and 1936, it struck down early New Deal recovery acts.

In the face of such discouragement, however, embattled citizens refused to give up. "Into their hearts," wrote the progressive Kansas journalist William Allen White, "had come a sense that their civilization needed recasting, that the government had fallen into the hands of self-seekers, that a new relationship should be established between the haves and the have-nots." Not content merely to wring their hands and cry "Woe is us," everyday citizens researched the issues, organized public events to educate their neighbors, held rallies, made speeches, petitioned and canvassed, marched and exhorted. They would elect the twentieth-century governments that restored the "general welfare" as a pillar of American democracy, setting in place legally ordained minimum wages, maximum working hours, child labor laws, workmen's safety and compensation laws, pure foods and safe drugs, Social Security and Medicare, and rules to promote competitive rather than monopolistic financial and business markets.

The social contract that emerged from these victories is part and parcel of the "general welfare" to which the founders had dedicated our Constitution. The corporate and political right seeks now to weaken and ultimately destroy it. Thanks to their ideological kin on the Supreme Court, they can attack the social contract using their abundant resources of wealth funneled—clandestinely—into political campaigns. During the fall elections of 2010, the first after the *Citizens United* decision, corporate front groups spent $126 million while hiding the identities of the donors, according to the Sunlight Foundation. The US Chamber of Commerce, which touts itself as a "main street" grassroots organization, draws most of its funds from about a hundred businesses, including such "main street" sources as BP, ExxonMobil, JPMorgan Chase, Massey Coal, Pfizer, Shell, Aetna, and Alcoa. The ink was hardly dry on the *Citizens United* decision when the Chamber organized a covertly funded front and fired volley after volley of missiles, in the form of political ads, into the 2010 campaigns, eventually spending approximately $75 million. Another corporate cover group—the Americans Action Network—spent more than $26 million of undisclosed corporate money in six Senate races and twenty-eight House of Representative elections. And "Crossroads GPS" seized on *Citizens United* to raise and spend at least $17 million that NBC News said came from "a small circle of extremely wealthy Wall Street hedge fund and private equity moguls," all determined to water down the financial reforms designed to avoid a collapse of the financial system that their own greed and reckless speculation had helped bring on. As I write in the summer of 2011, the *New York Times* reports that efforts to thwart serious reforms are succeeding. The populist editor Jim Hightower concludes that today's proponents of corporate plutocracy "have simply elevated money itself above votes, establishing cold, hard cash as the real coin of political power. The more you spend on politics, the bigger your voice is in government, making the vast vaults of billionaires and corporations far superior to the voices of mere voters."

Against such odds, discouragement comes easily. If the generations before us had given up, however, slaves would still be waiting on our tables and picking our crops, women would be turned back at the voting booths, and it would be a crime for workers to organize. Like our forebears, we will not fix the broken promise of America—the promise of "life, liberty, and the pursuit of happiness" for all our citizens, not just the powerful and privileged—if we throw in the proverbial towel. Surrendering to plutocracy is not an option. Confronting a moment in our history that is much like the one Lincoln faced—when "we can nobly save or meanly lose the last best hope on earth"—we must fight back against the forces that are pouring dirty money into the political system, turning it into a sewer.

How to fight back is the message of this book. Jeffrey Clements saw corporate behavior up close during two stints as assistant attorney general in Massachusetts, litigating against the tobacco industry, enforcing fair trade practices, and leading more than one hundred attorneys and staff responsible for consumer and environmental protection, antitrust practices, and the oversight of health care, insurance, and financial services. He came away from the experience repeating to himself this indelible truth: "Corporations are not people." Try it yourself: "Corporations are not people." Again: "Corporations are not people." You are now ready to join what Clements believes is the most promising way to counter *Citizens United*: a campaign for a constitutional amendment affirming that free speech and democracy are for people and that corporations are not people. Impossible? Not at all, says Clements. We have already amended the Constitution twenty-seven times. Amendment campaigns are how we have always made the promise of equality and liberty more real. Difficult? Of course; as Frederick Douglass taught us, power concedes nothing without a struggle. To contend with power, Clements and his colleague John Bonifaz founded Free Speech for People, a nationwide nonpartisan effort to overturn *Citizens United* and corporate rights doctrines that unduly leverage corporate economic power into political power. What Clements calls the People's Rights

Amendment could be our best hope to save the "great American experiment."

To find out why, read on, and as you read, keep in mind the words of Theodore Roosevelt, a Republican, who a century ago stood up to the mighty combines of wealth and power that were buying up our government and called on Americans of all persuasions to join him in opposing the "naked robbery" of the public's trust:

> It is not a partisan issue; it is more than a political issue. It is a great moral issue. If we condone political theft, if we do not resent the kinds of wrong and injustice that injuriously affect the whole nation, not merely our democratic form of government but our civilization itself cannot endure.

Introduction
What's at Stake?

his book is about how an audacious, long-term, and well-funded strategy created new constitutional rights for "things" such as corporations and money, at the expense of the rights of people and democracy itself. This might be a bleak tale, except that now, four years after *Citizens United*, this book also is about the remarkable success of so many Americans who insist on rewriting the end of the story and renewing the promise of our democracy.

America's story is one of defiant struggle against the odds for an improbable vision: that all people, created and born free and equal, can live and govern together "in the pursuit of happiness." This dream of a society of free people with equal rights, where people govern themselves, was unlikely indeed in the eighteenth century. In a world of empires, governed by royalty and divided by class, and in our own country, with millions enslaved, where women were considered the property of their husbands, and where land ownership was considered a prerequisite to participation in government, the pursuit—let alone the fulfillment—of this vision was far-fetched indeed.

Yet we Americans never let that vision go, despite dark days. In generation after generation, for more than two centuries, the power of this dream drove us and inspired the world. Despite all of

1

the contradictions, shortcomings, missteps, and failures along the way, this basic American story remains true, and it is an undeniable triumph of the human spirit. Cynics and critics will have their say, but Americans really did come together to defeat the British Empire; to overthrow the evil of slavery and work for justice; to secure equal voting rights for women; to insist that everyone, not only the wealthy, has an equal vote and voice; to suffer, work, and fight year after year to defeat fascist, communist, fundamentalist, and totalitarian challenges to our vision of democracy, equality, and freedom.

People are free. People are equal. People govern. We have lived by that and died for that, and whenever we fell short, we worked and sacrificed for that, to ensure, as Abraham Lincoln said in one of our darkest moments, ". . . that government of the people, by the people, for the people shall not perish from the earth."

To triumph again over powerful enemies of human equality, dignity, and freedom in our generation, we must properly identify the challenge and bring clarity of thinking and action to making our republic work again. As so often before, success and struggle begin with the simplest of propositions: Corporations are not people and every American is an equal citizen.

In *Citizens United v. Federal Election Commission* in 2010, the Supreme Court of the United States concluded, in effect, that corporations are people with First Amendment free speech rights and that democracy is for sale; it is a "marketplace." According to the Supreme Court, we cannot prevent corporations, unions, and billionaires from controlling who wins, who loses, and who gets a voice in elections and government—and who does not. In one stroke, the Court erased a century or more of bipartisan law and two previous Supreme Court rulings that affirmed the right, if not the duty, of the people to regulate corporate political spending to preserve the integrity of American democracy.

As a result, a small group of people, corporations, and unions have poured more than $20 billion into state and federal elections since the *Citizens United* decision. The global oil giant Chevron openly dropped $2.5 million into the Speaker of the House of Representatives' PAC, with only yawns from a Washington press corps incapable of seeing scandal at the end of their noses. Chevron even spent $1.2 million in a city council election in Richmond, California, a community of 100,000 people living in the shadow of a Chevron refinery that caused 15,000 residents to go to area hospitals.

The US Chamber of Commerce, working for global corporations, spent more than $35 million—the source of which is secret—in the 2012 election and has passed the $1 billion mark in lobbying spending since 1998. In case that kind of money was not enough to warrant politicians' attention, the Chamber president warned, "When we bite you on the ass, you bleed."

The "corporate capture of the courts," as Elizabeth Warren has put it, goes beyond the issue of money in politics. The same "corporate speech rights" fabricated by the Court in *Citizens United* now are used with regularity to strike down laws deemed unfriendly to corporate profits. In 2014, one business corporation with 13,000 employees and more than 500 stores, Hobby Lobby Stores, Inc., has even gone to the Supreme Court with a claim that it—the corporation itself—has a constitutional right of free exercise of religion so as to to deprive those employees of legally required insurance coverage for reproductive health care.[1]

Corporate-oriented courts now are creating astounding new corporate constitutional rights. The pharmaceutical industry has a right to traffic in private prescription information, driving up health care costs. Monsanto has a right "not to speak" to block GMO labeling. Utility corporations have a right to promote energy consumption in defiance of conservation policies. Cigarette corporations have a right to eliminate warning labels.

Corporations now have a right to deprive employees of information about whether they may join a union. Verizon and the telecommunications industry claim a constitutional right to secretly turn over customer data and information to the government.

Citizens United, then, is not merely a mistake easily corrected, nor is the case simply about campaign finance or money in politics. The Court's declaration in *Citizens United* that corporations have the same rights as people must strike most Americans as bizarre. To the five justices in the majority and to the corporate legal movement out of which they have come, however, it was more like a victory lap or an end zone dance for a three-decade-long campaign.

This campaign, begun in the 1970s, had already succeeded in creating a corporate trump card to strike down federal, state, and local laws enacted for the public's benefit. Even before *Citizens United*, the fabrication of corporate rights and the reality of corporate power controlled economic, energy, environmental, health, budget, debt, food, agriculture, and foreign policy in America.

The results? Massive job outsourcing abroad; destruction of our manufacturing capacity; wage stagnation for the vast majority of Americans and unprecedented enrichment of the very few; uncontrolled military spending and endless wars; out-of-control health care spending at the same time that millions of people cannot get health care at all; bloated and unsustainable budgets and debt at every level of government; national and global environmental crisis; loss of wilderness and open land, and the takeover of public hunting and fishing grounds; chain store sprawl and gutting of local economies and communities; obesity, asthma, and public health epidemics; and a growing sense that the connection between Americans and our government has been lost.

Not forever, though. Since *Citizens United*, millions of Americans have decided that we do not have to live with this and that we can put the American project back together again.

To most effectively respond, we need to see where *Citizens United* came from and how much we have lost to the triumph of corporate and money power. Most of the first six chapters of this book, therefore, examine these themes from different perspectives. In Chapter Three, I digress to examine what a corporation actually is as a matter of law and fact. This may be a digression, but it lies at the heart of why corporations can have no constitutional rights superior to the rights of the American people to make laws governing corporations. Corporations are not merely private entities, owing no duties to the public. Corporations are legal creations of government, with the duties as well as privileges that we, the people, decide upon in public debate.

In the latter part of the book, I describe a roadmap back to democracy, republican government, and balance in a sustainable economy. The heart of this road map is a strategy, already making significant progress, for reversing *Citizens United*, cleaning the swamp of our corrupted politics, and designing corporations that better serve our society.

We are well on our way to a Twenty-Eighth Amendment to the Constitution that will overturn *Citizens United* and corporate rights, and restore people's rights and equal citizenship. People, outside of Washington, D.C., anyway, are coming together across political, ideological, and cultural differences to work on bigger, more fundamental reforms in elections, voting rights, and anticorruption. And corporate law no longer is left only to corporate lawyers. People in business, people as customers, and people as citizens are insisting on corporate accountability and corporate law reform. They want corporations that better reflect the public policy reasons for which we allow the legal benefits of incorporation, such as limited liability, and they are making it happen.

Finally, a word about nomenclature: I am not "anticorporate," and this book is not "anticorporate," whatever that means. When

I refer to "corporations" and "corporate power" and the like, I am talking about large global or transnational corporations. Size matters. Complexity and power matter. Whether corporations operate in the economic sphere without dominating the political sphere matters.

Thousands and thousands of corporations in America are just like the corporation I set up for my business and just like the kinds of corporations that you may have set up or worked for. They are convenient legal structures for businesses to make economic activity more efficient, productive, flexible, and, we hope, profitable.

If I am "anti" anything, I am opposed to any force that takes God-given rights away from people and threatens one of the most remarkable runs of democracy and republican government in the history of humanity. Today that force is defined by the misguided ideology and unbalanced power that *Citizens United* represents and has let loose: insufficiently controlled global corporations empowered with "rights" and locked-in political inequality that leaves elections and government to those with vast sums of money. To succeed in making government of the people real in our generation, we will need to restore our right and duty to check, balance, and restrain that power.

Chapter One
American Democracy Works, and Corporations Fight Back

In 1838, a quarter century before he became the nation's sixteenth president, a twenty-nine-year-old Abraham Lincoln stepped up to speak at the Young Men's Lyceum in Springfield, Illinois. He spoke about what was to become the cause of his life: the preservation of that great American contribution to the human story, government of, for, and by the people. He insisted that the success or failure of the American experiment was up to us. "If destruction be our lot, we must ourselves be its author and finisher. As a nation of freemen, we must live through all time, or die by suicide."[1]

Lincoln's generation of Americans, and every generation since, has faced daunting questions of whether "destruction be our lot," and we certainly have our share today. Most people can point to a host of complex and related reasons for rising anxiety about our future. Global and national environmental crises seem relentless and increasingly related to energy, economic, military, and food crises. Our unsustainable debt and budgets—national, state, local, family, personal—seem beyond control, reflecting an economy that has not generated significant wage growth in a generation.

We have been locked in faraway wars for more than a decade, at war in one form or another for a half century. Despite our victory over totalitarian communism, we spend more on our military than all other countries combined. We, the descendants of republicans with great suspicion about standing armies, now maintain a costly military empire across more than one hundred countries and a sprawling secret government that collects the communications data of everyone. Many Americans now doubt that we are, in fact, a government of the people and no longer believe that our democracy and government are working.

We can point to an array of causes, and we can point fingers at one another, but a taproot of many of these related problems is our collective failure to do what generations of Americans before us did: choose to take responsibility as citizens to manage hyperconcentrations of political power among the largest corporations and the wealthiest few. We have lost sight of the implications in a republic of the extreme wealth and power of transnational corporations. The agenda of the largest corporations and those who control them is not the agenda of the American family and the American community. Yet the corporate agenda is now dominant at home and across the world.

The Impact of *Citizens United*

In 2010, in *Citizens United v. Federal Election Commission*, the Supreme Court proclaimed that the American people are not permitted to determine how much control corporations and concentrated wealth may have over elections and lawmakers. The Court, in a 5–4 decision, ruled that a federal election law designed to prevent corporations and unions from dominating elections and government violated First Amendment free speech rights.

The impact of the Supreme Court's folly now is beyond dispute. More money was spent by fewer donors in the 2012 election than ever before in history. As much as $10 billion in the federal election;[2] billions more in state and local elections.[3] "Dark money" from corporations, billionaires, and unions was run through secretive "social welfare" nonprofit corporations acting as partisan political operatives;[4] foreign money was run through corporate subsidiaries and trade associations;[5] and Super PACs, corporations, candidates, and operatives pretending to be "uncoordinated" unleashed saturation attack ads across the land, all to drown out other issues, candidates, ideas, and, ultimately, Americans' faith in effective democracy.

This spending is not "free speech," unleashed at last, nor is it a burst of democratic enthusiasm for electioneering. Instead, it is the deployment of power of, for, and by a very few.

How few? A few dozen donors contributed 60 percent of the Super PAC money, and almost all of the Super PAC money came from came from just 3,318 donors. That is 0.0011 percent of the American population.[6] One billionaire global casino mogul alone contributed $93 million.[7] One global oil corporation alone, Chevron, handed $2.5 million to the "Leadership PAC" of the Speaker of the House, who has promised to oppose cutting oil and gas subsidies and to block action on the climate catastrophe.

Almost all political contributions of any sort—80 percent— come from just 0.5 percent of the population. This "donor class," interwoven with corporations and lobbying firms, are largely concentrated in New York, Washington, Los Angeles, Chicago, and Boston.[8]

Political domination by the few has even overwhelmed state ballot initiatives, originally intended to check concentrated corporate and wealth power. A century ago, American government was "fast becoming a plutocracy," and an "invisible government" of large corporations overwhelmed government of the people.[9] Voters acted in many states to amend state constitutions, creating the citizen ballot initiative to enable more democracy to check the special interest lock on state legislatures. People in the states intended the initiative process to ensure that "this government shall be brought back to the real control of the people."[10]

Now the ideology of *Citizens United* has broken the check and balance of the citizen initiative. In 2012, "corporations and some of the wealthiest Americans" spent more than a billion dollars in initiatives in just eleven states, "an unprecedented explosion of money used to pass new laws and influence the public debate."[11] In the state of Washington, corporations such as Monsanto, Pepsico, Nestle, and Dupont spent more than $20 million to defeat a ballot initiative to require disclosure of genetically modified organisms (GMOs) in food. Of that $20 million, only $600 came from people or businesses in the state itself.[12]

Even small cities and towns have felt the impact of *Citizens United*. In Richmond, California, a community of 100,000 people, a single corporation—Chevron again—spent $1.2 million to control the outcome of the city council election. Richmond Mayor, Gayle McGlaughlin, says that Chevron will spend another $2 million in city elections in 2014. A Richmond citizen serving on the city council, Tom Butt, adds, "They want a city council loyal to them. I think it's wrong for a corporation to pour that kind of money into a local election. Nobody can match that."[13]

Most Americans agree, but that does not matter, according to *Citizens United*. Corporations and unions now have the same rights under the First Amendment as people. And if "free speech" means unlimited election spending by the powerful, that cannot be "infringed."

The *Citizens United* Decision

In *Citizens United*, the Court struck down the federal Bipartisan Campaign Reform Act (also known as McCain-Feingold, after its Republican and Democratic sponsors). The Bipartisan Campaign

Reform Act had banned electioneering spending by corporations and unions for or against specific candidates within sixty days of a federal election. The law was intended to prevent corporations and unions from bypassing election integrity and anticorruption laws dating back more than a century.[14]

The case is called Citizens United because a Virginia nonprofit corporation by that name sued the Federal Election Commission to challenge the corporate spending restriction in the Bipartisan Campaign Reform Act. Citizens United, the corporation, wished to use its corporate money and donations from for-profit corporations to make and distribute what the Court described as a feature-length advertisement against Hillary Clinton, who was running for president when the case began. Further, Citizens United sought to do this within the sixty-day period before an election when the law restricted corporate spending on electioneering activity. According to Citizens United, the law violated corporations' First Amendment rights of free speech because it prevented Citizens United, the nonprofit corporation, from engaging in electioneering activity and did not allow for-profit corporations to contribute to that campaign to influence the election.[15]

Of course, people are free to make a feature-length advertisement attacking a powerful senator running for president if that is what people wish to do, and people may pool their money to do this. That is essential for political participation. At first blush, the background to the case seemed to warrant concern about government restrictions on the free ability of people to pool resources to advocate views.

The Court majority in *Citizens United, however,* was not content to leave the case at first blush. Instead, they saw an opportunity to throw out a century of law they thought too restrictive of corporations. In the end, the *Citizens United* decision decreed that all corporations (and all unions) have a constitutional right to spend unlimited money in any American election—federal, state, local, and judicial.

The Supreme Court had rejected this argument only a few years earlier, when Justices William Rehnquist and Sandra Day O'Connor were still on the Court. In 2003, in the case of *McConnell v. Federal Election Commission*, the Court ruled that the very same corporate spending provision in the McCain-Feingold law did not violate the First Amendment. In McConnell, the Court agreed that Congress may make different election spending rules for corporations than for people. The Court in *McConnell* followed the 1990 case of *Michigan Chamber of Commerce v. Austin*, in which another majority of the Court had ruled that corporate money, aggregated with advantages that come from the government, is not the same as people's money pooled together. Corporate spending in elections can be restricted because government creates the advantages for corporations to make them effective in the economic sphere, and the same advantages pose dangers in the political sphere.

Now in *Citizens United*, the Court, with the additions of a new chief justice, John Roberts, and a new justice, Samuel Alito, threw out *McConnell* and *Austin*. The *Citizens United* Court said its earlier decisions were wrong. The Court struck down the McCain-Feingold law as a violation of free speech rights and invited billions of corporate dollars into American elections.

Justice Anthony Kennedy wrote the opinion in *Citizens United* for the Court. At first, Justice Kennedy's opinion sounds like a ringing defense of free speech and American democracy. He writes that the government may not "ban speech." Yes! All "speakers" must be allowed and no "voices" may be silenced. Yes! The government cannot restrict a "disadvantaged person or class" from speech. Yes! All "citizens, or associations of citizens," must have a right to get their views about candidates or anything else out to the people. Of course!

But wait. Who are these "voices," "speakers," and "disadvantaged persons"? They are corporations, particularly global corporations with trillions of dollars in revenue and profits. And what was this onerous "ban on speech"? A rather weak law that said a corporation may not, within sixty days of an election, spend its "general treasury" money to support or attack candidates for federal office. That's it.

The Court announced its decision on a cold January day in 2010 when most Americans were anxious about millions of job losses, angered by national debt and massive deficits deepened by corporate bailouts, and worried about our military and global strength overstretched by distant wars while China, Germany, and other economic powerhouses at peace charged ahead. Now the Supreme Court says corporations are "disadvantaged persons" with "rights" that trump and invalidate our laws?

The Initial Response

Immediately, four dissenting justices on the Court, led by eighty-nine-year-old Justice John Paul Stevens, sounded the alarm. Justice Stevens's ninety-page dissent, among his last work before retiring, may be his greatest legacy.

Stevens, born and raised in Chicago, had enlisted in the US Navy on December 6, 1941, the day before the Japanese attack on Pearl Harbor, and received the Bronze Star for his service in World War II. He then began a twenty-five-year career as a lawyer and represented numerous corporations in antitrust cases. In 1969, Stevens led the investigation and prosecution of corrupt judges in Illinois and was hailed for his fair, honest, and determined approach. A Republican, he was appointed to the Court by President Gerald Ford in 1975. It would be difficult to find a more honest, moderate, and balanced judge.

Alarmed by the majority's decision, Stevens took the unusual step of reading his dissent aloud in the Supreme Court's public chamber. Although the elderly judge's voice at times faltered, his words were unmistakable. Stevens called the Court's action in *Citizens United* a "radical departure from what has been settled First Amendment law." He blasted the Court's conclusion that corporations, "like individuals, contribute to the discussion, debate, and the dissemination of information and ideas that the First Amendment seeks to foster." Justice Stevens said that "glittering generality" obscured the truth about what *Citizens United* really meant for America, already suffering from undue influence of corporate power. Then Justice Stevens said this:

> *The Framers [of our Constitution] thus took it as a given that corporations could be comprehensively regulated in the service of the public welfare. Unlike our colleagues [on the Supreme Court], they had little trouble distinguishing corporations from human beings, and when they constitutionalized the right to free speech in the First Amendment, it was the free speech of individual Americans that they had in mind. . . .*
>
> *At bottom, the Court's opinion is thus a rejection of the common sense of the American people, who have recognized a need to prevent corporations from undermining self-government since the founding, and who have fought against the distinctive corrupting potential of corporate electioneering since the days of Theodore Roosevelt. It is a strange time to repudiate that common sense. While American democracy is imperfect, few outside the majority of this Court would have thought its flaws included a dearth of corporate money in politics.*

Rejection of the *Citizens United* decision crossed all political lines. President Obama called the decision a "strike at the heart of democracy." John McCain, the 2008 Republican presidential candidate, put it bluntly: "What the Supreme Court did is a combination of arrogance, stupidity, and naivete, the likes of which I have never seen."[16] Others, including members of Congress, labeled *Citizens United* the worst decision since the Supreme Court ruled in the 1856 case of *Dred Scott v. Sanford* that African Americans could never be American citizens. A founder of the Tea Party said, *Citizens United* "just allows them to feed the machine. Corporations are not like people. Corporations exist forever; people don't. Our founding fathers never wanted them; these behemoth organizations that never die. . . . It puts the people at a tremendous disadvantage."[17]

Polls confirmed that more than 75 percent of Independents, Republicans, and Democrats alike rejected the decision.[18] People formed groups to launch a constitutional amendment campaign to overturn the decision and corporate rights, and pushed for public funding of elections, disclosure, and other reform to lessen the damage of *Citizens United*.

Since that January day in 2010, millions of Americans have signed petitions calling on Congress to send a constitutional amendment reversing the Court's decision in *Citizens United* to the states for ratification. Many worked in their communities to enact constitutional amendment resolutions. By the beginning of 2014, constitutional amendment resolutions had passed by overwhelming margins in sixteen states and more than 500 cities and towns in every region of the country. Put on notice, more than 160 members of the House and Senate have cosponsored constitutional amendment bills.[19]

Why this reaction? The real people are not buying the metaphors of corporations as "speakers" or "disadvantaged persons." They do not agree that corporate and union money is simply another "voice."

Rather, most Americans understand two fundamental truths about our Constitution and system of government that the Court got wrong: First, corporations are not entitled to the inherent, human rights that "we, the people" wrote into our Constitution. Large corporations already have far too much power in America and across the world, and requiring that we allow that power to be deployed without limit in elections and government will be the death of democracy and republican government. Second, with respect to elections and representation in government, every American, rich or poor, has the same right to speak, participate, be represented in government, and serve if their fellow citizens so desire. At election time and in governing, Americans indeed are created equal. We are citizens, not mere spectators to arguments among factions of the rich.

Senator John McCain summed it up: "[We] need a level playing field and we need to go back to the realization that Teddy Roosevelt had that we have to have a limit on the flow of money, and that corporations are not people."[20]

Roots of *Citizens United*: Earth Day 1970

To see how the *Citizens United* disaster happened, we need to go back to the 1970s and the formation of the organized corporate campaign to put American democracy on a leash. First came a wave of engaged citizens and responsive government, then came the corporate reaction. *Citizens United* could not have resulted without the deliberate drive for corporate power and rights that began four decades ago.[21]

After a century of industrialization, Americans had by 1970 had enough of corporations using our rivers, air, oceans, and land as sewers and dumps, leaving most people and communities with the costs and giving the profits to shareholders. One day in April 1970, twenty million Americans of every age and political party came out into the streets and the parks to celebrate the first Earth Day. They demanded a better balance between corporations and people and better stewardship of our land, water, and air. Look at the photos from this first Earth Day and you will see families with children, men in suits and ties and neatly dressed women, working- and middle-class Americans, people of all ages and races.

These millions continued a longstanding American principle of guarding against concentrated corporate power that might overwhelm the larger interests of the nation. This nonpartisan tradition goes back not only to Franklin Roosevelt's New Deal, not only to Theodore Roosevelt's Square Deal, but to the founding of America. James Madison, a chief architect of the Constitution, wrote in the early 1800s that "incorporated Companies with proper limitations and guards, may in particular cases, be useful; but they are at best a necessary evil only."[22] Always willing to be more colorful, Thomas Jefferson said that he hoped to "crush in its birth the aristocracy of our monied corporations, which dare already to challenge our government to a trial of strength and bid defiance to the laws of our country."[23]

In the 1830s, President Andrew Jackson and his allies battled against the partisan activity of the Second Bank of the United States, a corporation. Jackson pressed the urgent question of "whether the people of the United States are to govern through representatives chosen by their unbiased suffrages or whether the money and power of a great corporation are to be secretly exerted to influence their judgment and control their decisions."[24] Even President Martin Van Buren, hardly a radical, warned of "the already overgrown influence of corporate authorities."[25]

That first Earth Day in 1970 again awakened our government to the necessity of restoring the balance of corporate power and public interest, of those who control powerful corporations and the rest of Americans. With a Republican president in the White

House and bipartisan support in Congress, the extent of reform that quickly followed in the months and a few short years after the first Earth Day remains astonishing:

- Environmental Protection Agency
- Clean Water Act
- Federal Water Pollution Control Amendments
- Clean Air Act Extension
- Toxic Substances Control Act
- Safe Drinking Water Act
- Wilderness Act
- Surface Mining Control and Reclamation Act
- Endangered Species Act
- Marine Mammal Protection Act
- Resource Recovery Act
- First fuel economy standards for motor vehicles

These 1970s reforms were long overdue. For a time, they worked, and they made a profound difference in the quality of life of the vast majority of Americans. No longer could dumping untreated sewage and toxic waste in our waters be considered a standard business practice; no longer could corporations walk away from hazardous waste and chemical sites; more wilderness areas preserved more of our birthright and that of future Americans; new laws rejected the industry view that we just had to live with the discharge of brain- and organ-damaging lead from millions of cars and the spread of lead paint in every building in the land; access to clean, safe water was assured for far more Americans; and much more.

The market did not do this. We did this by acting as citizens in a republic.

As with every time in American history, of course, the 1970s were times of crisis and challenge. Yet the American people worked the levers of democracy and saw a connection between those levers—voting, organizing, debating, petitioning, marching—and our government's conduct.

Environmental balance was not all. We often remember the strife and problems of the late 1960s and early 1970s but think of the progress for the country: in race and gender equality; ending the Vietnam War; real wage growth for average Americans; global leadership in trade and commerce and manufacturing; steady, comprehensive, creative, and effective resistance across the globe to dictatorial communism; public accountability when the president broke the law; more open government and better congressional oversight; manageable debt and budgets in Washington, D.C., and the states; employee rights and safety; and a constitutional amendment to enfranchise millions of Americans from eighteen to twenty years old. The people demanded change; our government delivered change.

The biggest corporations on the planet, however, did not celebrate the responsive democracy that followed Earth Day. Instead, they organized to fund a sustained program to take political power and rights for themselves and away from average Americans. With *Citizens United*, we see the end game of this project, but it has been years in the making.

1971: Lewis Powell and the "Activist-Minded Supreme Court"

In late August 1971, Lewis Powell, a mild-mannered, courtly, and shrewd corporate lawyer in Richmond, Virginia, soon to be appointed to the US Supreme Court, wrote a memorandum to his client, the US Chamber of Commerce. The next day, he traveled to the Chamber's offices in Washington, D.C., to meet with the leaders of the powerful lobby. There, Powell outlined a critique and a plan that changed America.[26]

Powell, like the *Citizens United* dissenter Justice John Paul Stevens, was a decorated World War II veteran who had returned home to build a respected law practice. By all accounts, he was a gentleman—reserved, polite, and gracious—and a distinguished lawyer and public servant. Commentators and law professors cite Powell's "qualities of temperament and character" and his "modest" and "restrained" approach to judging.[27] At his funeral in 1998, Sandra Day O'Connor, who had joined the Supreme Court in 1987, said, "For those who seek a model of human kindness, decency, exemplary behavior, and integrity, there will never be a better man."[28] Even the rare critic will cite Lewis Powell's decency and kindness.[29]

Much about these accounts must be true, but none tells the whole story of Lewis Powell. All of them, and even the principal Powell biography, omit the details of how he used his gifts to advance a radical corporate agenda. It is impossible to square this corporatist part of Powell's life and legacy with any conclusion of "modest" or "restrained" judging.

Powell titled his 1971 memo to the US Chamber of Commerce "Attack on American Free Enterprise System." "No thoughtful person," he explained, "can question that the American economic system is under broad attack." In response, corporations must organize and fund a drive to achieve political power through "united action." Powell emphasized the need for a sustained, multiyear corporate campaign to use an "activist-minded Supreme Court" to shape "social, economic and political change" to the advantage of corporations.

Powell continued:

But independent and uncoordinated activity by individual corporations, as important as this is, will not be sufficient. Strength lies in organization, in careful long-range planning and implementation, in consistency of action over an indefinite period of years, in the scale of financing available only through joint effort, and in the political power available only through united action and national organizations.

The roots of *Citizens United* lie in Powell's 1971 strategy to use "activist" Supreme Court judges to create corporate rights. "Under our constitutional system," Powell told the US Chamber of Commerce, "especially with an activist-minded Supreme Court, the judiciary may be the most important instrument for social, economic and political change."

Powell's call for "business to go on the offensive" should not be misunderstood as a "conservative" or "moderate" reaction to the excesses of "liberals" or "big government." Rather, to understand the perspective of Powell and his allies is to understand the difference between a conservative and a corporatist.

Powell and the Tobacco Corporations Show the Way

By 1971, Lewis Powell was a director of more than a dozen large corporations, including Philip Morris Inc., a global manufacturer and seller of cigarettes. Powell joined the Philip Morris board of directors in 1964, when the corporation sought to mitigate the US Surgeon General's report about the grave dangers of smoking. Powell remained a director, and an executive committee member, of the cigarette company until his appointment to the Supreme Court in 1971. Powell also advised the Tobacco Institute, a lobbying and misinformation shop that was stripped of its corporate charter in the 1990s after decades of using phony science and false statements to create a fraudulent "debate" about smoking and health.[30]

The cigarette corporations' response to public efforts to address addiction, smoking, and health is a big part of the larger story of how corporations undermined the Constitution and American democracy. The tobacco companies, with Powell's encouragement, began testing the ideas that Powell urged upon the US Chamber of Commerce in 1971. By a campaign of aggressive resistance to efforts to address the devastating social and public costs of its lethal products, the cigarette corporations created a model. As a director and an executive committee member of Philip Morris, Powell shared responsibility for the fraudulent attack on the conclusions of scientists and the surgeon general by the cigarette industry and for its false insistence for years that "no proof" showed cigarettes to be unhealthy.

Hints of this work can be seen in the Philip Morris annual reports issued during Powell's tenure as a director. We now know, thanks to recent findings of a federal judge, that many of the assertions in these annual reports were knowingly false. According to the reports themselves, these statements and others were made "on behalf of the board of directors," including Powell:

1964: "The industry continues to support major research efforts directed towards resolving the many unanswered questions on smoking and health."

1967: "The year 1967 was marked by an intensification of exaggerated claims made relative to the possible adverse health effects of smoking on health. . . . We deplore the lack of objectivity in so important a controversy. . . . Unfortunately the positive benefits of smoking which are so widely acknowledged are largely ignored by many reports linking cigarettes and health, and little attention is paid to the scientific reports which are favorable to smoking."

1967: "We would again like to state that there is no biological proof that smoking is causally related to the diseases and conditions claimed to be statistically associated with smoking . . . no proof that the tar and nicotine levels in smoke are significant in relation to health."

1970: "Often the scientific information which is relied on to indict cigarette smoking is of dubious validity."

Powell endorsed these false statements as a director and executive committee member. He also actively encouraged the disinformation campaign, congratulating the Philip Morris CEO for the company's "attacks" (as the industry called it) on the American Cancer Society and urging the CEO to "restrain" the "extremism" of the Cancer Society and scientists.[31]

Absent proof, it might be reckless to say that Philip Morris and the other tobacco corporations engaged in a willful, aggressive, wide-ranging conspiracy and racketeering enterprise so that the corporations could sell more products that kill people. Now that the evidence is in, however, we know that this is exactly what happened. *We know*, thanks to scientists, victims of the conspiracy, state attorneys general (both Democrats and Republicans), the US Department of Justice (under both Presidents Bill Clinton and George W. Bush), and Judge Gladys Kessler and a panel of US Court of Appeals judges appointed by Presidents Ronald Reagan, Bill Clinton, and George H. W. Bush.

In 2006, the US Department of Justice took the cigarette corporations to trial, alleging that they had engaged in a racketeering conspiracy. Eighty-four witnesses testified in the nine-month trial, and hundreds of internal corporate secrets were finally exposed. When the verdict came in, Judge Kessler concluded that "overwhelming evidence" proved that the cigarette corporations "conspired together" to fraudulently deny that cigarettes caused cancer, emphysema, and a long list of other fatal diseases; to manipulate levels of highly addictive nicotine to keep people smoking; to market addictive cigarettes to children so that the corporations would have "replacement smokers" for those who quit or died; and that they "concealed evidence, destroyed documents, and abused the attorney-client privilege to prevent the public from knowing about the dangers of smoking and to protect the industry" from justice.[32]

As counsel to the cigarette industry and as a Philip Morris director, Powell already had begun testing the use of activist-minded courts to create corporate rights. In one case in the late 1960s, Powell argued that any suggestion that cigarettes caused cancer and death was "not proved" and was "controversial." According to Powell, the Federal Communications Commission wrongly violated the First Amendment rights of cigarette corporations by refusing to require "equal time" for the corporations to respond to any announcement that discouraged cigarette smoking as a health hazard.[33]

Even the US Court of Appeals for the Fourth Circuit, based in the tobacco-friendly South, rejected this claim. Although Powell lost that time, he went on to win far more than he could have imagined after he got on the Supreme Court and helped change the Constitution.

Powell's 1971 memo to the US Chamber of Commerce laid out a corporate rights and corporate power campaign. The Chamber and the largest corporations then implemented these recommendations with zeal, piles of money, patience, and an activist Supreme Court. In equating corporations with "We, the People" in our Constitution, no justice would be more of an activist than Lewis Powell after he joined the Supreme Court in 1972.

1972: Powell Gets His Chance

In January 1972, the US Senate confirmed President Nixon's nomination of Lewis Powell to the Supreme Court. In a private farewell dinner, The Philip Morris CEO hosted a celebration of Powell's achievement and the corporation provided him with a judicial robe to wear during his service on the Court.[34]

President Nixon filled two Supreme Court vacancies that month, the other going to William Rehnquist, a conservative Republican lawyer from Phoenix, Arizona. Rehnquist had never been shy about his conservative views, which were well known and, to some, controversial. At the same time, neither Congress nor most Americans knew of Powell's corporatist views. In his Senate confirmation hearing, no one asked about his recent proposal to the US Chamber of Commerce recommending the use of an "activist-minded Supreme Court" to impose those views on the nation. No one asked because Powell, and the Chamber kept Powell's memo secret; neither disclosed the memo during his background check or confirmation proceedings.[35]

Once on the Court, these two Nixon appointees followed very different paths. Justice Powell would go on to write the Court's unprecedented decisions creating a new concept of "corporate speech" in the First Amendment. Using this new theory, the Court struck down law after law in which the states and Congress sought to balance corporate power with the public interest. With increasing assertiveness after Powell retired in 1987, the Supreme Court has used the new corporate rights theory to invalidate laws concerning food, the environment, public health and drugs, financial and insurance reform, and more.[36]

Powell helped shape a new majority, but several justices resisted the new model of "corporate rights." The most vigorous resistance came from the conservative Justice William Rehnquist. He grounded his dissents in the fundamental proposition that our Bill of Rights sets out the rights of human beings, and corporations are not people. For years, Rehnquist maintained this principled conservative argument, warning over and over again that corporate rights have no place in our republican form of government.[37]

Here Come the Foundations

Despite the Rehnquist dissents, Powell's vision of an unregulated corporate political "marketplace," where corporations are freed by activist courts from the policy judgment of the majority of people, won out. Powell, of course, could not have acted alone. He could not have moved a majority of the Court to create corporate rights if no one had listened to his advice to organize corporate political power to demand corporate rights. Listen they did—with the help of just the sort of massive corporate funding that Powell proposed.

Corporations and corporate executives funded a wave of new "legal foundations" in the 1970s. These legal foundations were intended to drive into every court and public body in the land the same radical message, repeated over and over again, until the bizarre began to sound normal: corporations are persons with constitutional rights against which the laws of the people must fall.

Huge corporations, including Powell's Philip Morris, invested millions of dollars in the Chamber of Commerce's National Chamber Litigation Center and other legal foundations to bring litigation demanding new corporate rights. In rapid succession, corporations and supporters funded the Pacific Legal Foundation, the Mid-Atlantic Legal Foundation, the Mid-America Legal Foundation, the Great Plains Legal Foundation (Landmark Legal Foundation), the Washington Legal Foundation, the Northeastern Legal Foundation, the New England Legal Foundation, the Southeastern Legal Foundation, the Capital Legal Center, the National Legal Center for the Public Interest, and many others.[38]

These foundations began filing brief after brief challenging state and federal laws across the country, pounding away at the themes of corporations as "persons," "speakers," and holders of constitutional rights. Reading their briefs, one might think that the most powerful, richest corporations in the history of the world were some beleaguered minority fighting to overcome oppression. The foundations and the corporate lawyers argued, "Corporations are persons" with the "liberty secured to all persons." They used new phrases like "corporate speech," the "rights of corporate speakers," and the "corporate character of the speaker." They demanded, as if to end an unjust silence, "the right of corporations to be heard" and "the rights of corporations to speak out."

This campaign sought to redefine the very role of corporations in American society. The message was insistent: We should no longer think of corporations as useful but potentially insidious industrial economic tools. We should no longer be concerned that corporations might leverage massive economic power into massive political power or trample the public interest for the profit of the few. Instead, we should think of corporations as pillars of liberty, institutions that Americans can trust. They would protect our freedom for us. They would stand up to "government" for us.

A 1977 brief written by the Chamber of Commerce, for example, argued that the Court should strike down a state law that limited corporate political spending in citizens' referendum elections because corporations help maintain our freedoms: "Business's social role is to provide the people a valuable service which helps maintain their freedoms. . . . The statute at issue prevents the modern corporation from fulfilling a major social obligation. . . ."[39]

By 1978, the millions of dollars that corporations invested in this campaign began to pay off. The first major victory came in 1978 with a successful attack on a Massachusetts law in *First*

National Bank of Boston v. Bellotti. Several international corporations—including Gillette, the Bank of Boston, and Digital Equipment Corporation—filed a lawsuit after the people of Massachusetts banned corporate political spending intended to influence a citizen ballot initiative. Justice Lewis Powell cast the deciding vote and wrote the 5–4 decision wiping off the books the people's law intended to keep corporate money out of citizen ballot questions.[40] For the first time in American history, corporations had successfully claimed "speech" rights to attack laws regulating corporate money in our elections.

With that success, an emboldened corporate rights campaign next attacked energy and environmental laws. In the 1982 case of *Central Hudson Gas & Electric Corporation v. Public Service Corporation of New York*, utility corporations and the new array of corporate legal foundations all argued that a New York law prohibiting utilities from promoting energy consumption violated the corporations' rights of free speech. The corporations won again, and again Justice Powell wrote the decision for the activist Supreme Court that he had imagined in his 1971 Chamber of Commerce memo. The corporate interest in promoting energy consumption for corporate profit trumped the people's interest in energy conservation.[41] Over a period of six years, Justice Powell wrote four key corporate rights decisions for the Supreme Court. These unprecedented cases transformed the people's First Amendment speech freedom into a corporate right to challenge public oversight and corporate regulation.

Powell led a majority of the Court to accept the repeated mantra that "corporations are persons" and corporate "voices" must be free, and the sustained attacks on the people's laws continued for the next two decades. Oil, coal, and utility corporations, tobacco corporations, chemical and pharmaceutical corporations, alcohol corporations, banking and other Wall Street corporations, and many others all successfully claimed corporate speech rights to invalidate federal, state, and local laws. As you will see in Chapter Two, corporations even succeeded in attacking the right of parents to know whether the milk they fed their children came from cows treated with Monsanto's genetically engineered recombinant DNA bovine drug.

In 2007, the Chamber of Commerce's National Chamber Litigation Center celebrated thirty years of using judicial activism on behalf of corporations and admitted that it was the "brainchild of former US Supreme Court Justice Lewis Powell." The brainchild, with its motto of "Business Is Our Only Client," bragged about such "victories" as convincing the Supreme Court to throw out a decision by a jury of people to impose punitive damages for the unlawful conduct of Philip Morris.[42]

The Consequences

The success of the Powell–Chamber of Commerce plan transformed American law, government, and society, with two devastating consequences for the country. First, corporations gained vastly increased political power at the expense of average citizens. Corporations poured out money to lobbying and election campaigns and to help friendly politicians and hurt unfriendly politicians. With even modest reform crushed by corporate rights decisions such as *First National Bank of Boston v. Bellotti*—and now much more so, *Citizens United*—corporations could threaten and deliver "independent expenditure" campaigns against politicians who did not bend their way. Corporate money to influence legislative votes and politician behavior lost its scandalous, shameful nature. Bags of corporate cash were no longer bags of cash; they were "speech." How could "speech" be corrupt or scandalous?

Washington, D.C., and many state capitals became playgrounds for corporate lobbyists, and our elected representatives became increasingly disconnected from the will of the people. With the new, organized corporate radicalism, staggering amounts of corporate money flooded Washington, D.C., and our political system. Between 1998 and 2013, for example, the Chamber of Commerce alone spent more than $1 billion on lobbying.[43] Pharmaceutical and health care corporations spent more than $5.7 billion on lobbying in those years.[44] Three corporations seeking military contracts—Northrop Grumman Corporation, Lockheed, and Boeing—spent more than $660 million on lobbying. GE Corporation ($298 million), AT&T ($162 million), the pharmaceutical lobby PHRMA ($246 million), ExxonMobil ($193 million), Verizon ($183 million), and many more corporations all joined the lobby-fest.[45] In the states, corporate-funded lobbying entities such as the American Legislative Exchange Council (ALEC) and the State Policy Network began to dominate legislatures.[46] Financial, labor, energy, environmental, health care, trade, and other policy tilted sharply in favor of corporate interests; the hurdles for advancing the public interest became much higher.

Second, "corporate rights" created a corporate trump card over public interest laws. If laws that were inconvenient to corporate business models somehow made it through the lobbyist machine, corporations now had constitutional "rights" to attack the laws in the courts. It no longer mattered if the majority of people and our representatives chose laws to curb pollution, require disclosure, protect the public health, or nurture small businesses and local economies. The democratic process was no longer enough to decide the issue. After the creation of "corporate speech" rights, it was now up to judges, rather than the people, to decide whether the law served an "important" interest and was not too "burdensome."

And not just any judges would make these decisions. As with the other branches of government, corporations have captured the courts. Several recent studies by legal scholars confirm that the current Supreme Court favors corporations over people more than ever before, and the impartiality of justice in the states is eroding rapidly.[47] After *Citizens United*, corporate interests began dumping ever more money into state judicial elections. In twenty state Supreme Court elections in 2012, the campaigns spent $56 million (compared with less than $6 million in 1990). Ten donors alone contributed $19.6 million, with much of the money coming from R. J. Reynolds Tobacco and other corporations.[48] According to the American Constitution Society, "The data confirm a significant relationship between business group contributions to state supreme court justices and the voting of those justices in cases involving business matters."[49]

The Lost Promise of Earth Day

On that long ago Earth Day in 1970, Americans reclaimed the water, air, land, and forests that belong to all of us and to our descendants. We reclaimed the promise of government of the people, where people and our representatives would weigh, debate, and decide the balance of private and public, corporate and human. Since that spring day in 1970, we have pushed resources and the ecological systems on which life depends to the breaking point. Even as the oil, gas, and coal corporations mimic the strategy of the cigarette corporations to create a fraudulent "controversy" and "open question" about the global warming "hoax," we have ripped past the point of no return on climate catastrophe.

Although the evidence of national and global environmental destruction at a level that will challenge our civilization and way of life is more compelling now than it was back in 1970, our leaders in government are not even debating, let alone enacting, possible solutions. Incredibly, the current debate in Congress is not what we can do to save our world but whether Congress should strip the Environmental Protection Agency of its authority to regulate pollution that causes the global climate crisis.

Corporate media might tell you that the reason for inaction is that Americans oppose environmental regulation and oppose drastic changes to address the energy and environmental crisis. Yet there is little reason to believe that this is true. In fact, try an experiment. Find a moment to talk seriously in a nonpolitical, nonconfrontational way with your friends, neighbors, or family members, regardless of what political party or philosophy they may favor. I bet that you will find that they, too, think that we cannot rely on corporations to protect freedom for us and that corporate business as usual will condemn us to disastrous energy, economic, and environmental policies and will ensure that we pass to our children a very bleak and weak nation and world.

This basic understanding of the connection between our state of decline and crisis on one hand, and our corporate-driven energy, environmental, economic, foreign, and military policy on the other, is one of the many points of consensus among the American people that the corporatist political elite ignores. According to an independent, nonpartisan 2010 Pew Research poll, for example, huge majorities of Americans favor better fuel efficiency standards for cars and trucks (79 percent), more funding for alternative energy (74 percent), more spending on mass transit (63 percent), and tax incentives for hybrid or electric vehicles (60 percent).

Similarly, for years, most Americans have supported, and still support, stronger, not weaker, environmental and energy policies. This is true even in times of recession, terrorism, and deep concern about budgets. From 1995 to 2008, when the independent multiyear Gallup poll question was last asked, through every variety of political environment, from good economies to bad, from terrorist attacks to war, the American people have been consistent in their response. More than twice as many Americans say we need "additional, immediate, and drastic action" to prevent major environmental disruption compared to those who say "we should just take the same actions we have been taking on the environment." The percentage of those identifying a need for "drastic, immediate action" was 35 percent in 1995, 38 percent in 2007, and 34 percent in 2008. When you add in those who say "we should take some additional action," the range of Americans who want better, stronger, tougher environmental protection stayed between 80 and 90 percent for more than a decade. The percentage of those who chose the status quo answer ("we should just take the same actions we have been taking on the environment") ranged from 13 to 20 percent. And even after years of corporate-funded confusion and denial about the environment, the vast majority of Americans still worried about the quality of the environment (69 percent) and global warming (58 percent) "a great deal" or "a fair amount"; only 16 percent believe that our government does "too much" to protect the environment.[50]

Polls are not infallible, but I suspect that these results would be duplicated in most family discussions around the dinner table. And I believe that we would see a similar disconnect between what people know about the state of our nation and the world and what the corporate-dominated government does. Whether the issue is the environment, the economy, the decades of wars in the Middle East, bloated military budgets, corporate agriculture subsidies and industrial food systems, or other corporate welfare, what most people think or want out of our government does not matter much anymore.

We have become accustomed to thinking that we cannot change, that our problems are too big, that our government cannot be effective. This was not always so, and it does not have to be so now. The choice we face in America now about whether to succeed or fail begins with our choice about whether we agree with Lewis Powell, the US Chamber of Commerce, and the corporate rights movement that massive, global corporate entities are the same as people.

Chapter Two
Corporations Are Not People—and They Make Lousy Parents

If the tobacco companies really stopped marketing to children, the tobacco companies would be out of business in 25 to 30 years because they will not have enough customers to stay in business.

—Bennett Lebow, cigarette corporation CEO[1]

"F#*k you." That (without the sanitizing symbols) is what Bad Frog Brewery, Inc., a corporation chartered under Michigan law, demanded the constitutional right to have on its labels. In the mid-1990s, the corporation wanted to market its beer with a foul-mouthed frog who, as the label said, "he just don't care." The corporation offered a mascot on the label, a large cartoon frog elevating its middle finger. Because New York law prohibits alcohol labels that are "obscene or indecent" and "obnoxious or offensive to the commonly and generally accepted standard," the state liquor authority refused to approve the label for sale in New York. The corporation balked at complying with the law and filed a lawsuit against the New York State Liquor Authority and the people who served on it.

At first, Bad Frog insisted that the up-yours gesture was a "symbol of peace, solidarity, and goodwill." After taking the case to the federal appeals court in New York, the corporation admitted that its beer label conveyed, "among other things, the message 'f#*! you.'" (The court decision helpfully explains that this was "presumably a suggestion of having intercourse with yourself.") Noting the "serious issues" in the case, the court ruled in Bad Frog's favor and voided the New York law, leaving the people powerless to stop corporations from spewing vulgarities from beer shelves across the land.[2]

OK, it's not the most serious case in the world. Maybe most people don't really care if lewd beer labels fill the shelves, although the people of New York cared enough to have a law preserving some decency in the beer aisle. Still, the case of the finger-waving frog reflects the hallmarks of the new corporate rights era: the shameless ("honest, the finger means peace, solidarity, and goodwill"), the irresponsible ("he just don't care," placed beside the health warning label), and the display of power over the people ("we will do whatever sells, and your law can't stop us"). These themes now run through far more serious areas of our national, community, and family life than beer labels.

Beyond Beer Labels

The fabrication of corporate constitutional rights has not only changed our politics and law; corporate rights and corporate power affect everything: the water we drink, the air we breathe, the food we eat, what our kids learn in school (and what they buy on the way home), what kind of health care we get, the wars we fight, and the taxes and debt generations to come will carry.

Do you want to know if your food is safe? Do you want to be able to choose milk, cheese, and yogurt from cows that are not injected with a genetically engineered drug that is banned in most of the world? Do you want to know if your water supply has been contaminated with diesel fuel, toxic chemicals, and radiation so that global energy corporations can "frack" natural gas? Do you want to stop toxic-pesticide manufacturers from claiming that their products are "safe for kids" in big letters on the label? Do you want the school to which you are required to send your kids to be inundated with youth-targeting advertisements? Do you want college education to be available without Wall Street corporations sucking billions of dollars of tax money into Ponzi-like for-profit student-debt schemes? In the new corporate rights era, the corporations say you can't.

The Right to Addict Kids

What should we do when a wealthy, suit-clad drug pusher sidles up to children and uses cartoon images and tricks to exploit teen insecurities and risk-taking to get kids hooked on a fatal drug? What kind of person would hang around a school yard trying to get teens and preteens hooked on an addictive drug known to kill hundreds of thousands of people a year? That's exactly what Philip Morris and the other cigarette corporations did for decades. When parents, lawmakers, prosecutors, and judges tried to stop them, the cigarette corporations self-righteously insisted on the corporate "free speech right" to say, well, to say what Bad Frog Brewery likes to say.

In the late 1990s, the people of Massachusetts tried to protect school kids from the cigarette companies' "youth-targeting" campaigns, banning cigarette ads within 1,000 feet of a school or playground. The US Supreme Court struck down the law in 2001, calling it a violation of the speech rights of the cigarette corporations. In many ways, this case shows how much our courts and our Constitution have shifted away from the people and to corporations in the years since the 1970s, before the Powell–Chamber of Commerce campaign began.

Back in 1971, Lewis Powell, as a private lawyer for the cigarette companies, argued that the corporations had a First Amendment right to spread corporate lies in response to what the corporations called propaganda about smoking and health. He and the cigarette industry were laughed out of court.[3] Back then (and in the two hundred years before that), the corporate legal foundations and the Supreme Court had not grafted the new concept of corporate speech into the Bill of Rights. Thirty years later, though, everything had changed. In 2001, the Supreme Court did exactly what the cigarette corporations asked, striking down the Massachusetts law that required cigarette advertisements to stay 1,000 feet away from schools and playgrounds.

Why Did We Need a School Playground Cigarette Law?

Inside the tobacco corporations, they referred to children as "replacement smokers." Corporate marketing plans and sales documents analyzed the need to replace smokers who died; children younger than eighteen years old were prime targets. The cigarette corporations had studies showing that if kids did not start smoking by the time they were eighteen, they probably never would become regular smokers. For decades, the cigarette corporations secretly researched nicotine, smoking, and the habits of teenagers. They spent millions of dollars on teenager tracking, marketing, and manipulation. Internally, the cigarette companies called addicting teens to cigarettes a "key corporate priority."[4]

For decades, cigarette corporations tried to dispute allegations like these. They can do so no more after the Court of Appeals affirmed the 1,000-plus-page decision of Judge Kessler, the federal judge who oversaw the 2006–2007 racketeering trial of the cigarette corporations. Judge Kessler concluded: "The evidence is clear and convincing—and beyond any reasonable doubt—that

Defendants have marketed to young people twenty-one and under while consistently, publicly, and falsely denying they do so."[5]

Judge Kessler's judicious reference to "young people under twenty-one" actually gives the cigarette corporations more credit than they deserve. Inside the companies, the term "younger adult" was a euphemism. Younger adult and YAS (meaning "younger adult smoker") are corporate-speak for child or teenager. Corporate marketing studies of YAS included children as young as ten years old, and the companies studied the percentage of "twelve- to seventeen-year-olds" who "smoked at least a pack a week." They called teens aged fifteen to nineteen the "new-smoker age group," and they noted with encouragement that "the thirteen-year-old age group 'shows the most dramatic increase in proportion of smokers.'"[6] The cigarette corporations knew that "YAS are the only source of replacement smokers—[fewer] than one-third of smokers start after age 18," and the companies spent hundreds of millions of dollars to increase sales to children between the ages of twelve and seventeen.[7]

According to Judge Kessler: "Defendants realize that they need to get people smoking their brands as young as possible in order to secure them as lifelong loyal smokers." She quoted dozens of internal corporate documents, including an "opportunity analysis" weighing how to exploit teen insecurities: "Socially insecure, they gain reinforcement by smoking the brands their friends are smoking, just like they copy their friends' dress, hairstyle, and other conspicuous things. To smoke a brand no one has heard of—which all new brand names are—brings one the risk of ostracism. It's simply not the 'in' thing to do."[8]

What makes people go to work each day, year after year, trying to figure out how to hook children on smoking? A cigarette executive provides the answer in a long-concealed internal document: the possibility of billions of dollars in corporate profit. "If we hold these YAS for the market average of 7 years," he wrote, "they would be worth over $2.1 billion in aggregate incremental profit. I certainly agree with you that this payout should be worth a decent sized investment."[9] By the 1990s, the "decent-sized investment" targeting kids for cigarette sales had succeeded in ensuring that 72 percent of six-year-olds recognized the cartoon symbol of Camel cigarettes.[10]

This is why several states, including Mississippi, Washington, and Massachusetts, began law-enforcement actions against the cigarette conspiracy. These cases began to uncover the truth about the conduct of the cigarette corporations, and by 1998, Massachusetts banned outdoor cigarette advertisements within 1,000 feet of a playground, elementary school, or secondary school.[11] Massachusetts attorney general Scott Harshbarger said the law was needed "to stop Big Tobacco from recruiting new customers among the children of Massachusetts."[12]

In response, the tobacco corporations did not apologize and change; they went on offense. They cried "Free speech!" and sued to block the law. They turned to the Powell-Chamber corporate rights theory that by 2000 had become a very potent tool for corporations to evade responsibility, accountability, and public oversight. The corporate legal foundations imagined by Lewis Powell and the Chamber of Commerce in the 1970s by now were fully funded and rushed into the fray. They filed briefs alongside the tobacco companies, demanding that the Supreme Court protect the "vital role in American society" of corporations. They quoted Henry David Thoreau and weirdly complained that during World War II, "Commercial speech became a casualty as surely as Veronica Lake's 'peekaboo' hairstyle."[13]

The corporate lawyers repeated the now familiar refrain that corporations are the same as people. They said that restricting the cigarette corporations' advertising around playgrounds and school yards violates corporate speech rights under the First Amendment.[14] The Supreme Court, by this time fully shaped by the legacy of Lewis Powell, agreed and struck down the Massachusetts law.[15] The law keeping Joe Camel and the cigarette ads away from schools and playgrounds was dead.

Now, a decade later, the cigarette corporations and those who lead them are unembarrassed by the federal verdict that they engaged in an illegal racketeering conspiracy. They are using *Citizens United* to go on offense. The usual corporate activists, including the Chamber of Commerce Litigation Center (which has described itself as Powell's "brainchild") has joined the cigarette industry in the courts to block implementation of the 2009 Family Smoking Prevention and Tobacco Control Act, which requires updated warning labels. In August 2012, the Court of Appeals in Washington struck down the new warning labels. Despite a strong dissent, the majority ruled that the required warning labels violated corporate First Amendment rights and a "broader concept of individual freedom of mind" for corporations and people alike.[16]

Cigarette Corporations Aren't People

Sometimes First Amendment cases frustrate Americans because the freedom at stake often is the freedom to say things that are unpopular, cause offense, challenge or undermine government policy supported by many, or inflict emotional pain. Infuriating though that can be, people usually appreciate that the Supreme Court's protection of someone's unpopular free speech also protects a core American value and benefits all of us. When the courts save the "right" of cigarette corporations to advertise around playgrounds and elementary schools, or to conceal product hazards, however, is a single human being made any more free? Is our public debate and state of knowledge any more expanded or enriched?

When the government suppresses the speech of real people, we all lose some of our freedom. Our ability to govern ourselves is compromised when ideas and information are restrained, even bad ideas and unpleasant information. When we regulate corporate economic conduct, though, what rights of anyone are lost? Is speech even at issue at all?

The Massachusetts law regulated corporate conduct, not speech. If the Massachusetts law curtails the youth-targeting strategies of cigarette corporations, sales might drop, but how does that create less freedom of speech for anyone? Any human being who had something to say about cigarettes and youth smoking remained free to say or write whatever that person wanted, wherever and whenever he or she wanted, about cigarettes, youth smoking, or anything else. The Massachusetts law about cigarette advertising had nothing to do with people or groups of people speaking, writing, or expressing their point of view in any way. Even if someone wanted to stand outside a public park or school with a sign saying, "I love cigarettes and kids should, too," the Massachusetts law did not touch them.

In the unlikely event that a real person actually did that, though, what would happen? Perhaps we would see how free speech is supposed to work in America: other people would talk with the miscreant and ask him or her to consider whether that was a decent thing to do. The creep might respond, and debate would ensue. At some point, the cigarette enthusiast or his or her opponents would get tired and move along. If the smoking advocate really had strong views about the merits of smoking, the debate might continue the next day when the person came back again or in writing, interviews, meetings, or wherever people wanted to talk, listen, and debate. The Massachusetts law prevented none of that.

Try talking or debating with Joe Camel; it doesn't work. It doesn't work because Joe Camel and the corporation that spawned him are not people. Corporations never get tired, and they never move along until the money stops or the law steps in. People speak. Corporations do not speak. With the Court's new corporate speech theory, corporations won a dangerous immunity from the will of the people, while real people and American freedom gained nothing. Indeed, we lost freedom and a tool of self-government.

Monsanto: Secret Genetically Modified Food

In 2013, people in the state of Washington brought a citizens' initiative to the ballot to enforce their right to know if their food contained genetically modified organisms, known as GMOs. As with 93 percent of Americans, they thought food containing GMOs ought to be labeled so that people can make their own choices.[17] With 93 percent favorability, victory might seem assured. Not after *Citizens United*.

The year before the Washington initiative, Monsanto, DuPont, PepsiCo, Nestle, and a few other corporations had spent $46 million to defeat citizen initiative for GMO labeling in California. The millions of corporate dollars saturated the state with a false and misleading portrayal of the initiative as a "deceptive scheme" and "a blank check paid by the taxpayers" that would "increase food costs by billions."[18]

In 2013, the chemical and GMO industry used the same playbook in the Washington State initiative, spending more than $20 million. Led by Monsanto, five international corporations alone contributed $14 million of the total.[19] The GMO labeling proposal failed by a narrow margin. Of the $20 million funding that defeat, only $600 came from individuals or businesses in the state.

People are not giving up on the right to know what is in our food and to preserve the right to choose what kind of farming and economy we wish to support. When a citizen initiative to label GMO food eventually prevails though, litigation about corporate rights to strike down the law is sure to follow. After all, that's exactly what happened to farmers and other people in Vermont.

When the people in Massachusetts were battling for the right to stop cigarette corporations from targeting children, people in Vermont were in a fight of their own. As in Massachusetts, the people of Vermont were about to learn that the rules had changed and winning the debate and overcoming corporate lobbyists in the legislative process is not enough anymore.

Monsanto is a transnational chemical, biotech, and industrial corporation with more than $14 billion in annual global sales. Monsanto's products have included DDT, saccharine, aspartame, sulfuric acid, Agent Orange, and various plastics and chemical products. Now Monsanto focuses on genetically engineered agriculture and an array of pesticides and herbicides. In response to questions about safety, Monsanto's spokesperson says, "Monsanto should not have to vouchsafe the safety of biotech food. Our interest is in selling as much of it as possible. Assuring its safety is the FDA's job."[20]

In the 1990s, Monsanto started selling a genetically engineered drug to be injected into the blood of dairy cows to force them to produce more milk. The drug was rBST (also called rBGH by some and labeled Posilac by Monsanto). Monsanto had used recombinant (meaning artificially created) DNA to fabricate rBST. BST stands for bovine somatotrophin, a naturally occurring hormone in cows, and BGH refers to "bovine growth hormone." The r in rBST and rBGH stands for "recombinant DNA" and refers to the Monsanto drug, which is not natural.

Because of safety and other concerns, most free, democratic countries in the world banned the use of rBST in any dairy product intended for human consumption. Canada prohibited the drug after "more than nine years of comprehensive review of the effects of rBST on animal and human safety, and consideration of the recent findings by two independent external committees."[21] All twenty-seven countries of the European Union, as well as New Zealand and Australia, banned rBST. In the United States, Monsanto got its way. The Food and Drug Administration (FDA) quickly approved the use of rBST in 1993, brushing aside the views of farmers, mothers and fathers, scientists, and other people who had opposed approval.

Dexter Randall, a sixty-five-year-old dairy farmer who has lived and worked in Vermont all his life, had joined others in trying to stop the FDA from approving Monsanto's drug. They presented studies showing elevated antibiotic residues in milk (increased antibiotics were needed because rBST increased disease in cows). They pointed to other studies showing higher levels in rBST milk of an insulin-like growth factor linked to breast cancer in humans, as well as other dangers. They cited the absurdity of forcing cows to produce more milk, driving milk prices lower, at a time when family dairy farms all over the country were failing and taxpayers were paying millions of dollars to keep milk prices high enough to prevent a collapse of farm communities.

"Organic dairy farmers were already not getting paid enough for their milk, and when rBGH went on the market they suffered even more," says Randall. "But in addition to these economic concerns there were the health impacts of the product—the possible harm it could cause to livestock and humans. No long-term studies had been done. None of the truth was brought out. Our government let corporations override everything that made sense to the people."[22]

The Vermont farmer says, "Zillions of studies were presented to the FDA, but anything they saw they just turned the other way." The FDA claimed that it lacked the authority to consider "social" or "economic" factors or to require a label on rBST dairy products. The FDA also reported that "a State that has its own statute requiring food labeling based on a consumer's right-to-know would not be preempted by FDA from requiring rBST labeling."[23]

Randall and many other people in Vermont went to work to ensure that Vermont law would protect the people's right to know. "We lobbied our state senators and representatives, sent letters to the editor, talked all over the place, made people aware of the problem," Randall says. "We basically held a protest in front of the statehouse, just to get our legislators and the public to take notice. We tried talking to our commissioner of agriculture and to other officials there."

Monsanto pushed back, and progress was slow. Randall says, "There was always money overriding us—the industry rules. The Grocers' Association was screaming bloody murder, having to put labels on their products. Is it such a crime? People were still going to buy their products, but now they had a choice. I've always been a person for choice—you need to choose what size pants you're going to buy, don't you?"

Finally, after organizing, researching, testifying at hearings, and letter writing, the people persuaded the Vermont legislature to pass, and the governor to sign, a law to protect the right to know about our food. The Vermont law said, "If rBST has been used in the production of milk or a milk product for retail sale in this state, the retail milk or milk product shall be labeled as such."[24]

In deciding how to implement the law in a balanced way, the Vermont Department of Agriculture held four hearings around the state, including one with interactive television. Ninety-nine speakers took the time from work and home to participate in the hearings, and 152 written comments were filed.[25] Monsanto and the industrial dairy and grocery groups certainly weighed in, but according to the commissioner of agriculture in Vermont, "Most individuals expressed that they felt they had a right to know what they wanted to purchase for themselves and their families."[26]

Monsanto and the industrial dairy corporations lost the public debate, lost the debate in the legislature, and failed to persuade the commissioner of agriculture to keep people in the dark about rBST. They were not done, though. Monsanto had Covington & Burling, a corporate law firm in Washington, D.C., to lead the attack.

For years, Covington & Burling had serviced the drive to shelter corporations from public oversight by creating new theories of "corporate speech." According to Judge Kessler in the federal racketeering trial of the cigarette corporations, Covington & Burling took a leading role among corporate lawyers in furthering the illegal cigarette industry scheme: "Two of those law firms," she said, "in particular Covington & Burling, became the guiding strategists for the Enterprise and were deeply involved in implementation of those strategies once adopted." She added, "What a sad and disquieting chapter in the history of an honorable and often courageous profession."[27]

In Vermont, Covington & Burling represented the interests of Monsanto and the industrial dairy lobby in trying to stifle knowledge and disclosure about milk products derived from rBST-treated cows. They claimed that corporate speech rights entitled the industry to disregard the new right-to-know law. They insisted that Monsanto and the industry could refuse to disclose when milk and dairy products came from cows treated with Monsanto's genetically engineered rBST.

The industry claimed that giving information to people would only cause "fear and uncertainty."[28] Employing odd euphemisms, the corporate lawyers called cows injected with the Monsanto drug "supplemented cows," while natural cows became "unsupplemented cows." Covington & Burling explained why "fear and uncertainty" would result from the truth: "Mandatory labeling of milk products derived from supplemented cows will have the inherent effect of causing consumers to believe that such products are different from and inferior to milk products from unsupplemented cows."

What about farmers or dairies that did not want to use the Monsanto drug; they should be free to tell people about the natural way they make their milk, right? Oh, no, said the corporate lawyers: "The industry's experience in recent months demonstrates that voluntary 'rBST-free' type labeling of milk and milk products has a high potential for misleading consumers and for sowing the seeds of uncertainty, distrust, and fear about the quality and safety of milk and milk products." According to Monsanto, it is your right to know about your food—not Monsanto and its drug that is banned in most of the world—that sows the "seeds of uncertainty, distrust, and fear."

Monsanto not only threatened to sue Vermont but also began to intimidate and silence farmers, dairies, and stores that tried to sell "rBST-free" milk.[29] Monsanto even filed a federal lawsuit against a Maine dairy to force it to stop stating on its labels, "Our Farmers Pledge: No Artificial Growth Hormones."[30]

Nevertheless, people such as Dexter Randall stood up to the intimidation, and Vermont went ahead with its right-to-know law. Covington & Burling and the industry then followed through on the threat to sue. Now that Vermont law supported the people's right to know about rBST, the cry of "Free corporate speech!" became the cry of "Corporations are like people and have the right not to speak!" Covington & Burling argued that the "public right to know" must fall to "a manufacturer's right to decide when to speak and when to remain silent." According to Covington & Burling's legal brief, "Corporations have the same rights to remain silent as individuals."[31]

At first, Vermont had some success in the case. The chief judge of the federal court in Vermont concluded that corporate rights do not overpower the people's right to know:

Apparently, a majority of Vermonters do not want to purchase milk products derived from rBST-treated cows. Their reasons for not wanting to purchase such products include: (1) They consider the use of a genetically-engineered hormone in the production unnatural; (2) they believe that use of the hormone will result in increased milk production and lower milk prices, thereby hurting small dairy farmers; (3) they believe that use of rBST is harmful to cows and potentially harmful to humans; and, (4) they feel that there is a lack of knowledge regarding the long-term effects of rBST.[32]

The industry appealed to the same federal Court of Appeals that had decided the Bad Frog beer label case. Once again the court sided with corporations, striking down the Vermont law. The appellate court decreed that the lower court judge had "abused his discretion" by failing to agree with the corporations that the law violated corporate speech rights. According to the Court of Appeals, the people of Vermont had caused a "wrong" to the industrial dairy manufacturers' "constitutional right not to speak."[33]

That was the end of the line for the Vermont law and for disclosure laws around the country. "It was a long, hard battle getting the legislation passed, and it wasn't in place for any length," says dairy farmer Dexter Randall. "We saw the end coming before it happened. I learned a lot about the power of corporations—about Monsanto's power."[34]

Corporate Rights Weaken People and Citizenship

Look again at how the Court of Appeals labeled what dairy farmer Dexter Randall and so many other Vermont people had done by deciding to participate in our government of the people. According to the court, by passing a right-to-know law, the people of Vermont committed a "wrong" to the constitutional rights of others, specifically, to the industry's "constitutional right not to speak."

This is how the fabrication of corporate rights hollows out American citizenship. A successful demand by a person or class of people for rights amounts to a declaration that such a person or class is equal to everyone else and has an equal share of sovereignty in our nation. Government then is accountable to that person, rather than the other way around. When we accept that people have constitutional rights, we quite properly have disdain for those who deprive our fellow people of rights, and we will resist. At a minimum, we are careful, or should be, not to press for government action that might hinder rights of others. After all, in a society of people with equal rights, when the government violates the rights of any of us, none of us is secure.

When courts strike down laws where they conflict with constitutional rights, they make a statement about who we are as a people and as a country. As we come to accept these judgments of the courts (or when we do not), our culture and politics, and even our way thinking and acting, can change. *Brown v. Board of Education* ruled that segregation violates the equality rights of African Americans; that helped transform who we are and how we act. *Reed v. Reed* ruled for the first time in 1971 that laws that discriminate against women are wrong; that contributed to a transformation of how we view gender in America. More recently, we are seeing the role of the courts in shaping how Americans perceive the freedom of all people to marry the person they love. Court cases about rights may reflect and accelerate, rather than cause, movements and change. Yet when the courts rule, an insistent proposition about American life begins to become a fact.

The same phenomenon tends to occur when courts declare that corporations hold the constitutional rights of people, as Dexter Randall found out. Lewis Powell's advice to the US Chamber of Commerce in 1971 sought not merely to propose policies but to change American society. As Powell made clear, the creation of corporate rights is an "instrument for social, economic, and political change."[35]

These corporate rights cases, then, mean much more than allowing the Bad Frog Corporation to say whatever it wants on its beer labels, or the cigarette corporations to target children for addiction to a fatal product, or Monsanto to deprive people of information about food. All of that would be bad enough. The impact of these cases goes beyond their specific facts; they push people back from exercising vigilance about corporate power and from acting as citizens in a republic. Even mild proposals that might serve the public good, from environmental stewardship to disclosure and transparency in the financial system, now get buried under savage attacks from corporate interests. Those who might serve as potential public champions are accused not merely of being "wrong" but of violating constitutional principles. Public champions retreat into defensiveness and uncertainty. As with other major developments of previously unrecognized constitutional rights, the fabrication of corporate rights is changing American culture.

The new metaphor of corporations as people in our Bill of Rights threatens to erode, perhaps we can say "corporatize," the American character. We can see this in many areas of American life, from the state of our media to declining civic participation and voting. What we thought of as public for generations, from the sublime, such as mountains or groundwater, to the utilitarian, such as prisons, is shifting away from us, and over to corporate control. Corporate power is shifting the law, our public assets, even how we think about ourselves and what we teach our children.

Learning to Be Corporate

Education in America is linked to our egalitarian vision of a free, democratic people who govern a republic. Thomas Jefferson wrote, "Of all the views of this law [for public education], none is more important, none more legitimate, than that of rendering the people safe as they are the ultimate guardians of their own liberty."[36] The Supreme Court relied on Jefferson's view of public education "as a bulwark of a free people against tyranny" to hold that "providing public schools ranks at the very apex of the function of a State."[37]

Now schools and children have joined the Constitution, legislatures, and courts as subjects for increasingly aggressive assertions of corporate influence. The critical civic function of our schools—teaching equality, citizenship, as well as the critical thinking and competence needed to participate in a vibrant, free society—is deteriorating to make room for corporate access to children's minds and wallets. More corporations seek to turn schools into marketing outlets; more corporations seek to teach children, regardless of the wishes of parents, to be consumers rather than citizens; and more corporations seek to make the curriculum itself reflect the corporations' position on public issues. As corporations increasingly "embed" in education, will the next generation recognize when the promise of American self-government has evaporated, let alone summon the will to restore it?

Joe Camel was not lurking alone outside the playground and school gates. Compared to some other corporate child-targeting efforts, Joe Camel was downright shy by waiting outside the gate. Ronald McDonald walked right inside. The McDonald's Corporation is a Fortune 150 global corporation in 117 countries, with $27.5 billion in revenue in 2012. The corporation sends employees or contractors dressed up as clowns with enormous shoes, bright clothes, and glistening red grins into schools to talk to children about "character education" and "fitness."[38] In 2008, some schools in Florida began "branding" report cards with the McDonald's logo and the clown-costumed pitchman promising a free Happy Meal to reward student performance.[39]

Eight thousand middle and high schools in the country have contracted with the Channel One Corporation. Channel One beams into classrooms ten minutes of video news and two minutes of mandatory advertisements, which children are compelled to watch. Channel One contracts require that the advertising content "must be shown when students are present in a homeroom or classroom (i.e., not before school, after school, or during lunch)" on at least 90 percent of the days in which school is in session.[40]

Most schools, to which we are required by law to deliver our children each day, now serve as corporate marketing outlets. In 1983, corporations spent $100 million per year on child-targeted marketing; they now spend $17 billion per year.[41] Virtually every school in the land now carries corporate advertising.[42] School districts such as Los Angeles negotiate corporate naming rights, logo placements, and "school visits" during which corporate representatives can pass out samples to the children. One Los Angeles school board member reluctantly voted for the corporate plan in 2010, but he knew that "the implications of doing this are really disconcerting and really bother me to the core."[43]

Corporations now spend billions of dollars on "embedding" advertising into the schools, including into the curriculum. They do so because "students are generally unable to avoid these activities; moreover, they tend to assume that what their teachers and schools present to them is in their best interest." According to the National Education Policy Center, "Advertising makes children want more, eat more, and think that their self-worth can and should come from commercial products. It heightens their insecurities, distorts their gender socialization, and displaces the development of values and activities other than those associated with commercialism."[44]

In school and out of school, corporations now spend billions of dollars to make kids fat and unhealthy. The food and beverage industry spends more than $12 billion per year to market to children, and the vast majority of advertisements on television shows watched by children are for snacks, fast food, and candy.[45] "Nearly 20 percent of caloric intake among 12-to-18-year-olds comes from fast food, compared with 6.5 percent in the late 1970s."[46] Since 1980, as those billions of dollars in youth targeting were spent, the number of overweight children and adolescents has soared.[47] In 2005, Congress requested that the Federal Trade Commission (FTC) conduct a study of food and beverage marketing to children and adolescents. The FTC found that forty-four companies alone spent $1.6 billion in a single year to advertise fast food, soda, snacks, and other food and beverages to children as young as two years old.[48]

The FTC mission is to ensure that people are not hurt by unfair business practices; so why doesn't the FTC do something to stop the unfair practice of exploiting children and undermining parents? Because Congress passed a law in 1980 saying that the FTC is *not allowed* to do something. The law says, "The Commission shall not have any authority to promulgate any rule in the children's advertising . . . on the basis of a determination by the

Commission that such advertising constitutes an unfair act or practice in or affecting commerce."[49]

Increasingly, corporations influence and embed marketing into the actual curriculum itself. BP and other corporations participated in the writing of California's environmental curriculum.[50] Materials provided to schools by Chevron suggest that global warming may not exist, while the American Coal Foundation class materials state that increased carbon dioxide levels in the earth's atmosphere could be beneficial.[51] The American Petroleum Institute (API), with 400 corporate members, offers "lesson plans" for kindergarten through twelfth grade, including "Progress through Petroleum."[52]

Kindergartners and elementary school kids will learn that "most of our energy needs are being met by nonrenewable energy sources—oil, natural gas, coal, and uranium (nuclear). This is because these energy sources are more reliable, affordable, and convenient to use than most renewable energy resources." The API lesson plan does not mention climate change, oil spills, toxic wastes, or any air, land, or water pollution issues. The lesson plan offers an "Environmental Progress Report" that promotes the industry's investment in "improving the environmental performance of its products, facilities, and operations—$11.3 billion in 2006 alone." What about offshore drilling and the environment? Didn't BP's Deepwater Horizon oil disaster in April 2010 nearly destroy the Gulf of Mexico? The API lesson plan instead teaches kids something a little different about offshore drilling and the environment: "Floating platforms, anchored to the ocean floor, allow energy companies to recover oil and natural gas reserves located under deeper parts of the ocean—and have proved to be valuable habitats for marine life."[53]

The Council for Corporate-School Partnerships says nothing is wrong with corporations embedding into children's education.

Then again, the council was founded and funded by the Coca-Cola Company, a corporation under Delaware law that operates in 200 countries with more than $35 billion in annual revenue. One need not be too cynical to think that the council's opinion might not be a good-faith assessment made with due regard for the American interest.[54]

On to College: The Subprime Student Loan Game

In the age of corporate bailouts, the Wall Street financial system privatizes huge profits and socializes big risks. That model of enriching a very few at the expense of the many has created a new "industry" of for-profit colleges. For-profit corporations now own more than 2,000 colleges or universities. The number of students enrolled in for-profit colleges has increased 500 percent in the past several years, to 1.8 million.[55] According to a 2012 Senate investigative committee report, "Virtually all of the revenues of for-profit colleges come directly from taxpayers."[56] In effect, operation of corporate universities transfers billions of dollars in federal student loans and government guarantees from American taxpayers to corporate executives and shareholders.[57]

Most of these students (1.4 million) attend for-profit colleges that are owned and controlled by fourteen corporations. Wall Street values the publicly traded corporations at $26 billion, due to huge revenue flows based on high tuition, minimal standards, and government backing for tuition payment. In 2009 alone, American taxpayers provided these corporations and others that operate for-profit colleges with more than $4 billion in Pell Grants and $20 billion in guaranteed student loans.[58]

Among for-profit schools examined by a Senate investigation, "over 87 percent of total revenues came directly from the federal government, but 57 percent of the students who enrolled between 2008–2009 have departed without a diploma but with a high probability of debt."[59] The sixteen largest for-profit schools had profits of $2.7 billion in 2009, with some corporations doubling profits between 2009 and 2010 alone.[60] In 2011, when the Department of Education proposed to apply minimal performance standards (based on actual student graduation rates) to corporations that take billions of taxpayer dollars, the corporations threatened a lawsuit challenging the constitutionality of such action.

A recent US Senate committee investigation focused on one school owned and operated by Bridgepoint Education, Inc., a Delaware corporation traded on the New York Stock Exchange. In 2005, Bridgepoint Education used financial backing from a global private equity firm to acquire a religious college in Clinton, Iowa. Bridgepoint bought the school, Franciscan University (originally Mount St. Clare College), from the Sisters of Saint Francis. At the time, the Bridgepoint CEO announced, "Bridgepoint Education and the Sisters of Saint Francis have much in common. We believe in quality academic training and in service to others."[61]

The new corporate owner then changed the name to Ashford University. Before the corporate acquisition, Franciscan University was spending $5,000 per student on instruction. After the buyout by Bridgepoint, Ashford University spent $700 per student on instruction. The savings were not passed on to students, who now are charged as much as $46,000 in tuition and fees. Most of the tuition payment actually comes from taxpayer-funded federal programs. In the 2009–2010 school year, Bridgepoint's Ashford University received $613 million in federal student aid funds. Most of the revenue (86 percent) at the university comes directly from the US government—in other words, from all of us. With all that revenue, how did instruction spending per student fall from $5,000 before corporatizing the school to $700 after?

From 300 students at Franciscan University in 2005, enrollment (including online students) at the newly corporatized

Ashford University zoomed to nearly 78,000 by 2010. Bridge-point Education spends $2,700 per student to recruit new students (who need new federal loans). Bridgepoint directed $1,500 per student to corporate profit. Most of the students who enroll quickly drop out. Fully 84 percent of students who enroll in an associate degree program at Ashford University are gone by the following year, and 63 percent of students in the bachelor's degree program do not return the next year. Bridgepoint employs more than 1,700 people to recruit new students; it employs one person to help students with job placement.[62]

Bridgepoint paid its CEO, Andrew Clark, $20.5 million in 2009, and another $11.5 million to four other top executives. The CEO refused an invitation to testify at the Senate hearing.

Corporate university companies are unapologetic about the betrayal of students and virtual theft of tax money. When the Government Accountability Office (GAO) simply reported facts about the for-profit corporate education industry, its corporate lobby group sued the GAO for "negligence" and "malpractice." They claim that the report is "biased" and "erroneous." When the government proposed reform that would require some actual education performance before the taxpayers sent billions of dollars to Wall Street investors and CEOs, the industry sued to block the Department of Education reform. The corporate school lobby argues that the rules are unconstitutional because they are "vague."[63]

No one can doubt that education is challenging and no model is perfect. Why, though, would corporations rush into a Wall Street model of university education that so clearly fails far too many students and costs American taxpayers far too much money? Why would corporations in this business pay their CEOs $20 million for such awful performance? Why does our government not stop this?

The answer to all three questions lies in the massive profit that a corporation can reap from recruiting thousands of unwary students, taking the proceeds of government-backed student loans, and shaving costs from the educational program. In Wall Street parlance, that was the "play," the opportunity. A CEO who executes the play and delivers that massive corporate profit has accomplished what the corporation was designed to do. From a corporate perspective, the CEO's performance was not awful, even if debt-burdened students drop out by the thousands and the transfer of government money to Wall Street and executives runs into the billions of dollars.

As currently operated, large public corporations (meaning those with shares that are actively traded on the stock exchanges) seek profit above all. Yes, socially responsible investing, responsible corporate conduct, and many efforts to "hardwire" corporations with ethical behavior matter a great deal. Nevertheless, the "market judgment" of global corporations measures profit into the share price and little else. And at least so far, we have not required a "character test" or imposed other responsibility requirements for corporate conduct.

Can we design a different corporation, an entity that engages in economic activity with more responsibility and ethical conduct? Can we conceive of corporations as holding public duties rather than constitutional rights? Or are we destined to become a corporate nation of underpaid hucksters in clown suits, trying to juice corporate profit and executive compensation by pushing school kids around?

I don't think Americans will accept the latter path for long. When we begin to insist that corporate money is not "speech" and that corporations are not people, we begin to take back power. Addressing the complex problem of corporate power requires, of course, more than recognition that corporations are not people.

We also need a shared understanding of what corporations are and what they should and should not be doing in our national life.

This is the topic for the next chapter. A corporation is not a person, nor is it simply an association or group of people. A corporation is a creation of law, a public tool of economic policy. If we appreciate this point, corporate "rights" are exposed as unconstitutional folly. Moreover, we can decide to create better corporations. We can require that corporations be much more effective, useful, and supportive instruments for the American people and our economy.

Chapter Three
If Corporations Are Not People, What Are They?

Metaphor . . . is the peculiarity of a language, the object of which is to tell everything and conceal everything, to abound in figures. Metaphor is an enigma which offers itself as a refuge to a robber who plots a blow, to a prisoner who plans an escape.

—Victor Hugo, *Les Miserables*[1]

I am compelled to say something about corporate "personhood." . . . Human beings are persons, and it is an affront to the inviolable dignity of our species that courts have created a legal fiction which forces people— human beings—to share fundamental, natural rights with soulless creations of government.

—Justice James Nelson,
Montana Supreme Court, December 30, 2011[2]

What is a corporation? One might expect to find a good description of a corporation in *Citizens United* or the other corporate rights cases, but the Supreme Court is strangely silent on that point. Instead, corporate rights decisions from the Court come packaged in metaphorical clouds. It is not corporations attacking our laws; it is "speakers" and "advocates of ideas," "voices" and "persons," and variations on what Justice John Paul Stevens called in his *Citizens United* dissent, "glittering generalities."

Corporations are economic tools created by state law; corporate shares are property. Yet the majority decision in *Citizens United* did not explain even the most basic features of a corporation, an entity created and defined by state laws. The Court did not examine why, for more than a century, Congress and dozens of state legislatures thought it made sense to distinguish between corporations and human beings when making election rules. One reading the *Citizens United* decision might forget that the case concerned a corporate regulation at all; the Court described the timid corporate spending rule it struck down as a "ban on speech," government "silencing" of some "voices," some "speakers," and some "disadvantaged classes of persons."[3]

Metaphor Marches On

The use of the "speaker" and "speech" metaphor in *Citizens United* follows the playbook dating back to the corporate rights pioneer, Justice Lewis Powell. In 1978, Powell wrote the *First National Bank of Boston* decision that created the new corporate rights theory to strike down a Massachusetts law banning corporate spending in citizen referenda. He sidestepped the question of what a corporation is, saying, "If the speakers here were not corporations, no one would suggest that the State could silence their proposed speech."[4] The people of Massachusetts, however, did suggest exactly that because corporations are not "speakers." And the corporations did not propose "speech." Rather, the corporations proposed to spend corporate money to influence a citizen referendum vote. A law prohibiting this did not "silence" anyone; it defined a prohibited activity of corporate entities in elections.

In a 1980 corporate rights case, Justice Powell described the Consolidated Edison Corporation as "a single speaker." The Court struck down a New York law regulating this corporate monopoly because, according to Powell, the law "restricts the speech of a private person."[5] Later that year, Justice Powell wrote the *Central Hudson* decision creating a "right" of utility corporations to promote energy consumption in defiance of a government policy of conservation. Justice Powell identified "the critical inquiry in this case" as whether or not the First Amendment allowed the state's "complete suppression of speech."[6] (Who's for the complete suppression of speech? If that is really the question, the answer is pretty easy: the Court struck down the law.) In a 1986 decision using the corporate speech theory to strike down regulation of utility corporations, Justice Powell identified the corporation as a "speaker," with an "identity" seeking to make "speech."

Justice Powell's successors on the Court have followed this pattern of euphemism and distortion. In the 2001 *Lorillard v. Reilly* case about cigarette advertising directed to school children, Justice Clarence Thomas explained that corporations selling cigarettes and targeting children are no different from "advocates of harmful ideas. When the State seeks to silence them, they are all entitled to the protection of the First Amendment."[7]

Justice Thomas wrote the Court's 1995 decision in *Rubin v. Coors Brewing Company*, which ruled that Coors has a First Amendment right to ignore a federal law banning the display of alcohol levels on beer labels. Coors, now part of Molson Coors, is an international conglomerate of corporations with billions of dollars in sales around the globe. At the time of the 1995 corporate speech case, Coors Brewing Company was, among other things, a Colorado corporation; a subsidiary corporation of a larger corporation listed on the New York Stock exchange; one of a web of corporations with international operations, including alcohol products in Spain and Korea, and a joint venture among corporations for an aluminum processing operation; it had sales of nearly $2 billion and had its corporate name on the largest sports stadium in Colorado.[8]

Writing the 1995 decision in *Coors Brewing Company*, Justice Thomas set out to describe exactly who or what it was that came before the Court claiming a free speech right to strike down a law passed by Congress and on the books for more than fifty years. Here is Justice Thomas's complete description: "Respondent brews beer."[9]

It is true enough, I suppose, that Coors "brews beer," but that is hardly the only relevant fact about a corporate entity created by the law of Colorado that demands that the Court invalidate a federal law. Why is the fact that Coors is a corporation relevant? Before the justices or the rest of us reach any conclusion about that question, it would seem useful first to define *corporation*. A definition would certainly seem in order before we attribute to the entity any capacity for "speech," participation in elections, and the constitutional rights with which humans are born.

What Is a Corporation?

A corporation is a government-defined legal structure for doing business, with "legal privileges that can only be provided by government."[10] Corporations are defined by state legislatures to advance what the state deems to be in the public interest. Corporate entities are government policy tools; only government makes incorporation possible.[11] Unlike other associations or ways of doing business, a corporation cannot exist by private arrangement.[12]

Many good reasons support state laws that permit ready incorporation of enterprises. The corporate legal entity is supremely effective at bringing together and channeling ideas, capital, and labor to make a productive, growing enterprise. The corporate form streamlines the making and enforcement of contracts; it encourages, secures, and rewards investment; it enables risk-taking as well as sustained operations, expansion, and innovation over long periods of time; and it can efficiently spread risk (and reward) over many diverse shareholders. All this and more makes incorporation a very useful tool to encourage and reward investment, innovation, job creation, and economic growth. That's why my business, the publisher of this book, and many thousands of other businesses take advantage of the privilege of incorporation.

Because the corporate entity is so useful and so prevalent, we can forget that it is a legal tool created by government to advance government policy. People can start and run businesses without government permission or a government form of organization. People can form advocacy groups, associations, unions, political parties, clubs, religious organizations, and other institutions without incorporating and without the government's permission or involvement. People, or even "associations of people," however, cannot form or operate a corporation unless the state enacts a law authorizing the formation of a corporation and providing rules for operations as a corporation.

Most modern incorporation laws provide attributes of a corporation such as limited liability, perpetual life, and legal identification as a unitary actor. These attributes encourage simplicity and efficiency for a corporation to own property, make and enforce contracts, sue and defend lawsuits in court, and so on. State law, not the Constitution, provides these attributes. That law offers, but does not require, a useful vehicle for the individuals involved in doing business. No one is required to use the corporate form, with its relative benefits and burdens, but if people decide to do so, the privilege of incorporation is a package deal. We cannot decide to comply with some of the law to get the benefits and defy the parts of the corporate laws we find inconvenient.

Some people mistakenly call corporations mere "associations of people" or a "product of private contract."[13] This is incorrect. Corporations are not private matters, and they are not mere "associations of citizens."[14] Corporations exist only because states enact laws defining exactly what a corporation is, what it can do, and what it cannot do. In virtually every state, it is illegal for people to do business as a corporation unless the corporation is incorporated or registered under the laws of that state.[15]

Most transnational corporations are incorporated under the law of Delaware. Three hundred of the mega-corporations listed on the Fortune 500 list are incorporated under Delaware law, as are more than half of all publicly traded companies in the United States.[16] The reason for this is a matter of some debate. Some say that giant global conglomerate corporations such as BP, Dow Chemical, and Goldman Sachs incorporate under the law of Delaware, where the corporations do little business, to ensure low corporate standards that benefit the few at the expense of the many.[17] Others defend the dominance of Delaware, arguing that by now the state has a detailed body of corporate law.[18] Either way, as with the corporate law of every state, none of the features of the Delaware corporation law are "required." Rather, they are policy choices made by elected legislatures.

Take shareholder limited liability, for example. The concept of limited liability for corporate shareholders means that if you invest in a company, you might lose your investment if things go badly, but you will not be responsible for paying all of the debts of the corporation or for compensating victims of any misconduct or neglect by the corporation. Imagine that you owned some shares in the BP corporation in April 2010 when the Deepwater Horizon oil well exploded in the Gulf of Mexico. If the corporation cut corners on safety, resulting in the death of eleven people and a catastrophe that ruins a vast ecosystem and fishery that had sustained millions of people for eons, are you as a shareholder to blame? If BP is liable for this death and destruction but the corporation runs out of money to pay its debts, why are the shareholders who own the company and who profited in the safety-cutting years not forced to sell their personal property, their houses, their cars, and their kids' college savings accounts to pay BP's bills? After all, the shareholders own and are presumed to control the corporation that caused so much damage in the pursuit of their profit. Why are the shareholders not held to account?

The rule of limited liability, that's why. Limited liability of corporate shareholders did not come down from on high. Only because people in the state of incorporation (in BP's case, Delaware) decided to include limited liability in their corporate laws, the shareholders are not responsible for the debts of the corporation. Here's how the elected state representatives in Delaware put limited liability into the law, which they call the Delaware Corporations Code: "The stockholders of a corporation shall not be personally liable for the payment of the corporation's debts except as they may be liable by reason of their own conduct or acts."[19]

As with many other features of incorporation law, I think limited liability probably is good policy because it encourages efficient, effective capital investment in economic activity that benefits all of us. Others disagree and make strong arguments that limited liability encourages excessive risk, "externalizes" losses and damage of all kinds onto society, and directs profits only to a few individuals.[20] Whether limited liability is good policy or bad policy, though, it is public policy that we decide on. It is not a private arrangement among people involved in the corporation.

The same is true of the other basic features of a corporation. How is it possible that the GE corporation keeps going on, decade after decade, long after every shareholder, director, executive, and other human being involved in forming and building GE has long since died? How does something called the GE corporation sign contracts, go into court, or prove to a creditor or a bank that it exists as an entity that will pay its bills, no matter how the people involved in the corporation may come and go? GE and other corporations can do that because we, the people in our states elect representatives in government who decide to make corporate "perpetual life" possible. Again, we very well could decide otherwise if we chose to do so.

Look at Delaware law again, by way of example. Corporations organized under Delaware law have "perpetual existence" because the Delaware legislature said so. Here's how the legislature of Delaware wrote the law: "A provision [may limit] the duration of the corporation's existence to a specified date; otherwise, the corporation shall have perpetual existence."[21] Notice that the Delaware law does say that "the duration of the corporation's existence" can be limited "to a specified date." This used to be the norm with corporate law. Years ago, traditional American distrust of concentrated power and caution about corporate dominance of government led most state laws to limit the life span of corporations. The period in which a corporation could exist was usually limited to a defined term of years, often twenty years.[22] Is it not strange that a thing that exists only by the policy of the state, a thing as to which the state can decide "the duration of the corporation's existence," can successfully take control of the people's Bill of Rights to strike down federal, state, and local laws?

Delaware Cannot Rewrite the Constitution

This brings us to the notion that some call "corporate personhood," the idea that under the law, corporations are treated as "persons." As with perpetual existence, limited liability, and other features of corporations, the source of this concept of a "corporate person" is not particularly complicated. We came up with it, or rather, our state and federal legislatures did, because treating the corporation as a legal "person" makes sense for certain purposes. That policy choice, though, is our choice and has nothing to do with the Constitution or corporate "rights."[23]

There are lots of good reasons why states and the federal government enact laws that say, in some instances, that the word *person* includes corporations. For example, the Clean Water Act prohibits unpermitted discharge of toxics and pollutants into the waters of the United States by any person. Congress wrote the Clean Water Act to create civil and criminal penalties for "any person" who violated the law. Obviously, we want to make sure those penalties apply to corporations that violate the Clean Water Act. For that reason, here's what Congress said in section 502 of the Clean Water Act: "The term 'person' means an individual, corporation, partnership, association, State, municipality, commission, or political subdivision of a State, or any interstate body."

Congress and the states take the same approach to include corporations when we say "no person shall violate another person's trademark" or "no person shall sell drugs that have not been approved by the FDA." Similarly, it makes sense as a matter of policy to treat a corporation like a "person" when a corporation makes a contract or is sued or brings a lawsuit or engages in any one of many activities that state law may authorize a corporation to do. We do this because we have decided as a matter of state law that the "person" metaphor can help make the corporation better as a tool of public policy. Yes, corporations create private wealth, and shareholders own shares as private property, but the corporation as an artificial entity, and the rules that define it are public choices.

The Constitution is different from state laws and federal statutes. Our Bill of Rights is not a "policy choice" that government can decide. Rather, the Bill of Rights defines the relationship between we human beings and our government. The First Amendment and our other rights in the Constitution are the natural human rights that we insist on ensuring to ourselves when we consent to the Constitution's plan of government.

When we decide, as we might, that under our state or federal laws, corporations are "persons" that can be prosecuted (or that can contract or be sued), that decision cannot transform corporations into "persons" under the Constitution's protections of rights. We can change state laws of incorporation anytime we can muster a majority in the legislature for a particular change. We do not change the meaning of the Constitution anytime a legislature, let alone the legislature of Delaware alone, decides it might be efficient to do so. The rights in our Constitution, including the rights of "life," "liberty," "property," and "equal protection" for all "persons" are human rights.

The Constitution cannot be changed by state or federal laws; it can be changed only by the process of amendment as set forth in Article 5 of the Constitution. The people have never added corporations to the definition of *persons* in the Constitution by using the amendment process. As the Supreme Court declared in the 1800s when rebuffing early corporate efforts to create corporate rights, "State laws, by combining large masses of men under a corporate name, cannot repeal the Constitution."[24]

To appreciate the distinction between *person* under state or federal law and *person* under the Constitution, consider Delaware law again. Recall that Delaware law declares that corporations can exist for a defined period of years or may have "perpetual existence." If a majority of the Delaware legislature wanted to delete that last part of the law and simply declare that corporations may exist for a period of twenty years, they could do so. In contrast, neither Delaware nor any other state or federal legislature in

America can decide that people shall have a limited period of existence. No matter how good the policy justification for such a law, that law obviously would violate the Constitution's due process clause protecting the life of all persons.

The Right Thing in the Wrong Place

Corporations, then, are policy tools; they are not people or holders of constitutional rights. As economic tools, corporations are highly effective. Yet the same traits that make corporations such useful economic policy tools can also make them dangerous to republican government and democracy if people and lawmakers do not watch and restrain abuses. Corporations can aggregate immense power, corrupt government, drive down wages, trash public resources, concentrate markets to squeeze out competitors, and more. As Justice William Rehnquist said in one of his many dissents from the corporate rights decisions in the late 1970s and the 1980s, a "State grants to a business corporation the blessings of potentially perpetual life and limited liability to enhance its efficiency as an economic entity. It might reasonably be concluded that those properties, so beneficial in the economic sphere, pose special dangers in the political sphere."[25]

As with all tools, use of the corporate entity requires oversight and care. Gasoline is fantastic. It is also dangerous. I enjoy working with a chainsaw or taking out guns for hunting or practice, but I know that care and rules are necessary to prevent potentially disastrous consequences of using either one. Great tools, but we would not hand them out to anyone without having some clarity about how they will be used.

The problem of corporate power is not the personal failings of the many good and decent people who work for corporations, often creating wonderful products or services that benefit us all. Rather, corporate power is now subverting our democracy because we have forgotten that corporations are just tools, and we have forgotten our duty to keep an eye on them. Until the corporate rights offensive of recent years, the idea of restraining corporate power was a mainstream, basic American proposition, not a fringe viewpoint.

The Southern Pacific Case

Occasionally, the 1886 Supreme Court case of *Santa Clara County v. Southern Pacific Railroad Company* is cited to claim that corporations are constitutional "persons" with rights. In that case, the Southern Pacific Railroad Company tried to avoid state and county taxes by claiming that it was a "person" under the recently adopted Fourteenth Amendment to the Constitution. The Fourteenth Amendment had been enacted after the Civil War to ensure that freed slaves and all people in America had equal rights to due process, liberty, property, and equal protection of the law. The Southern Pacific Railroad corporation sued Santa Clara County, California, arguing that a tax assessment violated its rights as a "person" under the Fourteenth Amendment because the tax was not "equal" with taxes applied to other "persons."

The Court decided the case in favor of the railroad, but not for the reasons for which the case became known. In fact, in the *Santa Clara* decision, the Court did not discuss Southern Pacific's Fourteenth Amendment argument at all. Instead, the outcome of the case rested on California law rather than a constitutional question.[26] Nevertheless, the Gilded Age courts, almost as corporate-oriented as today's Court, repeatedly used *Santa Clara* as authority to fabricate corporate rights and strike down workers compensation, child labor, conservation, and other laws.[27]

Following *Santa Clara* in 1886, the Supreme Court faced a wave of cases in which large corporations and the infamous corporate monopoly "trusts" demanded constitutional rights to shield them from the growing movement for laws to protect employees (including child labor), the environment, fair taxes, and other public interests. On several occasions in the 1890s and early 1900s, the Supreme Court agreed with the corporations. The cases stated, without any explanation whatsoever, that "a corporation is a person under the Fourteenth Amendment," as if saying that with a straight face would make it true.[28] Could it be true?

Not a chance. Absolutely no evidence suggests that corporations were intended to be included in the Fourteenth Amendment or in the Constitution generally. Indeed, the evidence is exactly to the contrary. Since the beginning of our country, virtually every generation of Americans has acted to prevent corporate power from being leveraged into political power at the expense of the people. During the colonial era, only "a handful of native business corporations carried on business . . . four water companies, two wharf companies, two trading societies, and one mutual fire insurance society," and only twenty business corporations were formed by 1787, when the American people convened the Constitutional Convention in Philadelphia.[29] Legislatures, however, increasingly permitted the creation of corporations in the new republic to facilitate and expedite all kinds of public purposes, such as the building of roads, dams, and bridges.[30] Yet it remained clear that corporations were legal instruments of the state, defined and controlled by the state, with limitations on their purposes and their duration.[31]

It would be bizarre if the generation that defiantly declared to the world that "all men are created equal" and that "they are endowed by their Creator with certain unalienable Rights" and who wrote a constitution opening with "We, the People" would have tolerated corporate constitutional rights. Founders such as Thomas Jefferson and James Madison could not have been more clear about the danger of unregulated corporations and the need for, as Madison put it, "proper restraints and guards." Another founder, James Wilson, a Pennsylvania man who signed the Declaration of Independence, served in the Continental Congress, helped draft the Constitution, and was nominated by George Washington to be one of the first six justices on the Supreme Court, agreed. He well expressed the prevailing view of the time that corporations can be useful tools of the state but must always be controlled by the people:

> A corporation is described to be a person in a political capacity created by the law, to endure in perpetual succession. . . . It must be admitted, however, that, in too many instances, those bodies politick have, in their progress, counteracted the design of their original formation. . . . This is not mentioned with a view to insinuate, that such establishments ought to be prevented or destroyed: I mean only to intimate, that they should be erected with caution, and inspected with care.[32]

The Supreme Court at the time knew that any "rights" of corporations come from the state charter, not from the Constitution (let alone from our Creator). The corporate legal form today is not fundamentally different than when Chief Justice Marshall explained in 1819 that a corporation, as a "mere creature of law . . . possesses only those properties which the charter confers upon it, either expressly or as incidental to its very existence."[33] A corporation today is chartered from the state just as in 1809 when a unanimous Supreme Court held that "a body corporate as such cannot be a citizen within the meaning of the Constitution."[34]

For nearly two hundred years, the Supreme Court rejected the argument that corporations were entitled to the rights of citizens under the Constitution's "privileges and immunities" clause. In 1839, the Court said, "The only rights [a corporation] can claim are the rights which are given to it in that character, and not the rights which belong to its members as citizens of a state."[35] Fifty years later, the Court said that the term *citizens* in the Constitution "applies only to natural persons, members of the body politic owing allegiance to the state, not to artificial persons created by the legislature, and possessing only such attributes as the legislature has prescribed."[36]

At least until recently, the vigilance of American leadership about corporate power did not waver as corporations became more dominant in our economy. "Corporations, which should be the carefully restrained creatures of the law and the servants of the people, are fast becoming the people's masters," warned President Grover Cleveland.[37] Theodore Roosevelt sought to end "a riot of individualistic materialism" and successfully called for a ban on corporate political contributions: "Let individuals contribute as they desire; but let us prohibit in effective fashion all corporations from making contributions for any political purpose, directly or indirectly."[38] President Roosevelt said he "recognized that corporations and combinations had become indispensable in the business world, that it is folly to try to prohibit them, but that it was also folly to leave them without thoroughgoing control."[39]

This vigilance did not mean that powerful corporations simply accepted or cooperated with the public's "thoroughgoing control." As those who came before us understood, the opportunity for using the advantages of corporate privileges to concentrate power and aggregate wealth have always led corporations to seek to evade control or oversight by claiming "rights." In a democracy, an assertive, vigilant citizenry and leadership always is needed to push back.

Until the success of the Powell–Chamber of Commerce plan, Americans knew this. That is why the *Santa Clara* line of "corporate person" cases was rendered largely meaningless by the people's rejection of corporate rights throughout the twentieth century. Under Theodore Roosevelt, a Republican, Americans restrained corporate power with effective antitrust enforcement, labor laws, environmental laws, and laws banning corporate political spending. In Roosevelt's words, "There can be no effective control of corporations while their political activity remains."[40] Under Woodrow Wilson and Franklin Roosevelt, both Democrats, Americans likewise regulated corporate power to ensure the strength of the people and the country as a whole. Republicans, Democrats, and Independents came together to amend the Constitution twice in 1913 to weaken the hold on government by corporations and the extreme wealth of the few: first, by overturning a Supreme Court case striking down the federal income tax, and second, by requiring senators to be elected by the people rather than appointed by state legislatures.[41]

Finally, in a 1938 dissenting opinion, Justice Hugo Black, a former Alabama senator, demolished the idea that corporations were "persons" with rights under the Constitution's Fourteenth Amendment. Although he wrote in dissent, the clarity of his expression about corporations and persons sounded a warning to any justice who might try to slip corporate rights into the Constitution with "glittering generalities" and glib citation of *Santa Clara*. His lengthy dissenting opinion examined the words, history, meaning, and purpose of the Fourteenth Amendment:

> *I do not believe that the word "person" in the Fourteenth Amendment includes corporations. . . . A constitutional interpretation that is wrong should not stand. I believe this Court should now overrule previous decisions which interpreted the Fourteenth Amendment to include corporations.*
>
> *Neither the history nor the language of the Fourteenth Amendment justifies the belief that corporations are included within its protections.*

Certainly, when the Fourteenth Amendment was submitted for approval, the people were not told that the states of the South were to be denied their normal relationship with the Federal Government unless they ratified an amendment granting new and revolutionary rights to corporations. . . . The records of the time can be searched in vain for evidence that this amendment was adopted for the benefit of corporations.[42]

With Justice Black's warning shot that there would be no more free rides for corporate rights on the Supreme Court, *Santa Clara* "corporate personhood" was a dead issue for decades. Indeed, the Court said little more about corporations' "rights" until Justice Lewis Powell and his Chamber of Commerce plan came to the Supreme Court following the death of Justice Black in September 1971. Through most of the twentieth century, the Court returned to the basic American understanding that corporations were economic, not political, entities.

For example, in rejecting the claim of corporations for privacy rights in 1950, the Supreme Court said:

Corporations can claim no equality with individuals in the enjoyment of a right to privacy. They are endowed with public attributes. They have a collective impact upon society, from which they derive the privilege of acting as artificial entities. . . . Law-enforcing agencies have a legitimate right to satisfy themselves that corporate behavior is consistent with the law and the public interest.[43]

For more than a century until *Citizens United*, most states and the federal government banned corporate political contributions and spending. Some states, such as Kentucky, even made the control of corporate political activity part of their state

77

constitutions.[44] This basic understanding of the place of corporations in American democracy guided the Supreme Court, even as Justice Powell's "corporate speech" cases worked away at creating the new corporate rights doctrine.

The one time before *Citizens United* when the Supreme Court went off the rails with respect to corporate political spending occurred with Justice Powell's maiden corporate rights decision in *First National Bank of Boston*, striking down a state law banning corporate spending in referendum elections. That exception should have proved the rule, in large part because of the force of Justice Rehnquist's dissent. Rehnquist concluded that the "Fourteenth Amendment does not require a State to endow a business corporation with the power of political speech."[45] Instead, Rehnquist forcefully pressed the truth that corporations are not people with rights but are entities defined by the states, with restrictions that the legislatures find appropriate. Congress, he wrote, and numerous

> States of this Republic have considered the matter, and have concluded that restrictions upon the political activity of business corporations are both politically desirable and constitutionally permissible. The judgment of such a broad consensus of governmental bodies expressed over a period of many decades is entitled to considerable deference from this Court.[46]

Again, the different opinions of these two Richard Nixon appointees—William Rehnquist and Lewis Powell—showed the stark gap between the corporatist and the conservative understanding of our American republic. For a time, the conservative Rehnquist was able to form a majority on the Court. In 1990, the Chamber of Commerce in Michigan attacked a law restricting corporate political spending and lost. The Court upheld the right of the people to keep corporations out of politics. In that case, *Austin v. Michigan Chamber of Commerce*, Justice Rehnquist's dissenting views in the corporate speech cases became the majority view.[47]

Rehnquist joined Thurgood Marshall, who wrote for the Court in affirming Michigan's regulation of corporate spending in elections. Marshall's words for the Court were drawn from the earlier Rehnquist dissents:

> *State law grants corporations special advantages. . . . These state-created advantages not only allow corporations to play a dominant role in the Nation's economy, but also permit them to use "resources amassed in the economic marketplace" to obtain "an unfair advantage in the political marketplace."*[48]

Even as late as 2003, before Chief Justice John Roberts and Justice Samuel Alito replaced Chief Justice Rehnquist and Justice Sandra Day O'Connor, the Court agreed that the same corporate election spending law that the Court would later strike down in *Citizens United* was perfectly fine under our Constitution. In that 2003 case, *McConnell v. Federal Election Commission*, the Court affirmed that the people's representatives in Congress were entitled to "the legislative judgment that the special characteristics of the corporate structure require particularly careful regulation."[49]

Citizens United: Corporations Back on the Track, People to the Back

We then come to *Citizens United* a mere seven years later, posing again this fundamental question of American democracy: Can Congress and state legislatures make laws to ensure that government of the people does not become government of the corporations? What had changed since 2003, 1990, the New Deal, Theodore Roosevelt's presidency, the 1800s, or the days of

Madison, Jefferson, and President Washington's Supreme Court justice and national founding father James Wilson?

Is *Citizens United* different because that case involved a nonprofit corporation? Although that point may have been worthy of examination, it made no difference to the Court. The Court in *Citizens United* made very clear that its decision applied to all corporations (or, as Justice Kennedy's decision called them, all "voices" and "speakers"). That is why Chevron, Koch Industries, Target, News Corporation, and other global, for-profit corporations have funneled hundreds of millions of dollars into elections since *Citizens United*.

Although the claims of a nonprofit corporation seeking to express the views of its members are more sympathetic, all corporations, whether for-profit or not-for-profit, are creatures of the state. Take *Citizens United*, for example. *Citizens United* is a corporation organized under Virginia law. It exists as a nonprofit corporation because the people of Virginia passed an incorporation law. Under this law, people may create a nonprofit corporation only if they file with the state a set of articles of incorporation containing elements that the state requires, pay a filing fee of $75, designate a registered agent to deal with the state's annual assessment packet, and comply with recordkeeping and other requirements set out in the Virginia law.[50]

Without all of these steps, *Citizens United* (or any other nonprofit corporation) does not exist. In fact, the state provides the equivalent of the corporate death penalty for noncompliance with these laws. No one forced people to incorporate their activity as *Citizens United*, the nonprofit corporation, but once they chose to do that, is it too much to ask that the corporation comply with the laws on the books?

That does not mean that the people who support *Citizens United*, who work there, or who believe in its mission lose any rights whatsoever. They have all the same rights they had before they decided to incorporate and the same inalienable rights of all Americans. The corporation, however, does not, and we are not required to pretend that the corporation is the same as the people.

Once we recall that the rules for corporations come from us, for the betterment of our nation, the idea of "corporate rights" will be exposed as ridiculous. If we return to recognition that corporations are policy tools, rather than people with constitutional rights, we can then begin to realize many possibilities to improve the tool so that it better serves the purposes for which we Americans permitted the corporate entity in our laws in the first place. We can begin to rethink and reinvigorate our incorporation laws.

We might decide that the 315 million Americans who do not live in Delaware ought to have as much say about corporate law as the 900,000 people who live in Delaware now have. We might decide to create new and better corporate entities under the law, such as for-benefit "B Corporations," and options for sustainable "low-profit" hybrids between for-profits and nonprofits. We can change the rules to make real shareholder democracy and to make corporations justify their corporate charters and show how they have served the public and complied with the law. We can use the corporate chartering and charter revocation process and other features of corporate law to prevent and punish corporate crime and misconduct. We can insist on accounting for externalities—the dumping onto society of costs from pollution, destruction of our global ecosystem, and financial bailouts.[51]

That's not all. When people—voters, legislators, businesspeople, everyone—take responsibility for the public tool of incorporation, we are not only saving our republic; we may also be saving our economy. With new corporate rules, we can make corporations more effective at business, protect innovation and competition, create more jobs, and free human creativity.

In Chapters Seven and Eight, I will explore these ideas in more detail, along with the tools to restore our Constitution based on human rights, and our elections and government based on equal representation of the people. This will succeed because so many Americans know just how badly corporate power and the imposition of the Powell-Chamber vision of a "corporate market-place" republic has corroded our nation.

Chapter Four
Corporations Don't Vote;
They Don't Have To

The strength of America is in the boardrooms, country clubs and Lear jets of America's great corporations. We're saying to Wal-Mart, AIG and Pfizer, if not you, who? If not now, when?

—Murray Hill Inc., candidate for US Congress[1]

Not long after the *Citizens United* decision, a corporation chartered under Maryland law announced its campaign for Congress. Leading with the slogan "Corporations Are People Too," Murray Hill Inc., proposed to "eliminate the middleman" of the human Congresspeople and simply govern directly. The corporation promised to run "an aggressive, historic campaign that puts people second, or even third." The campaign would use Astroturf lobbying, avatars, and robocalls to reach voters, concluding with a call to all corporations to join the "struggle": "It's our democracy. We bought it, we paid for it, and we're going to keep it."[2] As with all good satire, the jest works because it hits so close to the truth.

"When It Bites You in the Butt, You Bleed"

International corporations now dominate our government. That statement should shock us, yet it is now a commonplace with which few Americans would disagree.[3] In the words of an Iowa Republican who served in Congress for thirty years, "Why in a corporatist political system would a politician want to speak up against the drug companies or gambling interests or investment banks if corporate monies can quickly be shoveled into campaigns?"[4]

Uncontrolled corporate money and power in politics are fast transforming our republic of people into what can be described as a corporate state. People may no longer need precise numbers to appreciate the government takeover by narrow corporate interests, but the numbers remain shocking (see Table 1).

The top twenty spenders alone have spent nearly $5 billion over the past decade and a half to gain or keep advantage in Washington, D.C. Those numbers do not include the massive lobbying and campaign spending in the states, or the funding of corporate "grassroots," "foundation," and "think tank" front groups that now proliferate across the land.

Corporations spend these billions not to advance any special interest, at least if "special" is meant in any ideological sense. The interest is not business, jobs, free market, or anything quite so noble. Corporations spend those billions of dollars to block reforms or enact favors for the profit interest of a very few specific corporations and the people who control them.

Lewis Powell's strategy memo had insisted that the "role of the National Chamber of Commerce is . . . vital" to the corporate assertion of power that he had in mind. And so it is.

As Table 1 shows, the US Chamber of Commerce now is the biggest lobbying spender by far (more than $1 billion as of 2013). In addition to its lobbying spending, the Chamber has spent at least

Table 1

Top 20 Spenders on Lobbying in Washington, 1998-2013

Lobbying Client	Total Spent
US Chamber of Commerce	$1,018,910,680
General Electric	$297,960,000
American Medical Assn	$295,057,500
American Hospital Assn	$249,433,008
Pharmaceutical Rsrch & Mfrs of America	$246,386,420
National Assn of Realtors	$245,760,858
AARP	$229,932,064
Blue Cross/Blue Shield	$220,956,832
Northrop Grumman	$202,685,253
Exxon Mobil	$193,022,742
Boeing Co	$183,432,310
Verizon Communications	$183,090,043
Lockheed Martin	$181,643,954
Edison Electric Institute	$180,356,789
Business Roundtable	$179,640,000
AT&T Inc	$162,630,644
National Cable & Telecommunications Assn	$155,650,000
Southern Co	$155,070,694
Altria Group	$145,815,200
National Assn of Broadcasters	$143,540,000
Total	**$4,870,974,991**

Source: Center For Responsive Politics, Top Spenders
http://www.opensecrets.org/lobby/top.php?indexType=s&showYear=a

$68 million since the *Citizens United* decision to influence the outcome of various elections. The Chamber is a tax-exempt corporation, but pays its president, Tom Donahue, more than $5 million per year.[6] It vows to defeat any law that would require disclosure of corporate election spending.

Despite its innocuous name and self-description as a "business" lobby, the US Chamber of Commerce does not promote a positive American business environment. Rather, it is an effective tool for the largest corporations in the world to influence our government. As the *Wall Street Journal* has reported, the Chamber offers "individual companies and industries the chance to use the Chamber as a means of anonymously pursuing their own political ends."[7] Nor does the Chamber of Commerce defend "conservative" points of view. Indeed, in 2014, the Chamber began to deploy big corporate cash to defeat Tea Party and conservative candidates; the Chamber sought to have a "more governable Republican party."[8]

The US Chamber of Commerce brags that it is a $200 million "lobbying and political powerhouse with expanded influence across the globe." Donohue, the Chamber president, says the Chamber is "so strong that when it bites you in the butt, you bleed."[9] This biting is not done to benefit most American businesses or communities but to promote the interests of the largest transnational corporations in the world. The interests of the Washington, D.C.–based US Chamber of Commerce are so far removed from main street interests in any American towns that since 2009 more than sixty local chambers of commerce have disassociated themselves from the US Chamber.[10]

In recent years, 83 percent of the Chamber's contributions were $100,000 or more; 40 percent came from just twenty-five contributors; the top three contributors provided 20 percent of the Chamber's dollars—anonymously.[11] In 2009, a single contribution accounted for 42 percent of all contributions to the Chamber. That came from the health insurance corporate lobby, which funneled $86.2 million to the Chamber to make sure no public option or other reform would hurt insurance company profits.[12] Trevor

Potter, a former member of the Federal Election Commission, explained why the insurance groups would use the Chamber as a front: "They clearly thought . . . it would appear less self-serving if a broader business group made arguments against it than if the insurers did it."[13]

Self-serving? Ten of the for-profit health insurance corporations paid their CEOs a total of $1 billion in compensation between 2000 and 2009.[14] One "nonprofit" health insurance corporation, Blue Cross and Blue Shield of Massachusetts, fired its CEO in 2011 with a $12 million severance and compensation package. CEOs of the ten largest publicly traded health insurance corporations earned a total of $118.6 million in 2007. Now, with mandated customers and no public option under the Affordable Care Act (or "Obamacare" to its friends and foes alike), health insurance corporations have further ramped up CEO enrichment. Whether profit or nonprofit corporations, they continue to pay CEOs and top executives millions of dollars.[15] One company, UnitedHealth Group, paid its CEO $49 million in 2012.[16]

Meanwhile, back in the public sector, "the Administrator of the federal Center for Medicare and Medicaid Services, who manages the health care of forty-four million elderly Americans on Medicare and about fifty-nine million low-income and disabled recipients on Medicaid," is paid $176,000.[17] It is hard to see how the Chamber serves the interests of America's businesspeople and employees who pay towering health insurance premiums to help fund exorbitant executive salaries and multimillion-dollar lobbying campaigns to block public health care.

In addition to protecting bloated health insurance companies, the Chamber works in other areas to protect the few and hurt the many. Bailed-out Wall Street corporations use the Chamber to block financial reform. Subsidy-collecting fossil fuel corporations pay the Chamber to block energy reform. In fact, the US Chamber of Commerce opposition to any effort to address the climate crisis is so extreme that even other global corporations such as Apple, Nike, and PG&E have resigned from the Chamber in protest.[18]

What about Union Spending?

"What about unions?" Anyone who questions the impact of staggering amounts of corporate money in our democracy will hear that from time to time. The question makes sense: Americans distrust excessive concentrations of power and potential corruption, regardless of the institution in which the power is concentrated.

We should seek transparency and accountability, checks and balances for any institution that has concentrated power, whether governmental, corporate, union, or otherwise. And we should be concerned when a union secretly funnels money into an election, as happened in the Boston mayoral election in 2013.[19] But we also should consider some facts about unions before accepting false equivalency with corporations.

The US Chamber of Commerce says not to worry, *Citizens United* "provided unions with the same political speech rights as corporations."[20] David Bossie, who brought the *Citizens United* case, says the "newfound freedom" for corporations makes a "level playing field" with unions and interest groups.[21] Perhaps they think that unions will somehow balance out corporate power.

Unfortunately, they won't. First, under the federal law that *Citizens United* struck down, corporations and unions were covered by the same restrictions on election spending. That had been true since 1947. If you are concerned about union political spending, then *Citizens United* is a disaster for you, too, as *Citizens United* blocks restrictions on union election spending. In that sense, Bossie is correct: *Citizens United* means that democracy is for sale to any and all who have the cash to bid in the $10 billion game.

Behind this bleak vision of a pay-to-play democracy is a deeply flawed premise that Americans are not citizens who govern; instead, we are told to be mere spectators, or consumers, as corporations and unions throw money around to decide our elections. That assumption, however, is not the only thing wrong with the "level playing field" viewpoint about unions. In real life, there is no such thing as equality between unions and corporations, just as there is no equivalence between most people and the CEOs of large corporations.

A union is very different from a corporation. A union is an organization of employees. The employees agree to be represented by an elected leadership of the organization. The leadership negotiates with employers to reach terms of employment on behalf of all of the workers, terms that are approved by the workers, as well as by management of the business. People who decide to form unions may choose to incorporate the union, or they may not. Some unions are corporations, but many other unions are not. Unincorporated unions are simply voluntary associations of workers or federations of local "chapters." The largest labor organizations, such as the AFL-CIO, are federations of smaller unions.

That difference does not make unions perfect, and it is true that union corruption has been a problem at times, as in any human institution. When unions worked well, though, as they usually did and continue to do, unions offer some counterbalance to corporate power. They provide an employee voice into the question of how corporate profits should be allocated among all of the people who contribute. In the long-gone heyday of unions, when corporations profited, everyone did well. Shareholders still gained, and CEOs and executives still made a fine living, but unions helped employees get a fair share, too.

Strong unions helped create the middle class. In the 1950s, when unions represented more than 35 percent of American workers in the private sector, wages rose. More people who worked hard had a chance to have health insurance and to retire in something better than poverty. For a variety of reasons, though, including corporate union suppression tactics, the rate of union membership declined steeply. By 1970, only one in four private sector workers was in a union. This number kept falling until today, when unions represent only 6.5 percent of private sector employees.[22] That means that 93 percent of private sector employees are not in unions.

So one answer to the question "What about unions?" is "What unions? They don't count anymore." That's not a complete answer, however. While private sector unions have declined significantly, public sector unions have grown over the same years. About 35 percent of public sector employees—firefighters, police, teachers, and the like—now belong to unions.[23] Though the data are mixed, unions in the public sector have probably helped those employees retain slightly more of what all Americans seek—a decent wage, health care, some possibility of retirement, and some level of security.

To be sure, unions are taking advantage of *Citizens United* and are spending millions to influence state and federal elections.[24] Public and private unions also spend money to influence government and policy. Union members pool contributions through political action committees (PACs), and unions have political influence, particularly in the Democratic Party. In 2010, members of SEIU (Service Employees International Union) contributed more than $11 million, members of teachers' unions contributed $15 million, and the teamsters, electrical workers, and carpenters unions also contributed millions of dollars. Thus, unions should not be exempt from any examination of the influence of money in politics.

Upon examination, however, the falsity of assertions about union-corporation parity is apparent. Unions do not have the membership, money, or influence to come anywhere close to balancing corporate power. The high ground for union members in politics comes at election time. Apart from union PAC spending (which itself is dwarfed by corporate money), unions can mobilize members to help get out voters and rally for favored candidates. Then, however, the election is over, and regardless of the winner, corporate influence in government overwhelms unions as much as it overwhelms every other interest.

If you go back and look at that top-twenty list of lobbying spenders (Table 1), you will see not a single union or federation of unions on the list. Not one. If we pull back from the top-twenty list to see all lobbying spending, including unions, corporate industries, and "special interests," the corporate domination remains clear (see Table 2).

Table 2
Top 20 Spenders on Lobbying in Washington, 1998-2013

Sector	Total Spent
Miscellaneous business	$5,815,757,543
Health	$5,760,020,799
Finance/insurance/real estate	$5,738,003,937
Communications/electronics	$4,730,941,613
Energy/natural resource	$4,268,300,046
Other	$3,076,689,869
Transportation	$2,947,569,032
Ideology/single issue	$1,894,591,537
Agribusiness	$1,736,175,743
Defense	$1,654,187,912
Construction	$631,315,233
Labor	$573,322,887
Lawyers and lobbyists	$408,016,748
Total	**$39,234,892,899**

Source: Center For Responsive Politics, Ranked Sectors,
http://www.opensecrets.org/lobby/top.php?indexType=c&showYear=a

In summary, corporate spending on lobbying came to around $40 billion; union spending, $0.5 billion. The financial industry alone spent $5 billion more than all of the unions combined, in every field, in the public and private sectors. Even by Wall Street accounting, $40 billion and $0.5 billion are not close to equivalent.

Apart from the overwhelming magnitude of corporate money, the type of money from a union is different. Jon Youngdahl, national political director of the SEIU, explains where that $11 million that SEIU put into the 2010 elections came from:

> About 300,000 janitors, nurses' aides, child-care providers and other members who voluntarily contribute on average $7 per month to SEIU's Committee on Political Education (COPE). . . . We are a union of working people, and the money we spend on politics is money donated by workers.[25]

Finally, in lobbying spending as elsewhere, the outputs reflect the inputs. If unions are using whatever power they have to drive into our government the union agenda—enlarged union membership, better wages, health care, and pensions for union members, and in the private sector, a more equitable division of corporate earnings among executives, shareholders, and employees—they have failed miserably.

Indeed, one recent exception to the string of union setbacks proves the rule. In 2011, the National Labor Relations Board finally required corporations to provide notice to employees of their rights to freely discuss working conditions with fellow employees and to decide for themselves whether to join a union. The required notice was no different than that which informs employees of their rights to workers compensation, minimum wages, and the like. You may be wondering why you have not seen this notice in your workplace. A corporate lobbying group, the National Association of Manufacturers filed a lawsuit, and in

2013, a federal court in Washington, D.C., struck the law down, finding it to be a violation of corporations' new constitutional right "not to speak."[26]

What Corporations Get for the Money

Virtually every significant issue now reflects a corporate agenda, with the possible exception of social issues of limited economic impact, such as abortion or lesbian and gay rights. Consider two macro issues: public spending and debt, and energy and the environment. Whether Americans can find a way to manage these two issues wisely may have the most impact on whether we face precipitous decline as a nation and as a world. On both, the well-financed corporate agenda overwhelms the public national interest.

Corporate Power Drives Deficits and Debt

Admiral Michael Mullen, chairman of the Joint Chiefs of Staff, has identified the growing national debt as one of the most significant national security issues.[27] As of January 2014, the national debt amounted to $17.3 trillion.[28] Total public debt is now 100 percent of gross domestic product (GDP), a historic level that cannot be attributed only to the financial crisis that began 2008.[29]

Four main factors contributed to the rapid debt increase since 2001: trillions of dollars in tax cuts enacted in 2001–2003 and largely extended in 2012; (2) the costs of the wars in Iraq and Afghanistan (estimated at $4–$6 trillion);[30] (3) the 2006 enactment of a massive prescription drug benefit called Medicare Part D with no revenue to pay for it; and (4) the 2008 collapse of the global financial system, followed quickly by the government bailouts to Wall Street and financial firms.[31] (Perhaps surprisingly, the Affordable Care Act has a net effect of somewhat reducing federal spending.[32])

The national debt reflects accumulated borrowing over the years. The budget deficit, on the other hand, reflects the amount of government spending in excess of government revenue in any given year. Continued deficits contribute to rising national debt.

Recent federal budgets of roughly $3.5 trillion break down as follows: Medicaid and Medicare, 21 percent; military, not including veterans benefits, 19 percent; Social Security, 22 percent; "mandatory" spending (veterans' compensation, unemployment, food stamps, and so on), 17 percent; "discretionary" spending (law enforcement, roads, student aid, energy, and the like), 16 percent; and interest payments on the national debt, 6 percent.[33] More accurate measures that include all government spending for military purposes, not merely that counted in the Pentagon's budget, show federal spending on the military and war much closer to 50 percent of the budget.[34] On the revenue side, tax receipts have fallen to the lowest level since 1950.[35]

What does any of this have to do with corporations? The corporate stranglehold on Washington, D.C., drives huge corporate subsidies and earmarks. Diverse organizations from Public Citizen to the Cato Institute calculate "corporate welfare," defined as unnecessary federal spending and subsidies for specific corporations, at $92 billion to $125 billion per year.[36]

The Cato Institute describes subsidies for corporate agribusiness (approximately $30 billion per year) as "a long-standing rip-off of American taxpayers."[37] The vast majority of agriculture subsidies do not go to "family farms" but to the biggest corporate producers. In fact, only 10 percent of the largest producers collected 75 percent of the nearly $300 billion in subsidies since 1995, and 62 percent of all farmers got nothing.[38] These subsidies cannot be justified on any measure of public policy merit; they are bad for the health of the American people and an unfair business advantage for large corporations over small business. Taxpayer subsidies for corn production and industrialized byproducts make unwholesome and fattening foods and drinks artificially cheap and place locally grown, organic, and otherwise healthy unprocessed food in an unfair competitive position.

Why does a practice that is bad for people and the country continue? Look back at Table 2; "agribusiness" is one of the largest lobbying machines in Washington, D.C., spending more than $1.7 billion since 1998.

Corporate interests also distort military spending, now as high as the defense budgets of every other country in the world combined. The Pentagon budget includes billions of dollars of corporate handouts, weapons systems that even the Pentagon does not want, and a troubling expansion of corporate contractors for every aspect of military activity, from supply to mercenary corporations such as Haliburton or Blackwater (which changed its name to XE, after infamous activity in Iraq, and is now called Academi. In 2000, the US military budget was $294 billion. In recent years, annual military spending has soared to between $600 and $700 billion.[39]

Consider General Electric's "alternative engine program" for the F-35 fighter jet. The engine is called "alternative" because it is not really the engine for the F-35. Pratt & Whitney, not GE, already makes the F-35 engine. The Pentagon says GE's proposed engine is not necessary. For years, the military has said that it does not want the "alternative" engine and that the money spent on it is a waste. President Bush urged Congress to kill the program in 2007, and President Obama did the same in 2009. No matter. GE kept spending political money, and Congress kept approving spending for the "alternative" engine program. The cost to taxpayers for this unwanted "zombie" program came to $3 billion.[40] If you go back to Table 1, you will find GE near the top, spending more than $297 million on 1998–2013 lobbying.

Corporate power also drives deficits in indirect ways. Corporate lobbyists ensure that even programs intended to benefit the public interest must be warped to enhance corporate profit, at the expense of the government and the American people. This is usually accomplished by writing the law to require hundreds of billions of dollars diverted to corporate revenue. One example is health care reform that mandates customers for private health insurance corporations and that prohibits the government from negotiating pharmaceutical prices.

Health care costs are among the primary drivers of the deficit. Although domination of government by corporations is partly a fiscal issue, the health care area also shows the terrible price many people pay in their personal lives for the disconnection of our representatives from the interests of the people.

Corporations in the Health Care Business Pervert Reform to Preserve Profits

The reason our government spends so much on health care is not because we are unduly generous for too many of our fellow citizens. Exactly the opposite: We are the only developed country in the world that relies on an expensive, wasteful, private sector, employer-sponsored health insurance system that leaves millions of citizens with nothing.[41] Our health care costs include billions of dollars of CEO pay and corporate profit that other countries do not need to add into the bill. We pay twice as much on health care as other developed democracies—about 17.4 percent of GDP versus 9.3 percent—with far less to show for it.[42] American babies born in 2013 have life expectancies lower than those in fifty other countries; we are below Guam and just ahead of Bahrain.[43]

The recently enacted health care reform has not altered this expensive corporate control of American health care. Indeed, the

Affordable Care Act has followed the pattern of building on this reality rather than confronting and changing it.

When President Clinton tried to change this unsustainable system in 1993, the health insurance and pharmaceutical companies spent hundreds of millions of dollars to defeat reform. The system only got more dysfunctional over the next fifteen years, and the corporate lobby got stronger, spending even more in 2009 and 2010 to ensure that massive corporate profits defined the boundaries of permissible reform or even debate.

With the Affordable Care Act, powerful health insurance companies won what most corporations could only dream of: 100 percent of Americans required to be customers, while the costs for those likely to be unprofitable customers (the older or poorer ones) shifted to the taxpayers. At the same time, international pharmaceutical corporations, cutting a private deal with the White House, made sure that Americans would continue to pay the highest drug prices in the world.[44]

Health care policy surely is complex and challenging, but other democracies seem to benefit by having a wider range of possible approaches to consider. What is mainstream and conventional throughout the world—cost-effective, single-payer health care—was never given a second of consideration, despite the fact that a majority of Americans favor that approach.[45] The so called public option, which at least would have allowed people to choose to take our business from profit-driven corporations to a public coverage pool to help keep costs down, never had a chance, despite support from three-quarters of the American people.

We saw a preview of this type of corporate-dominated health care lawmaking in 2003, when Congress enacted and President George W. Bush signed the Medicare Part D prescription drug program for senior citizens. The law provided no means for paying for this expensive program, which effectively transfers hundreds of billions of dollars of (borrowed) money from the federal government to global pharmaceutical corporations. Much worse, the 2003 Medicare law actually made it illegal for the government to negotiate fair drug prices. The law also banned the import of cheaper drugs from Canada and made generic alternatives more difficult to obtain.[46]

The federal government now pays 30 percent more for pharmaceuticals as a result of the 2003 law, resulting in overcharges to the government of billions of dollars per year. How did this happen? A Republican congressman from North Carolina explains: "The pharmaceutical lobbyists wrote the bill."[47]

A few months after the Medicare Part D law was enacted, the leading congressman who worked on the bill, Representative Billy Tauzin, who had been both a Democrat and a Republican over the years, left Congress. He took a job as president of the pharmaceutical corporations' lobby group, the Pharmaceutical Research and Manufacturers of America (PhRMA), at a salary of more than $2 million a year. "As a member of Congress, Billy negotiated a large payout to the pharmaceutical industry by the federal government," said another congressman. "He's now about to receive one of the largest salaries ever paid to any advocate by an industry."[48]

Olga Pierce, a journalist for ProPublica, reviewed what had happened to others in government who worked on that 2003 payout to the pharmaceutical corporations:[49]

- Former senator John Breaux, D-La., fought against allowing drug prices to be negotiated in Medicare Part D. A year after the bill passed, he left the Senate to begin his lobbying career. He now has his own lobbying firm, Breaux Lott Leadership Group, which this year has received $300,000 to lobby for the pharmaceutical industry.

- Former senator Don Nickles, R-Okla., who helped negotiate the final version of Part D, then left to form his own lobbying firm. Bristol Myers-Squibb paid the Nickles Group $120,000 this year to lobby for, among other things, "health care reform issues related to Medicaid and Medicare."

- Thomas Scully, the former Medicare chief who helped design Part D, obtained a waiver allowing him to discuss job offers before he left his government post. Less than two weeks after the bill passed, he went to work for the lobbying firm Alston & Bird, where he works on behalf of drug companies.

- Raissa Downs, a top legislative aide in the Department of Health and Human Services, helped spearhead the agency's efforts to shape Part D. Now she's a partner at Tarplin, Downs & Young, a consulting firm, where she is lobbying against changes to Part D.

- John McManus, staff director of the House Ways and Means health subcommittee when Part D was created, now has his own lobbying firm. Between 2004 and June 2009, the McManus Group earned about $6 million lobbying for PhRMA and various drug companies.

In 2009, the Obama White House secretly negotiated a deal with the pharmaceutical lobby, headed by the former congressman Billy Tauzin. The Obama administration promised not to touch the ban on the government's negotiating fair Medicare pharmaceutical prices. In exchange, the international drug corporations promised not to block other reforms and offered some unspecified "savings" of $80 billion over the next decade. The deal was so good for the pharmaceutical corporations that the industry ran (allegedly at the request of the White House chief of staff) a $70 million campaign through phony front groups with names like "Americans for Stable Quality Care" to promote passage of Obamacare.[50]

Apart from the unseemly elevation of a corporate lobby into a branch of government requiring negotiation with the White House, the deal was bad for Americans: if Medicare simply paid the same price that the government pays for the same drugs under the Medicaid program, taxpayers would save $150 billion.[51] As former Secretary of Labor Robert Reich says, "Perhaps the White House deal with Big Pharma is a necessary step to get anything resembling universal health insurance. But if that's the case, our democracy is in terrible shape."[52]

The Human Cost

The impact of the corporate takeover of government lawmaking in health care contributes to huge deficits and drains small business capital, but we should also remember the human cost. Health care is about lives of real people, as one health insurance executive discovered when he went back home to Tennessee.

Wendell Potter had been a high-level public relations executive for the Cigna health insurance corporation. Cigna is a Fortune 500 for-profit corporation, incorporated under Delaware law; in 2012, Cigna had profits of $1.6 billion and paid its CEO more than $20 million.[53] After *Citizens United*, Cigna admits that it now "regularly supports federal and state officials, candidates, parties, and other political groups and organizations where the Company believes it can advance its mission, business objectives and goals. . . ."[54] Despite this opaque disclosure, Wendell Potter says that "millions more—probably billions more—are spent secretly every year by corporations and their trade associations to shape policy discussions and actions."[55]

As Potter describes, after more than two decades in the health insurance industry, he quit in a moment of conscience. His life was changed by his visit to a "health fair" at a county fairground in Tennessee, where Potter had grown up. A nonprofit medical group that usually brings needed health care to Third World regions had made its eighth annual trip to the fairgrounds to help Americans who had no other option for treatment.

Potter stepped into a "war zone" at the health fair. Hundreds of soaking-wet Americans waiting all day in lines to be examined and treated in barns and animal stalls; teeth being pulled in open-sided tents; people "lying on gurneys on the rain-soaked pavement"; hundreds more turned away at the end of the day before they could be treated.

These are Americans. They were not waiting all day to be treated in animal stalls because they are shirkers. Two-thirds of them had jobs but no health insurance because, as Potter explains, they worked for small businesses that could not afford for-profit health insurance or, in many cases, the health insurers had "purged" unprofitable small business coverage from their rolls.[56]

The Affordable Care Act, if implemented effectively, could significantly improve the worst of this injustice. Unfortunately, effective implementation may not happen when politicians seek to achieve overdue reform by using, rather than confronting, entrenched corporate interests, and by forcing massive public payments for private gains.

Beyond Health Care

American strength has come from resiliency coupled with practicality, determination coupled with distrust of zealotry. Our eighteenth-century republic has prospered into its third century because we have been able to endure and adapt to tremendous changes and challenges. Now *Citizens United*, by locking in both an elite donor class and a run-up of unbalanced corporate power, is ossifying our government, blocking reform, and preventing our adaptation to fundamentally new circumstances in the world.

Citizens United turns uncontrolled corporate lobbying and corruption of government into uncontrollable corporate lobbying and corruption of government. Any attempt to control that problem, now says the Supreme Court, violates the right of free speech. The dynamic that culminated in *Citizens United* of corporate rights feeding corporate power, and of corporate power building corporate rights, makes the practical balancing effect of a political process that represents all interests increasingly difficult or even impossible to achieve.

This danger is particularly acute in the energy sector. Just as we can have no real health care reform until we contain corporate power, we can have no real energy reform. That has catastrophic consequences, given our dependence on fossil fuels. Multibillion-dollar oil, coal, and gas subsidies grow, our costly ensnarement and overextension in the Middle East further weakens our own country, alternative technologies are developed elsewhere, and the resources and environment that we need to sustain life and security are rapidly destroyed.

Empires and societies usually fail not because of a sudden, surprising blow but because of a long-term unwillingness or inability to adapt.[57] Decline proceeds apace, as all can see the plainly perilous conditions, but candor and action are blocked by zealotry, denial, or force. What can it mean except fatal, corporate-fueled zealotry when the rallying cry of a major political party in America becomes "drill, baby, drill" and modest regulation of deadly pollution is called a "war on coal"?

Energy, Deficits, and the National Interest

In a real sense, our entanglement in seemingly endless wars in the Middle East (Iraq-Kuwait, 1990–1991; Iraq no-fly zone, 1991–2003; Iraq War, 2003–2009; Afghanistan, 2001–2016 (maybe); Libya, 2011; Yemen 2010–2011; ongoing near-war with Iran;

billions of dollars in military aid to Pakistan, Israel, Egypt, Saudi Arabia, and others in the region) is a multitrillion-dollar subsidy to protect the oil on which we have depended for too long.

Even apart from this indirect, military subsidy for fossil fuel corporations, the oil, coal, and gas industry is among the biggest corporate welfare recipients. Corporations such as Exxon, BP, Chevron, Peabody Energy, and others receive billions of dollars in tax subsidies, liability caps, bargain-basement leases on public lands, and other government assistance, not to mention the subsidy of massive highway funds and minimal funds for transportation other than auto and truck. Annual federal subsidies to the hugely profitable oil and gas corporations exceed $10 billion. Bills that would repeal or reduce these subsidies were defeated in Congress in 2012 and 2013, after the companies spent millions to buy political influence, including a multi-million dollar pay-off from Chevron to the PAC of the House Speaker.[58] Of the $100 billion in direct subsidies to the energy sector between 2002 and 2008, approximately $72 billion went to the fossil fuel industry.[59]

Do the global oil companies need these handouts to obtain oil? Oil corporation profits are extraordinarily high and keep setting new records, so that seems unlikely. Take it from a Texas oilman, George W. Bush: "I will tell you with $55 [per barrel] oil, we don't need [to provide] incentives to oil and gas companies to explore."[60] With oil now costing nearly twice as much per barrel, we continue to subsidize oil companies, which already have the massive built-in subsidy of benefiting from the price-fixing of the global OPEC cartel.

The rising costs of our fossil fuel dependence for families, communities, and the environment, have moved from inconvenient to dangerous and are approaching catastrophic. When crises occur, as in the Gulf of Mexico when BP's Deepwater Horizon oil rig exploded in 2010 or when the Exxon Valdez ripped open in Alaska or when oil refineries exploded as in Texas and Washington State in recent years or when another war in the Middle East begins or an old one enters its second decade, we see the death of people, ecosystems, businesses, and livelihoods. What we sometimes fail to see right in front of us is the growing and terrible price that we place on families, communities, and our environment everywhere, every day. In some ways, oil is not the worst of it.

We burn what the coal corporate lobby calls "clean coal" for nearly 40 percent of our electricity.[61] There is, however, no such thing as "clean coal." Coal-burning utilities emit toxic pollution. Coal causes tens of thousands of premature deaths each year in the United States, as well as many thousands more cases of lung and other cancers, asthma attacks, upper respiratory illness, heart attacks, and hospitalizations.[62] Coal combustion pushes forty-eight tons of mercury, a neurotoxin, into the air each year.[63] Mercury and other coal pollutants contaminate the air we breathe and are deposited with the rain into our rivers, lakes, and streams. Thousands of water bodies where people used to fish now are poisoned. Forty-five states now have health warnings about the toxicity of eating fish from local waters.[64]

Coal is not cheap, either. The coal industry, like other nineteenth-century industries that leverage improper political power from their old economic power, takes billions of dollars each year from American taxpayers. As with oil, massive government subsidies prop up outdated coal energy, while Arch Coal, Peabody Energy, Patriot Coal, Massey Energy, and Alpha Natural Resources take record profits for themselves. Since 1950, the coal industry has received direct subsidies of $72 billion from the US government. Congress added $9 billion in subsidies as recently as 2005. The so called stimulus bill in 2009 added another $3.4 billion to help the coal industry figure out—so far unsuccessfully—how it could stop emitting massive amounts of carbon pollution.[65]

Coal corporations pass on, or to use the economists' term, *externalize*, huge costs onto American society. Annual costs of thousands of coal-caused disease, land devastation, and destroyed water resources are conservatively estimated at $333 billion.[66] Coal, along with oil, is the principal cause of the very real climate crisis. Fossil fuel emits polluting greenhouse gases such as carbon dioxide, which trap heat in the atmosphere due to absorption of sunlight. The climate disaster we now face is due to human-caused emissions, 80 percent of them stemming from the burning of coal, oil, and natural gas. The increased emission of these gases, based on thermometer measurements going back to 1880, has led to an average global rise in temperatures of 1.5 degrees Fahrenheit—twice as much in the Arctic—and an additional warming of 2.0 to 11.5 degrees is predicted over the next century if emissions go unabated. Likely effects of this rise include diminished water supplies; vanishing of snow and ice; rising sea levels endangering coastal populations; increased frequency of droughts, floods, and more devastating hurricanes and storms; and long-term decline in agricultural production and increased incidence of malaria, cholera, and other disease.[67]

Corporate Power Blocks Alternatives

Are we unable to change and adapt because we have no alternative? No, alternatives are available now. We do next to nothing to tap the vast energy resources in our buildings and homes, where 70 percent of energy is consumed, much of it wasted. For a small fraction of the cost of new power plants, we could have retrofit programs for insulation, windows, electricity-saving devices, and other efficiency steps that would save many more billions of barrels of oil, pounds of coal, cubic feet of gas, and American dollars. People may want that, but in contrast to oil, coal, and gas, we do not have a string of multibillion-dollar corporations lobbying to get our government moving on that.

105

We are falling farther behind. Denmark and Spain generate 21 percent of their electricity demand from wind power alone. Spain is on target to generate an additional 10 percent of its electricity from solar power and has a large export business in solar technology, though behind the leaders in this lucrative business—China and Germany. Three states in Germany generate 40 percent of their electricity from wind power. Scotland recently moved its 2020 target of 50 percent of power from wind up to 80 percent. The Philippines derives 28 percent of its energy needs from geothermal sources. In the United States, we generate less than 3 percent of our electricity from solar, wind, biomass, geothermal, and the like (an additional 6.5 percent comes from hydropower).[68]

BP's offshore oil drilling operation that nearly destroyed the Gulf of Mexico took a little over a month to receive government permits.[69] By 2012, two years after the explosion and oil deluge into the Gulf, twice as many offshore oil operations are drilling in the Gulf as there were on the day of the disaster.[70] Meanwhile, for more than twelve years, the nation's first offshore wind power operation off the Massachusetts coast has been trying to get approval for operation.

Why do we fail to do what we know we need to do and what other countries seem fully capable of doing? We do not change because old-line corporations that profit from preventing change have extraordinary and growing power to resist. After all, those first "corporate free speech" cases involved power struggles between the people and utility corporations such as Central Hudson, Consolidated Edison, and PG&E, and with the Supreme Court's creation of corporate rights, the people lost.

Thanks to the successful efforts of the US Chamber of Commerce and Lewis Powell and his allies to enlist the power of the Supreme Court, it is now illegal—a violation of "free speech"—to prevent utility corporations from promoting energy consumption.

After *Citizens United*, it is illegal for us to regulate corporate spending in politics and elections.

Oil, gas, and coal companies have long been among the biggest corporate spenders to gain and keep corrupt political influence in Washington, D.C., and state capitals. Oil and gas corporations spend well over $100 million per year on lobbying in Washington, D.C., and electric utility corporations match them.[71] In contrast, all alternative energy companies combined managed to come up with $16 million to lobby in 2013.[72]

After *Citizens United*, the American Petroleum Institute announced that it would spend millions of dollars to support friendly candidates and attack perceived opponents of the oil companies. "This is adding one more tool to our toolkit," said an API official. "At the end of the day, our mission is trying to influence the policy debate."[73]

And so they have. Oil corporations such as Chevron spent millions to buy influence and control debate in elections from the speaker of the US House of Representatives to city council. Koch Industries and the billionaire family that controls it run a vast, secretive funding network ($400 million in 2012 alone) to win elections and preferential policies.[74] Oil and gas corporations also spend millions to dominate (and eliminate) the political debate in many states, and are even spending millions in city council races.[75]

Symbolic of Our Fall: Mountaintop Removal

To fully appreciate the ecological, moral, and social disaster of corporate domination of government, you could go to Appalachia and see the impact of mountaintop removal coal mining. You should hurry, though, if you want to see mountains; they are going fast. To get coal more cheaply than it would cost to hire more miners, vast swaths of Kentucky, West Virginia, Tennessee, and Virginia, with some of the richest, most diverse ecosystems in the world, have been destroyed.

Global coal corporations have blown up and flattened more than 500 mountains, dumping the toxic debris into valleys and obliterating more than 2,000 of miles of headland streams—literally, they no longer exist. As Robert Kennedy Jr. points out, if you filled twenty-five feet of a stream in your town, you could go to jail.[76] Coal corporations have filled 2,500 miles of streams in Appalachia. Towns and communities have been destroyed, drinking water poisoned, disease incurred, and local economies ruined by this most destructive, irresponsible, and shortsighted form of extracting energy in the history of humanity.[77]

If you cannot go to Appalachia, you can still see and hear some of the brave people working to stop this by going to websites for organizations such as I Love Mountains (http://ilovemountains.org), a coalition campaign to end mountaintop removal, or Appalachian Voices, the Kentucky Riverkeeper, or the Waterkeeper Alliance.[78] The I Love Mountains website has a What's My Connection link that lets you type in your ZIP code and see how the destruction of Appalachia connects to you.

I live in Concord, Massachusetts, and felt glad about our lower-cost municipal utility pursuing alternative energy and conservation. When I put in my ZIP code at the I Love Mountains Web site, however, I discovered that when I turn on a light, coal from obliterated mountains in Appalachia is burned in the AES Thames power plant in Connecticut, which feeds into the New England grid and into the Concord Light & Power system.

Knowing this makes it hard to visit the people in West Virginia and Kentucky who cannot drink what used to be clean mountain water, whose coal-dust-covered homes shake with explosions, whose children go to schools and get sick from the toxic dust settling over them; the people who are pitted against one another by coal companies who destroy jobs and threaten to destroy the rest of them if anyone complains.

I did visit, and one must see it to believe that this is happening in America. Bill Haney, a businessman and film director, has documented the terrible crime going on across Appalachia in the film *The Last Mountain*. To watch it is to understand the sad, dangerous consequences of unchecked corporate power. Or watch Robert Kennedy Jr. in Blair, West Virginia, where he connected mountaintop removal extraction, *Citizens United*, and the destruction of American democracy.[79]

Or you can hear the voice of Elmer Lloyd, a retired coal miner in Harlan County, Kentucky.[80] After he retired, Lloyd built a fish pond because the local streams had been ruined. "When I was small, kids could go down to the river to fish; I could go down to the river, put a line in, and catch all the fish I wanted. But over the years, I mean, it became where you couldn't even find a minnow, or a fish, or nothin' in the river, because they were all gone. So I figured I'd build me a pond, you know, you'd have something in the area where the kids could fish."

When the mountaintop removal started, "people told me, when they start stripping behind your house, they're going to destroy your home. I said no, I believe there's enough laws out there to make 'em do it right. Well, they said, you wait and see." Toxic runoff from the operations destroyed the stream and Lloyd's fish pond, killing all the fish. When Lloyd complained, the coal company sent people over: "They were kinda laughing about it. Saying, there's one that might make it. There's one that didn't make it. And they were saying it like they thought it was funny."

Lloyd called the Kentucky Department of Fish and Wildlife, which told him to fill in the pond because with mountaintop removal coal mining, there was no hope for it. Lloyd says, "It just ain't right for companies to try and come in here and get a dollar and destroy the place, destroy people, and leave because they don't have to worry about it next year because they're gone looking for something else to make money on and destroy."

Lloyd's right when he says, "I believe there's enough laws out there to make 'em do it right." Many of those laws are the laws that we demanded after the first Earth Day in 1970, such as the Clean Water Act, which the government once vigorously enforced. The Clean Water Act has a "citizens' suit" provision so that when the government fails to do its job, people can bring a case of their own. People in West Virginia, Kentucky, and Tennessee did this, exposing widespread illegality by the coal corporations, from Clean Water Act violations (12,000 violations by one company at one mine alone) to falsified water-monitoring reports. Joe Lovett, a West Virginia lawyer who brought one of the first cases, says he "naively believed that we would just go to court, point out what was wrong, and that the United States government would fix it."[81] In four different cases, a federal judge in West Virginia found that the coal corporations, and the government that was supposed to regulate the coal corporations, were violating the law. Mountaintop removal mining had "cracked the walls" of nearby homes and "made the air so dusty that [people] cannot sit out on the porch comfortably." Even inside, people "cough from dust particles and their furniture is constantly layered with dust." Judge Haden also heard testimony from people who could no longer paddle up a favorite tributary "because it no longer existed, having been covered and destroyed by mining activities."

Judge Haden flew over southern West Virginia and saw the impact himself:

> *Mined sites were visible from miles away. The sites stood out among the natural wooded ridges as huge white plateaus, and the valley fills appeared as massive, artificially landscaped stair steps. Some mine sites were twenty years old, yet tree growth was stunted or non-existent.*

*If the forest canopy of Pigeonroost Hollow is leveled . . .
and aquatic life is destroyed, these harms cannot be undone. If
the forest wildlife is driven away by the blasting, the noise, and
the lack of safe nesting and eating areas, they cannot be coaxed
back. If the mountaintop is removed, . . . it cannot be reclaimed
to its exact original contour. Destruction of the unique topogra-
phy of southern West Virginia, and of Pigeonroost Hollow in
particular, cannot be regarded as anything but permanent and
irreversible.*[82]

Four times, the Court of Appeals reversed Judge Haden's decisions and allowed the mountaintop removal and valley fills to continue. The court noted that the coal corporations, United Mineworkers, and "the West Virginia State political establishment" all were allied against the citizens groups and the Environmental Protection Agency, as if the job of the court of law is to add up the weight of political influence before deciding a case.[83] When Judge Haden again ruled that mountaintop removal and the obliteration of streams violated the Clean Water Act, the Bush administration rewrote the rules to try to make what was illegal "legal." Judge Haden ruled that maneuver, too, was illegal because only Congress has the authority to rewrite the Clean Water Act, and "the rule change was designed simply for the benefit of the mining industry."[84] The Court of Appeals reversed that decision, too.

The power that leads government to aid and encourage illegal activity is not because of the great number of jobs and livelihoods at stake. Coal corporations favor mountaintop removal precisely because it requires fewer jobs and is therefore more profitable. There are fewer than 20,000 coal-mining jobs in West Virginia today, compared to 145,000 in the 1950s. Underground mining requires many more miners than mountaintop removal mining.

The political force that obliterates the very Appalachian Mountains themselves is not driven by the people of Appalachia demanding the destruction of their homes, communities, woods, mountains, and streams for all time but from the power of corporate money. The vast majority of the people in West Virginia want mountaintop removal mining stopped now, yet not a single West Virginia politician will stand for those people because of the political power of the coal corporations.[85]

Recently, the Environmental Protection Agency said it may begin to enforce the Clean Water Act on mountaintop removal. The coal corporation executives and hired hands went ballistic, calling this possibility a "regulatory jihad," a "regulatory assault," and "out of control." Indeed, if you search the Internet on "EPA out of control," you will encounter a well-funded corporate campaign spread out across the land, the blogosphere, the "think tanks" and "foundations," and the airwaves.

After *Citizens United*, the coal corporations are moving in for the kill. A leaked letter from one coal corporation executive to another shortly after *Citizens United* described the plan: "With the recent Supreme Court ruling, we are in a position to be able to take corporate positions that were not previously available in allowing our voices to be heard." (There are those corporate "voices" again.) He suggested that representatives of the corporations meet to discuss "developing a [political-spending] 527 entity with the purpose of attempting to defeat anti-coal incumbents in select races, as well as elect pro-coal candidates running for certain open seats." He proposed "a significant commitment to such an effort."[86]

This is what government of, for, and by the corporations looks like. If we want to live with it, the American experiment in freedom and government of the people is doomed. Fortunately, millions of Americans, from the mountains to the prairies and to the oceans, too, are saying "Enough!" To win change, though, people will need to be prepared for the implicit blackmail of corporations threatening "jobs" if we try to restrain or balance corporate power. For that reason, the next chapter looks more closely at the idea that we must quietly accept corporations as our rulers if we want to make a living.

Chapter Five
Did Political Inequality and Corporate Power Destroy the Working American Economy?

Who are to be the electors of the federal representatives? Not the rich, more than the poor; not the learned, more than the ignorant; not the haughty heirs of distinguished names, more than the humble sons of obscure and unpropitious fortune. The electors are to be the great body of the people of the United States.

—James Madison, Federalist No. 57

Crony capitalism is usually thought of as a system in which those close to the political authorities who make and enforce policies receive favors that have large economic value. . . .

—Stephen Haber, "The Political Economy of Crony Capitalism"[1]

"**D**emocratic capitalism is threatened as never before . . . . Not from without but from within." That's the conclusion about *Citizens United* from Robert Monks, a businessperson, corporate governance expert, and former chair of the Republican Party in Maine.[2] He has spent eight decades in business, and now has joined more than 2,000 business leaders with "Business For Democracy," a project of Free Speech For People and the American Sustainable Business Council, in working to overturn *Citizens United*. Other business leaders in this work include entrepreneurs such as Yvon Chouinard, founder of Patagonia; Ben Cohen and Jerry Greenfield, founders of Ben & Jerry's Ice Cream; Amy Domini, founder of Domini Social Investments; Gary Hirschberg, founder of Stonyfield Farm; Nell Newman, founder of Newman's Own Organics; Wayne Silby, founder of Calvert Social Investment Fund, and many more.[3] They recognize that democracy, freedom, and a sustainable world depend on a bill of rights for people, not corporations. And they know that government dominated by factions of corporations and the wealthy alone is terrible for American innovation and business.

The Hoover Institution and others have probed the problem of "crony capitalism" and how it hampers economies in other parts of the world. These studies tend to associate pay-to-play crony capitalism with Indonesia, Russia, Egypt, and other countries with less of a tradition of freedom and democracy. It may be time to look closer to home. In a 2013 study by the Committee on Economic Development, 75 percent of American business executives surveyed describe our current condition as a "pay-to-play," system. Eighty-seven percent believe our campaign finance system needs "major reform."[4]

Now even the most gifted economists probably could not definitively answer the question that titles this chapter. Nevertheless, two propositions are worth serious consideration: First, the *Citizens United* vision of American government as a corporate marketplace, where citizens are reduced to consumers, rewards large entrenched corporations that can leverage their last-generation economic muscle into political power to delay and obstruct new rivals. Innovative businesses and nascent industries waste precious capital trying to keep up politically, rather than economically. As with unions, however, new businesses, small businesses, or disfavored businesses do not have a prayer in the multibillion-dollar corporate lobbyist playground or in the corporatized courts. As a result, opportunity wanes, politically favored corporations shift costs to the public or onto potential competitors, and economic vitality declines.

Second, *Citizens United*'s elimination of the last modest restraint on corporate power and the lock-up of government by a ruling elite—elimination of fair spending rules in elections—is likely to complete the transformation of our economy into one where only a few people, rather than most people, have a shot to prosper. In our present corporatist era, good wages, benefits like health care or pensions, and notions of craftsmanship and job stability have changed from goals to bad things that should be crushed. They are costs to be reduced, or eliminated altogether, rather than good things to which society might aspire. It may be hard to remember, but we once thought that higher wages with more benefits for working people was a worthy goal, rather than a problem to overcome so that corporations can be more "competitive." Now CEOs who find a way to eliminate jobs and benefits or destroy a union are celebrated and paid tens or even hundreds of millions of dollars, while the stock price rises and the analysts and media cheer.

Entrenched Corporations Gain Inefficient Advantage

If we accept the false metaphor of corporate money as a "voice" and the fantasy that big corporations are no more of a threat to our political life than big people, you can count on coal and oil corporations prospering and solar, wind, tidal, and geothermal energy corporations struggling. When you call government for help after coal corporations crack your walls and poison your fish pond, you can count on being told to fill in your pond and move on. And we all can count on a low-wage, low-benefit economy with a great divide between the rich and everyone else.

In crony capitalism, distorted policies corrupt and tilt markets to favor connected, rather than good, businesses. Too often corporate interests exploit free-market advocates concerned about government or excessive regulation to support the elimination of regulations on even the most complex and potentially destructive businesses.[5] The elimination of regulation, or other manipulation of regulatory advantage, is the essence of inefficient, pay-to-play corrupt capitalism.

The perceived absence of regulations is neither the absence of government nor the presence of a market economy. The choice is not between regulation and no regulation; the choice is between a government that regulates in service of the public interest or one that regulates in service of powerful corporate interests. Sometimes it's more regulation (as in the case of laws prohibiting Medicare from negotiating with pharmaceutical companies for market rates), sometimes less regulation (as in passing a law prohibiting regulators from regulating the derivatives market), sometimes different regulations (as in expanding the rights of patent protection to delay increased competition and lower prices). Under any of these scenarios, government action shifts public assets and benefits to a favored slice of powerful people and interests while allocating huge costs to powerless people and interests.

Unremitting hostility to regulation that serves the public does not create more efficient business—just the opposite. Weak government oversight of transnational corporations rewards bloated enterprises that use political power to dump their inefficiencies off their balance sheets and onto society at the expense of new and more efficient enterprises.

Coal is a good example. Corporate and investor calculations about energy production will differ if the cost of coal does not include the cost of preventing the destruction of what belongs to other people—water, air, mountains, and valleys, not to mention fish ponds and house foundations. Coal appears "cheaper" than wind, solar, or other sources of power only if its costs do not include the very large costs—externalities—that coal corporations and coal burning utilities can, in the absence of effective regulation, displace onto others outside of the business. This is the corporate "externalization" problem.

According to Monks, "The corporation is an externalizing machine in the same way a shark is a killing machine."[6] That is just what it does. If it is legal to dump untreated waste or toxic pollutants into a river or the air, corporations will do so. They will do so not because corporations are evil or because the people who work for corporations are bad; they will do so because it is legal. If it is legal to dump pollution onto others, then the market price assumes "free" pollution disposal. If one corporation does not do that, another will. The one that dumps wastes and emits pollutants may have lower costs than the one that spends money to treat or prevent pollution. The one with higher costs will go out of business because it cannot compete, and "the market" then will require dumping waste into rivers and toxins into the sky.

In theory, this is a human problem, not a corporation problem. In the real world, it is a corporation problem. Corporations fund campaigns against the "out-of-control EPA" and "regulatory jihad" because they seek more profit. If allowed, coal corporations pour money into electing whomever they consider "friends of coal" and to defeating whomever they regard as enemies because the corporations seek more profit. Without government regulation to control greenhouse gas emissions, the destruction of mountains, the poisoning of streams, and so on, we can be sure that someone else (or everyone else) will bear the cost while the corporation reaps the profit.

What makes the hostility to regulation more perverse is that those problems—global environmental catastrophe, for instance—are caused in large measure by government's creation of the corporate entity and its advantages in the first place. Without the laws permitting incorporation, conferring limited liability, and other advantages, it would be difficult to marshal the scope of investment and operations capable of eliminating 500 mountains in a few years (unless the government itself coerced the capital for such operations, as in the Soviet Union or other state-enterprise regimes). Would you invest in Massey Energy or the Alpha Natural Resources coal corporation if you were personally held responsible for its actions?

That is not to say that we should not have corporations. Rather, we should not pretend that corporations are natural products of "the market" and that government has no business regulating them. As Theodore Roosevelt wrote about corporations a century ago, it is "folly to try to prohibit them, but . . . also folly to leave them without thoroughgoing control."[7]

So crony capitalism may be un-American, but do not fall for the idea that government or regulation is un-American. A true libertarian might not want any government or any regulation, but such a libertarian would not stoop to ask government for a corporate charter and would not hide behind limited liability and other government favors. Maybe we could live with a true libertarian society if we could get there, but we cannot live with a government that creates, protects, and serves corporate power but leaves corporations unsupervised and unregulated.

Jobs, Taxes, and Wealth

A lot of data suggest that the success of the corporate drive to power in our country in recent decades has helped transform our economy from a broad-based growth engine for all into "oligarchy" and "corporatism," in the words of former Iowa Republican congressman Jim Leach.[8] It now is very difficult for any but the rich to prosper in healthy, strong communities.[9]

In the corporate era, most Americans no longer make enough money. Median income is now around $28,000, and "household" income (i.e., husband and wife both working in many cases) is around $53,000.[10] Wages for most people have been flat for three decades. Personal savings have plummeted, and debt has soared.

This was not true in the previous thirty years: from 1950 through 1980, when the economy was growing, wages for most people grew, too. The average income for nine out of ten Americans grew from $17,719 to $30,941 in that period, a 75 percent increase in constant 2008 dollars. Since 1980, however, the economy continued to grow but the gains went overwhelmingly to the top fraction of Americans. The top 1 percent received 36 percent of the income gains between 1979 and 2008. The top sliver (again, 1 percent) received 53 percent of income gains from 2001 to 2006.[11] By 2012, the percentage of the nation's economic gains going to the top 1 percent reached levels not seen since 1913.[12]

For average Americans, income went from $30,941 in 1980 to $31,244 in 2008, a gain of only $303 dollars in twenty-eight years.[13] Total household income rose a little more than that, but only because most households required two paychecks and more women entered the workforce.[14] Since the Great Recession began in 2008, median income has fallen every year for five years.[15]

The top 1 percent of income-earning Americans now take a larger share of income than ever before. Between 1993 and 1997, "corporations enjoyed double-digit profit increases for five years in a row. . . . Meanwhile, over the 1990s, hourly wages fell for four of every five workers."[16] CEO pay rose 600 percent in the same decade.[17]

In the past decade, the United States has lost thousands of factories, and thousands more are on the precipice.[18] By 2009, fewer Americans worked in manufacturing jobs than at any time since 1941.[19] Most other measures of the American middle class are just as bad. Hours worked? Since 1979, married couples with children are working an additional 500 hours (equivalent to more than sixty-two eight-hour days).[20] Vacation time? We have by far the lowest standard for vacation time in the developed world. Debt? With incomes stagnating and savings rates are near zero, most Americans live under pressing burdens of credit card, mortgage, auto, school, and other debt. Affordability of housing? Ability to pay for college? Retiring with a safe pension? Health care? Most people have it much worse on these measures than thirty years ago.

Some people say that this steady decline is just the way it is, "globalization and all that," as if globalization were a meteor from outer space rather than a result of policy choices and a trend that democratic societies can shape. Secret, "fast-track" trade policies, negotiated by representatives of corporations (the North American Free Trade Agreement [NAFTA], the Trans-Pacific Partnership [TPP], and many more) shift a lot of work to low-wage countries by design. The downward pressure on wages in America, increased corporate profits, and enrichment of those who own shares in, or run, large corporations, are the intended result of these policy choices.

The intentional offshoring of American jobs to low-cost countries has taken a terrible toll. An accountant in India makes $5,000 per year, compared to an American accountant's average salary of $63,000. And as one well-paid CEO noted, "If you can find high-quality talent at a third of the price, it's not too hard to see why you'd do this."[21] Even if that is true as a mathematical calculation, should our government really enable, encourage, and reward so richly those who "do this"?

Could the struggles of American workers be a productivity problem? That might be an explanation; if American productivity (how much is produced per unit of labor, capital, and other inputs) steadily declined in those years, then noninflationary income gains for American workers would be unlikely. The problem with that explanation is that American productivity did not decline but instead continued to improve. Productivity continued to rise after 1979, but we distributed the gains from that rise differently in the corporate era than we did before. According to a 2005 analysis of data from the Bureau of Labor Statistics, between 1947 and 1973, productivity and the median income rose by almost exactly the same amount (productivity increase, 100.5 percent; median income increase, 100.9 percent). Between 1973 and 2003, however, things changed. Now even though productivity continued to increase (71.3 percent), median incomes increased much less (21.9 percent). In other words, the gains were no longer going to all Americans but were increasingly going disproportionately to a very few people at the top.[22]

This did not "just happen." Gains from economic growth that used to be widely shared now go disproportionately to the extraordinarily wealthy because government chooses that outcome. Those choices may not make sense to a lot of people, but they make sense to many in the small but wealthy "donor class" that has so much say in Washington, D.C. Most of these political donors really do have different interests and preferences than the vast majority of Americans.[23]

The crony capitalist "intermingling" of political and economic elites and the success of the corporate campaign envisioned by Lewis Powell work to enrich a very few individuals and to prevent choices that previously distributed wealth and opportunity more evenly. Tax policy is another good example.

Corporations, People, and Taxes

Although corporations are not people, people control corporations, and a very few people control the largest, richest corporations. As Stephen Haber noted regarding crony capitalism elsewhere in the world, "The intermingling of economic and political elites means that it is extremely difficult to break the implicit contract between government and the privileged asset holders."[24] That intermingling is on full display in Washington, D.C., and state capitals when government allocates the tax burden.

Gross income disparities are an enemy of successful market economies.[25] Nevertheless, shifting income to the very top lies at the heart of the corporatism agenda. In fact, the first of the modern corporate rights decisions arose from organized corporate opposition to a modest proposal in Massachusetts to tax the wealthy at a slightly higher rate than the middle-class and the poor. The 1978 decision in *First National Bank of Boston v. Bellotti* (a 5–4 decision written by Justice Powell) struck down a Massachusetts law banning corporate funding for or against citizen referendum campaigns. The referendum at issue in that case would have allowed Massachusetts to have a graduated income tax instead of one where the poor paid the same rate as the rich. That was the question that galvanized corporations such as Bank of Boston, Gillette, and Digital Corporation to sue for corporate speech rights to block a citizen referendum.

These corporations demanded that the Supreme Court guarantee them the right to spend as much corporate money as their executives decided was necessary to defeat the citizen tax referendum. According to the argument used by the corporations in the case, a slightly higher tax rate for very high incomes would make it more difficult for corporations to recruit talented executives in

Massachusetts. The corporations won. Now, thirty years later, Massachusetts still does not have progressive income taxes.[26]

What happened to the companies that got the Supreme Court to give corporations "speech" rights to spend unlimited money to defeat a citizen vote in Massachusetts? Without Powell's Supreme Court decision, the companies might not have been able to recruit the talented executives who would have avoided Massachusetts if the state had progressive income taxes—right?

Massachusetts should have been so lucky. Here's an update on each of the corporate plaintiffs in the case since the 1978 *Bellotti* decision. Gillette sold itself to Procter & Gamble in 2005, with the loss of more than 1,000 jobs.[27] The Gillette CEO who engineered the deal, James Kilts, made $188 million on the sale.[28] Bank of Boston sold itself to Fleet (5,000 lost jobs; $25 million for the CEO), which then sold itself to Bank of America (13,000 lost jobs; $35 million for the CEO).[29] Digital sold itself to Compaq in 1998 (15,000 lost jobs; $6.5 million for the Digital CEO who sold the company).[30] The tax rate for those CEOs and the laid off employees remains equal.

CEO Pay, Political Spending, and Corporate Government

It approaches a state of what Robert Kerr has called "cognitive feudalism" to imagine that there are no connections among corporate power, wealth disparity, and the erosion of democracy.[31] The same CEOs and executives who decide to spend corporate lobbying money and corporate "independent" campaign money also make substantial personal contributions directly to candidates. They also decide how much to pay themselves, advised by a sympathetic board compensation committee, and disconnected from meaningful shareholder review.[32] In the corporate era of today, that pay is now much, much more than it used to be, so that millions of dollars in CEO personal campaign contributions are relatively easy to make.

Between 2000 and 2008, CEO pay ranged from 319 to 525 times the average employee's pay. Even after the 2008 financial meltdown, the average CEO salary (nearly $14 million) remains 354 times higher than the average employee salary.[33] In 1980, the average CEO made only forty-two times the salary of the average employee.[34]

This is how the two prongs of *Citizens United*—corporate "rights" and unlimited political spending by the wealthiest—reinforce each other. The nonpartisan Center for Responsive Politics (CRP) provides data showing contributions to candidates and political parties from individual "heavy hitters." The CRP defines a *heavy hitter* as someone who has given federal political candidates and parties more than $50,000 during a single election cycle. That $50,000 giveaway to politicians is more than the annual income of 75 percent of Americans.

The CRP heavy hitter list includes dozens of CEOs and executives of global financial corporations that received billions of dollars in taxpayer-funded bailouts or other government aid during the recent financial crisis, including Goldman Sachs, Citigroup, AIG, JPMorgan Chase, UBS, Credit Suisse, Wachovia, Merrill Lynch, and Bank of America. The list of $50,000 campaign contributors also includes executives from global energy, media, tobacco, telecommunications, and pharmaceutical corporations that benefit from government policy decisions (or inaction) to the tune of billions of dollars in corporate profit.[35]

Another CEO, Sean McCutcheon, runs a mining engineering corporation in Alabama. He has decided to join the heavy-hitter club, and in 2014, he brought a case to the Supreme Court in another attack on America's campaign finance laws. He claimed that the limitation of $123,000 per year for his aggregate contributions to congressional campaigns "severely" limits his freedom of speech. Citing *Citizens United*, he argued that the principle of political equality for every American. According to McCutcheon's lawyers, contribution limits may not be upheld as a means of limiting disparities in the extent to which people of different economic backgrounds are able to participate in the political process and exercise their First Amendment rights."[36]

In another 5-4 decision, the Supreme Court agreed, and struck down the contribution limits.[37] In response to widespread outrage and protests in 140 cities and towns across the country, the corporate funded Manhattan Institute hastily explained that all is well because rich people vote more, may be better informed, and prefer better policies.[38]

For "heavy hitter" political donors and their companies, the large "investments" in politics pay off. Both receive coddling tax treatment that makes no sense from the perspective of national interest or sound fiscal policy in times of high deficits. Despite large profits and multimillion-dollar executive payouts, bailed-out Bank of America has paid zero taxes since 2009. GE ($14 billion in profits) paid zero taxes and instead claimed a $1 billion tax credit. The wars go on, Medicare and school budgets are cut, and "temporary" tax cuts for those making more than $250,000 (2 percent of American households) remain sacrosanct.

Then there's the "hedge fund loophole." In 2009, twenty-five hedge fund managers paid themselves a total of $25.3 billion—yes, that is billion, with a B. If these twenty-five billionaires paid income taxes like everyone else, one would expect those billions in earnings to be taxed at 35 percent, the federal income tax rate for the highest-paid Americans, or at 38 percent if the "temporary" tax cut enacted after the September 11 attacks had been allowed to expire in 2010. As the late billionaire Leona Helmsley famously said, however, "Only the little people pay taxes."

Hedge fund managers do not pay income taxes like other people do. Hedge fund managers take a fee in the form of a "carried interest" in the performance of the fund or, in other words, a designated percentage of the profits from investing other people's money. Hedge fund managers call this a "gain" rather than "income" and hence claim the right to pay a low capital gains tax rather than a normal income tax. For years, the top capital gains tax rate was 15 percent, and was only raised to 20 percent with the "fiscal cliff" deal at the end of 2012. Compared to income tax, that 15 percent or 20 percent is the same as the lowest income tax rates possible, available only to those with income of $36,000 or less. To put this in perspective, 75 percent of Americans make less than $50,000 per year. Say you are doing much better than most, have a high combined income with your spouse, and together make $146,000 per year. You would pay federal income tax at a 28 percent rate. Yet if you are a hedge fund manager who makes $1 billion, you pay a 20 percent tax.[39] That's the hedge fund loophole.

Unsurprisingly, this loophole outrages regular taxpayers (that is, almost everyone). Perhaps good arguments may be made, as a general proposition, for taxing capital gains at a lower rate than general income taxes. Lower capital gains taxes may encourage investment, generating economic growth, jobs, and wealth. The lower rate reflects risk-taking: investments might result in a gain, but they might also result in a total loss. But do hedge fund managers who make billions of dollars need the additional encouragement of a tax discount to do what they do? Are they going to stop making billions of dollars unless we promise not to tax them at more than 15 percent? Hedge fund managers do not have a risk of loss because they are investing other people's money, not their own. Hedge fund managers' compensation is in fact much closer to income than it is to investment gain.

Congress considered proposals to close the hedge fund loophole in 2007, 2009, 2010, and 2012. Each time, people thought that the loophole did not have a chance to survive because it is so indefensible. Undaunted, the hedge fund and private equity industry drove up millions of dollars in lobbying expenses to defeat reform.[40] The US Chamber of Commerce rushed out "studies" claiming that economic disaster would befall America if the hedge fund managers paid taxes like other people, and corporate-funded front groups with names such as American Crossroads and Crossroads GPS shouted "liberty" and inveighed against "taxes and wasteful government spending." With that snap of the leash, Congress did nothing.[41] At the end of 2013, a hedge fund manager paid himself $3 billion for the year's work or, as he would prefer, a year's "gain."[42]

The Intermingled Elite and the Economic Crisis

Perhaps nothing illustrates the "intermingled elite" of crony capitalism and its devastating consequences for the American economy better than the creation of the Citigroup financial conglomerate in 1998 and its decade-long dance into financial apocalypse.[43] Citigroup is the largest and perhaps the most dysfunctional of the "too big to fail" financial conglomerates. In 2007, it fired its CEO but paid him $105 million.[44] In 2009, the federal government bailed out Citigroup with a $306 billion guarantee of its toxic assets and a $20 billion cash infusion.

Citigroup is a monument to virtually every component of corporate misconduct that wiped out millions of jobs, homes, retirement funds, and other assets of middle-class America in the 2008 financial crisis. These components include incestuous relationships with high government officials, subprime mortgage scams, unregulated derivatives and credit default swaps, misleadingly inflated assets, securities packed with junk loans and stamped with bogus ratings, wildly excessive and irresponsible CEO and executive compensation, billions in government bailouts, unapologetic resistance to regulation or oversight, and millions of dollars in lobbying and campaign spending to continue the flow of government favors.

Almost as a bonus, Citigroup has also been a leader in corporate outsourcing of thousands of American white-collar jobs to what it calls "lower-cost locations" such as India.[45]

Back in April 1998, Citigroup, at the time one of the largest bank corporations in the world, announced its merger with Travelers Group, also a large financial and insurance conglomerate. The merger would create the largest financial company in the world. According to reports at the time, "Much of Wall Street liked the deal," and the share price of both companies soared.[46] There was only one problem: the corporate conglomerate they had in mind was illegal.

The law of the United States for at least fifty years had banned this kind of financial conglomerate. The law, known as Glass-Steagall, was passed after the 1929 stock market collapse and the ensuing financial panic that led to the Great Depression. Requiring separation of commercial and investment banks, Glass-Steagall created "firewalls" that had successfully prevented a repeat of the financial panic and Great Depression for half a century.

Illegality, though, was no deterrent. The CEOs and leaders of Citigroup and Travelers privately consulted with President Bill Clinton, Federal Reserve chairman Alan Greenspan, and Treasury secretary Robert Rubin (former chair of Goldman Sachs) to get assurances that they would help change the law.[47] Announcing the merger, Sanford Weil, CEO of Travelers said, "we are hopeful that over that time the legislation will change."[48]

They were right; the legislation did change. Congress dutifully repealed Glass-Steagall with the Financial Modernization Act of 1999 soon after the merger. A few days after Secretary Rubin's Treasury Department and the White House paved the way for Citigroup by supporting the repeal of Glass-Steagall, Rubin announced that he would be leaving government to become a top official and senior adviser at Citigroup. In the next decade, Citigroup paid Rubin $126 million.[49] Upon leaving the company in the midst of the meltdown and bailout in 2009, Rubin said he regretted that he did not "recognize the serious possibility of the extreme circumstances that the financial system faces today."[50]

At least Rubin acknowledged regret. The same cannot be said for former senator Phil Gramm, who as chair of the Senate Banking Committee drove the repeal of Glass-Steagall and was a longtime antiregulatory zealot. In Congress from 1983 to 2002, Gramm, like the corporate pharmaceutical lobbyist Billy Tauzin, was flexible enough to be both a Democrat and a Republican, depending on the winds. Gramm led the way to repeal Glass-Steagall's stabilizing regulation for Wall Street and the financial industry. A year later, he led the way to enact a law to exempt derivatives from government oversight.[51] Consensus opinion, apart from Phil Gramm, links the financial meltdown in 2008 directly to this rash abandonment of responsible government. Congress essentially surrendered the country's fortunes to the "years-long, massive lobbying effort by the banking and financial services industries to reduce regulation in their sector."[52]

Economists say this deregulation of the financial services industry and the related failure of oversight created a "less competitive and more concentrated banking system" that directly contributed to the financial crisis of 2008.[53] Conservatives and libertarians such as Robert Ekelund and Mark Thornton at the Ludwig von Mises Institute say, "This 'deregulation' amounts to corporate welfare for financial institutions and a moral hazard that will make taxpayers pay dearly."[54] Investigative journalists at *Mother Jones* agree:

> *Because of the swap-related provisions of Gramm's bill . . .*
> *a $62 trillion market (nearly four times the size of the entire*
> *US stock market) remained utterly unregulated, meaning*
> *no one made sure the banks and hedge funds had the assets*
> *to cover the losses they guaranteed. In essence, Wall Street's*

biggest players (which, thanks to Gramm's earlier banking deregulation efforts, now incorporated everything from your checking account to your pension fund) ran a secret casino.[55]

Where is Phil Gramm now? In 2002, while still serving in the Senate, he announced that at the end of his term he intended to join the UBS corporation, an international investment bank headquartered in Switzerland, as vice chairman. Since then, UBS has added a new twist to Citigroup's long list of misdeeds, folly, greed, and misconduct that led to the financial crisis: in 2009, as a result of a federal criminal investigation, UBS admitted that it participated in a years-long criminal scheme to defraud the United States by helping rich people hide assets so as to illegally evade taxes.[56]

Gramm, still with UBS, now lives in Texas with his wife, Wendy, who chaired the Commodity Futures Trading Commission (CFTC) from 1988 until 1993 and who herself is an intermingled corporate-government player. Back in 1993, just before leaving the CFTC office, she granted a "midnight order" that barred CFTC oversight of the trading in derivatives (called "weapons of mass destruction" by Warren Buffett). Mrs. Gramm then joined the board of directors of Enron, a major beneficiary of unregulated derivatives trading and a major financial supporter of Phil Gramm's political campaigns. She remained on Enron's board and its audit committee until the company's collapse due to systemic, repeated, and egregious accounting fraud in late 2001. Her Enron salary and stock income amounted to between $915,000 and $1.8 million.[57]

Phil Gramm is unrepentant. He says that he has seen "no evidence" that the financial crisis was caused by deregulation. In the summer of 2008, as the financial crisis began to unravel the nation and the world, he explained that the economy was not the problem. Rather, Americans were the problem. "This is a mental recession," he said. "We have sort of become a nation of whiners."[58]

Chapter Six
Corporations Can't Love

Only a virtuous people are capable of freedom.
—Benjamin Franklin[1]

No free government can stand without virtue in the people, and a lofty spirit of patriotism.
—Andrew Jackson[2]

Virtue may be defined as the love of the laws and of our country. As such love requires a constant preference of public to private interest, it is the source of all private virtue. . . . A government is like everything else: to preserve it we must love it. . . . Everything, therefore, depends on establishing this love in a republic.
—Thomas Jefferson[3]

In America, we are equal and free not because we have the same material goods, power, and interests as one another but because we are people. We believe that freedom and rights, as well as the responsibility of self-government, are our birthright. Now *Citizens United* has reopened ancient questions: How can a republican government of free and equal people survive in the real world of massive inequalities of wealth and power? How can all Americans participate in government on equal terms? How do we prevent the corruption of government and the destruction of liberty by what James Madison called "faction"?

Madison defined *faction* as "a number of citizens, whether amounting to a majority or minority of the whole, who are united and actuated by some common . . . interest, adverse to the rights of other citizens, or to the permanent and aggregate interests of the community." Madison and the other Founders well understood that faction was part of life. Because we are people, we might grasp for power and seek advantage for ourselves, for our families, and for our friends. The Constitution incorporates the truths of human liberty and equality and of human faults.

Our Constitution seeks to increase the odds for the success of liberty and self-government by diluting faction, balancing powers, and declaring rights. Even with better odds, government of the people requires a trait that only people can seek: virtue. "To suppose that any form of government will secure liberty or happiness without any virtue in the people, is a chimerical idea."[4]

Americans have kept this improbable run of human possibility going one generation after another, overcoming grievous injustice and brutal challenge, because of love: love of country and family, of justice and freedom. As Americans and human beings, we cannot help but believe and sacrifice for this miracle that has nothing to do with the corporate marketplace. In *Citizens United*, the Court forgot this human underpinning of our Constitution and, in thrall to its imprecise corporate metaphors, forgot the essential relationship of speech and other human rights to a virtuous republic of people. Corporate money is not speech, and corporations do not have the capacity for virtue—nor are they designed for it.

This point lay at the heart of Justice Rehnquist's repeated objections to Justice Powell's creation of corporate rights in the

1970s and 1980s. Whether or not the states or Congress regulate corporate political spending, Rehnquist wrote, "All natural persons, who owe their existence to a higher sovereign than the Commonwealth, remain as free as before to engage in political activity." He added, "In a democracy, the economic is subordinate to the political, a lesson that our ancestors learned long ago, and that our descendants will undoubtedly have to relearn many years hence."[5]

Virtue, Patriotism, and the Corporation

We are relearning at last. Distorting our Constitution and its Bill of Rights to create corporate, rather than human, rights destroys virtue and strengthens faction. Rather than balance or dilute Madison's faction, the fabrication of corporate rights promotes and strengthens the most formidable faction the world has ever known. Then it disables the constitutional mechanisms of controlling such faction by invalidating inconvenient laws and inserting corporate money and influence between lawmakers and their constituents. That is why, in America, there can be no such thing as "corporate speakers," "corporate voices," or "corporate citizens."

Corporations do not have voices or rights; they have no virtue or shame; and they do not love America. I am not saying, and do not believe, that people who work at corporations do not love our country and would not sacrifice for the nation, but corporations are not people. People in the corporation come and go, but the corporation (and again, here I am speaking primarily of large, global corporations) goes on and on (so long as it is making money). Corporations do not love (or hate) anything, including countries or humanity. It is not that corporations are disloyal to our country. Rather, it is more that they are "aloyal." Loyalty is not a trait that has any meaning or applicability to corporate charters or corporate entities or transnational corporate conglomerates, no matter how many flags General Motors or Anheuser Busch may use in advertisements. Indeed, despite its flag waving, Anheuser Busch and its "Great American Lager," Budweiser, are part of the Belgium-based global corporation called Anheuser Busch InBev.

After *Citizens United* ruled that Americans are not permitted to limit corporate spending in elections, some of the grave concern focused on "foreign corporations." But what does "foreign corporation" even mean today? The global corporations that dominate the US Chamber of Commerce agenda and spend billions on lobbying are not American or any other nationality. They have trillions in revenues and profits from around the world. They operate everywhere but are citizens of nowhere. Their largest shareholders are institutions, extremely wealthy people, or even other countries, anywhere in the world. They may have a cluster of corporate charters out of Delaware (and in various countries), but to global corporations, including what we might think of as "American corporations," the United States is just another market to control and manipulate and, if possible, in which to eliminate government oversight.

By way of example, News Corporation, the parent corporation of Fox News, now funnels millions of dollars into elections. Prince Waleed bin Talal's Kingdom Holding Company of Saudi Arabia is the second-largest shareholder, with $2 billion in shares. UBS, the bailout recipient and employer of former senator Phil Gramm, is headquartered in Switzerland, operates in fifty countries, and has as its largest shareholder the government of Singapore. Exxon, one of the biggest spenders on Washington, D.C., lobbying ($195.8 million from 1998 to 2013), operates in 200 countries. Exxon derives most of its revenues outside of the United States, and fewer than 25 percent of its employees work in this country. BP, formerly known as British Petroleum, is based in London, operates in eighty countries, and has twice as many employees outside the United States as in the country. GE (which spent $298 million in Washington, D.C., lobbying from

1998 to 2013) operates in 100 countries and has more employees and more production plants outside the United States than here. Apple, which has experienced explosive growth and enriched its shareholders, assembles virtually every one of its products in China and other parts of Asia.

It would have been bizarre and dangerous indeed if the Supreme Court of earlier times had ruled that Rockefeller's Standard Oil Corporation or the Union Pacific Railroad Corporation had "free speech" rights to spend corporate money in elections, no matter what the people or Congress thought about that. Now, in the modern age of giant corporations with byzantine international structures and international institutional shareholders, the ruling in *Citizens United* borders on assisted national suicide.

We Americans may disagree vehemently on many things. We may lose our tempers and perspectives in political fights and say terrible things about one another, but at bottom, I think, most Americans know that we all love our country and we all want America to succeed. We share values. We are family members, sometimes literally, sometimes figuratively. Our children will live together. And we take the future, nature, patriotism, and other nonmonetary considerations into account when we vote, support parties or candidates, and do what people in a republic must do. We know we will not be here to see the America our grandchildren will grow old in, but we all hope to make decisions and live in ways that will leave a free, strong country and world behind for them.

Corporations do not, and cannot, do that. The owners and executives and other people in the corporation do that, as people, on their own behalf outside of work. Almost certainly, however, any decision to spend corporate money to influence an election or to make up a constitutional corporate right to eliminate a law regulating the corporation will not reflect these diverse human considerations but will reflect only a calculation of possible corporate profit.

The virtue that so concerned the founders of our nation is a human aspiration, if not always a human trait. We all know that no one is perfect, but it is impossible to observe a jury deliberate a case, talk to people in polling places at election time, watch cops, nurses, firefighters, teachers, and soldiers do their jobs, or go to a school parent meeting, blood drive, food kitchen, or any local volunteer group and not see how strong virtue remains in America. That is civic virtue, and it happens because of human, not corporate, love.

Crime and Punishment

No matter how forgiving we may be, it is very hard to think of those who commit crimes against people and against the community as virtuous. People may be rehabilitated, and eventually, in some states, former felons may participate fully in civic life again. We usually expect, however, some combination of jail time, shame, and repentance before someone can earn back the right to be a full participating member of the community after committing crimes against it.

Not so with corporations. Shame, repentance, community condemnation, and redemption are for people. Bank of America, General Motors, Credit Suisse, General Electric, Deutsche Bank, BP, Exxon, Boeing, WellCare Health Plans, Alcoa, Volvo, Pfizer, and many, many more large corporations are criminals.[6] I don't say that as a provocative insult. I say that as a fact for consideration in evaluating whether it makes any sense to conceive of corporations as bearers of the people's constitutional rights. Those corporations have all admitted crimes or, in the case of General Motors, have been convicted of crimes after trial. If these corporations were people, they might not be allowed to vote, coach Little League, or head a scouting troop. They would not be trusted. Yet after *Citizens United*, nothing restricts their dominating political influence in our national life.

These convicted corporations are not people, so they did not go to jail, feel shame, or let down their parents, children, or neighbors. They paid some money and went back to making more money. They went back to paying hundreds of millions of dollars to lobbyists to block laws, preserve tax breaks and subsidies, and otherwise ensure favorable government policy. In some instances, they went back to committing more crimes.

In most cases, the corporation itself suffers no lasting damage after pleading guilty to crimes and, indeed, may even profit from breaking the rules. In the corporatist era, some even claim that is just fine and is as it should be. As Kent Greenfield describes in *The Failure of Corporate Law*, some of the leading scholars argue that corporate managers "do not have an ethical duty to obey economic regulatory laws just because they exist. They must determine the importance of these laws. . . . The idea of optimal sanctions is based on the supposition that managers not only may but also should violate the rules when it is profitable to do so."[7]

Crime and the Corporate Charter

Betty Harrah never imagined she would have reason to walk into the attorney general's office in Wilmington, Delaware. On a sunlit September morning in 2011, however, Ms. Harrah, a forty-four-year-old case manager for a children's care center, left her home in Beckley, West Virginia, to travel to the Delaware state capitol. She intended to make a complaint, to bear witness, and to seek justice. She would ask Attorney General Beau Biden to do what the Delaware Constitution and Delaware law obliges the attorney general to do: bring proceedings to revoke the corporate charter of the Massey Energy Company corporation, a $2.5 billion coal company incorporated under Delaware law.

In Delaware, as in every state, corporate charters are granted only "subject to dissolution or the revocation or forfeiture of the corporate charter."[8] The Delaware Constitution requires that the General Assembly "shall, by general law, provide for the revocation or forfeiture of the charters or franchises."[9] Delaware law requires that the attorney general "shall" bring an action in state court to "revoke or forfeit the charter of any corporation for abuse . . . of its corporate powers, privileges or franchises." The law defines *abuse* of corporate privileges or charters as "a sustained course of fraud, immorality or violations of statutory law. . . ."[10]

It is hard to imagine a better candidate for such action than the Massey Energy corporation. Betty Harrah and others from West Virginia joined Free Speech For People and Appalachian Voices in meetings at the attorney general's office because her brother, Steve, and twenty-eight other men were killed in a West Virginia coalmine explosion that never should have happened.

Betty's younger brother, whom she had always called Stevie, had worked for Massey Energy's coal operations for many years. He was forty years old, an army veteran, and he liked to hunt, fish, and play cards with his friends, Most of all, he loved the time he had with his six-year-old son. Toward the end of his life, Steve had told his sister of his worries about conditions in Massey Energy's Upper Big Branch mine. He had good reason to worry.

By April 5, 2010, when the mine exploded, Massey Energy had committed 62,923 federal mine-safety violations over a decade, including more than 25,000 violations deemed "significant and substantial." On top of that, the corporation violated the Clean Water Act 13,000 times. Fifty-nine men who worked in Massey's mines had been killed in recent accidents.[11] The United Mine Workers called the Upper Big Branch explosion "industrial homicide," and attorney and law professor Robert F. Kennedy Jr., deemed Massey a "criminal enterprise."[12]

After the Upper Big Branch mine explosion, an independent commission appointed by the West Virginia governor conducted a thorough investigation. The commission concluded that the explosion and twenty-nine deaths occurred because Massey Energy systematically violated the law and deployed its money and power to corrupt West Virginia government and the courts.[13] According to the commission, Massey Energy provided "a graphic illustration of the intertwining of coal and government. . . ."[14] The "ability of the government to rigorously enforce those laws is a hard-earned right paid for with the blood of coalminers;" Massey's corporate money and power in elections, lawmaking, and the courts had defeated that right.[15] In short, the commission concluded, Massey had "normalized deviance."[16]

With Massey, overwhelming evidence of a "sustained course of fraud, immorality, and violations of law" clearly warranted the revocation of its Delaware corporate charter, yet Delaware has done nothing to enforce its own law. While Betty Harrah and others wait for justice and accountability for the corporation that caused so much harm, Massey Energy shareholders and its chief executive officer, Don Blankenship, walked away from the disaster with massive profit.

After the explosion, Massey Energy sold itself to an even bigger coal company, Alpha Natural Resources, Inc., for $7.1 billion. Blankenship, the Massey CEO, had engineered the corporation's defiance of the laws; the breaking of worker safety standards, wages, and benefits; the corruption of West Virginia courts and government; and the imposition of a "code of silence" among executives. For that, in the three years before the explosion, the company paid him $38 million. When Alpha bought Massey after the explosion, Blankenship received an $86 million golden parachute, including a deferred compensation package, a $5 million pension, a house for life, stock options, and more. In total, eighteen Massey executives and board members received $196 million.[17]

Betty Harrah came to Delaware because she wanted justice for her brother, Steve, and for all of the families who lost so much to Massey and the government's abdication of duty. Although federal criminal prosecutions in West Virginia continue to move forward against some at Massey, Ms. Harrah and 30,000 other Americans who backed her up in a petition to the Delaware attorney general know that the corporation and shareholders also must be held accountable. They have demanded only what Delaware law requires: that the Delaware attorney general begin proceedings to revoke the corporate charter of Massey Energy for abuse of the privileges of incorporation. Although they are still waiting for action from the attorney general, they are not going away.

Massey Energy is not the only one. The global oil giant BP is another of many examples of the lack of public accountability and control over the transnational corporations that now dominate so much of our lives. BP is a web of corporations. The corporation was founded in the United Kingdom as British Petroleum in 1909. The parent corporation is now called BP plc and maintains its headquarters in London. BP operates in the United States through numerous subsidiary corporations that have been granted corporate charters under Delaware law. These include BP America, BP America Production Company, BP Products North America, BP Corporation North America, BP Exploration (Alaska) Inc., BP West Coast Products, Standard Oil, BP Amoco Chemical Company, and more.

Only a few weeks after the Massey explosion in April 2010, BP's Deepwater Horizon oil rig in the Gulf of Mexico exploded, killing eleven men. The resulting massive oil inundation into the Gulf waters created an environmental and economic catastrophe for people living and working in and along the Gulf. BP has concealed, evaded, or misrepresented the facts about the amount of oil that has poured into the Gulf. Even when scientists implored BP to allow them to monitor the flow of oil that created massive underwater plumes, BP stonewalled: "The answer is no to that. We're not going to take any extra efforts now to calculate flow there at this point."

BP has since pleaded guilty to thirteen counts of criminal provisions of federal law in connection with the explosion.[18] For months, though, BP illegally tried to shift the blame and evade accountability, including withholding documents and lying to Congress.[19] BP's CEO complained, "I'd like my life back."[20]

BP's criminal conduct in American waters in the Gulf was only the latest of its crimes. On one day alone in October 2007, BP admitted to a virtual crime spree.[21] First, BP Products North America Inc., pleaded "guilty to a felony" for causing a 2005 refinery explosion in Texas that killed fifteen people. BP admitted, "If our approach to process safety and risk management had been more disciplined and comprehensive, this tragedy could have been prevented." The criminal plea agreement required BP to pay a fine of $50 million and serve three years of probation.

Second, on the same day, BP admitted that it engaged in criminal conduct that caused "the largest oil spill ever to occur at Prudhoe Bay" in Alaska. As a result, BP Exploration Alaska Inc., pleaded guilty to violating the Federal Water Pollution Control Act.

Third, BP admitted to a criminal conspiracy, mail fraud, and wire fraud after BP America and several other BP subsidiary corporations "manipulated the price of February 2004 TET physical propane and attempted to manipulate the price of TET propane in April 2003." As a result of BP's criminal price manipulation, BP was required to pay $303.5 million in fines, penalties, and restitution.

And even these crimes were not the first. BP's other recent violations of law include the following:

- A guilty plea in Alaska related to the illegal disposal of hazardous waste, including paint thinner and toxic solvents containing lead, benzene, toluene, and methylene chloride, on Alaska's North Slope[22]

- $25 million in penalties in California due to "significant and numerous violations" at a BP refinery[23]

- $900,000 in penalties after producing and distributing gasoline that threatened public health[24]

- $87,430,000 in proposed penalties to BP Products North America Inc., "for the company's failure to correct potential hazards faced by employees." OSHA found that despite the death of fifteen people and the injury of 170 in its Texas oil refinery explosion and despite its promises to change its ways, BP continued to commit "hundreds of new violations."[25]

- $3 million in additional fines to BP North America when OSHA "found that BP often ignored or severely delayed fixing known hazards in its refineries"[26]

- Thirteen "serious safety violations" at a BP refinery near Blaine, Washington. A Washington official stated in 2010 that "we are disturbed that more than ten years after the explosion that killed six workers at the Equilon refinery, our inspectors are still finding significant safety violations every time we inspect one of the refineries in the State of Washington."[27]

BP's oil refinery operations account for 97 percent of all "egregiously willful" and "willful" violations found by government safety inspectors over the past three years.[28] Despite (or perhaps because of) this record of crime and misdeeds, in the first quarter of 2010 alone, BP made $5.6 billion in profit. And what happened to the CEO who wanted his life back after BP ruined the Gulf of Mexico and killed workers on the Deepwater Horizon? BP gave him a salary and bonus of $6 million in 2010 and awarded him $18 million when he left the company.

As with the Massey corporation, the Delaware attorney general has ignored a petition backed by thousands of Americans to request that he enforce the law and begin an action to revoke the Delaware corporate charters of BP, a serial criminal.[29]

Too Big to Tell the Truth

Large corporations defy even mild controls of health, environmental, and consumer protection laws and then seek shelter from the Supreme Court's corporate rights regime. Not long before *Citizens United*, the corporate "speech" campaign reached the point of claiming the right of corporations to lie, or at least to have the constitutional right of "breathing space" to protect them from charges of lying.

A California law allowed people to bring consumer fraud charges alleging that Nike fraudulently launched a campaign of lies about why no shoes were made in America anymore and whether Nike's shoes were made by badly exploited poor people in brutal overseas sweatshops. Nike went all the way to the Supreme Court arguing that the transnational corporation had a "free speech right" to block the law. Again, the global corporations and corporatist "legal foundations" rallied to the cry that corporations are people, and the Constitution prevents any restriction on corporate "speech."

Covington & Burling (remember them from the cigarette conspiracy and Monsanto GMO milk cases?) filed briefs for ExxonMobil, Microsoft, Morgan Stanley, and GlaxoSmithKline to support "corporate speakers' " First Amendment rights to block laws holding corporations accountable for massive deceptive disinformation campaigns. Covington & Burling wrote, "If a corporate speaker must limit its factual statements on matters of public concern to statements that no one could possibly challenge, or that the speaker could be certain it could prove as 'true' in a court of law or before a regulatory body, the result will be a deterrence of speech which the Constitution makes free."[30] The Washington Legal Foundation brief went straight to the heart of the matter: the Court should not allow anything that might cause the corporate share price to fall. Washington Legal Foundation, one of the largest of the Powell-Chamber–inspired corporatist legal groups, argued that a corporation must be able to block a law like California's or otherwise it would risk a "shareholder suit alleging negligence for the drop in stock values resulting from its failure to defend itself in the court of public opinion."

The theme of all of these corporate arguments is only partly that corporations should have the same First Amendment "breathing space" as people do to debate public issues with passion, hyperbole, and even scurrilous attacks and arguable falsehoods. An additional theme is that global corporations are just too big, too powerful, and in too many countries to be subjected to judgments of state law when they launch fraudulent feel-good campaigns in response to criticism or when they spew lies about cigarettes, global warming, sweatshops, the rainforest, or anything else.

In the Supreme Court brief, the global corporations argued that Nike could not possibly guarantee "truth" (the brief itself uses quotation marks around the word *truth*) when Nike has "736 facilities located in the 51 countries in which 500,000 workers are used by its subcontractors to manufacture its products."[31] In other words, Nike is too big, too global, and in too many countries exploiting cheap labor to possibly operate without getting sued by someone. And we can't have that, can we?

Why can't we have that? If that really is a problem, it is an economic problem for Nike and its shareholders, not a constitutional problem for Americans. The slippery slope argument that the Court and the Constitution must step in to make sure that Nike does not find itself in court having to defend its false statements implies that Nike not only has a "right" to its corporate charter and privileges but also has a "right" to operate in fifty-one countries and outsource jobs to impoverished areas of the world and the "right" to wage PR campaigns if people question the human impact of Nike's decisions. Each of those, however, is a corporate policy preference, not a right.

Nike's arguments state a business problem, not a constitutional problem. Nike could solve its business problem in a number of ways without fabricating constitutional rights to block the law. It could make its shoes in the United States. It could be smaller. It could price into its shoes the cost of defending itself from global human rights campaigns about its overseas sweatshops. It could ask the legislature to create an exception in the law for global corporations operating overseas sweatshops. Whether these options are unattractive or might raise the price of Nike sneakers or, God forbid, lower the share price has nothing to do with the Constitution. There is no constitutional right to cheap overseas labor and false marketing campaigns to make Americans feel better about lost jobs, human rights abuses, and immoral conduct. In the end, the Supreme Court declined to hear the Nike case, but we know how this story ends in *Citizens United*.

The Consequences of Corporate Amorality and Crime

Corporate crime and allowing corporate power to slip out of control of the people have consequences. WellCare Health stole millions of dollars from a children's health program in Florida. BP's many crimes killed fifteen people in a Texas refinery and eleven people in the Gulf of Mexico. Massey Energy killed twenty-nine people. Volvo supported Saddam Hussein's regime in Iraq by committing crimes to get heavy trucks and equipment around a United Nations sanction, and Credit Suisse criminally moved money around to evade American economic sanctions against dangerous regimes in the world.

Unchecked corporate power poisons food, water, and air, and people get sick and die. Workplaces are more dangerous, and people die. Markets are corrupted, people lose their savings, and jobs are wiped out. Taxes for most people are higher because corporations and the rich do not pay their share and hide money "offshore," abetted by criminal international bank corporations.

In *Citizens United*, the majority failed to consider whether the problem of serial corporate crime and the reality of global corporate power exposed the fallacy of excess metaphorical thinking when it comes to corporations. Had the Court considered why Congress might have distinguished between corporations and people in the Bipartisan Campaign Reform Act and the 1907 law banning corporate money in politics, the Court would have inquired into how corporations might be different from people.

In doing so, the Court might have connected "speech" to "virtue" as essentially human characteristics and recognized the relationship of both to a self-governing republic of free people. This virtue, as Jefferson and the other founders knew, is not only "love of the laws and of our country" but also a love that "requires a constant preference of public to private interest."[32]

Corporations are incapable of virtue, not because they are bad but because they are mere tools. A hammer has no virtue, either. And we would not call a hammer a "speaker" or its noise banging nails a "voice." We could design a better tool, but for most of the large public corporations, the risk of crime and fraud runs high because we do not sufficiently conceive of the corporation as a tool to aid the progress of the many. Instead, we have allowed our courts, our public officials, maybe ourselves, to view the corporation simply as an enrichment machine for a few in control of the corporation.[33]

Sadly, the failure to control corporate power corrodes and destroys virtue itself in too many American people. Think of those CEOs who reaped millions to destroy jobs or the public servants who sell out the country for corporate dollars or position. Think of the self-effacing Lewis Powell described by Sandra Day O'Connor and all those decent, patriotic, kind, hardworking people who went off to work each day on behalf of the long cigarette conspiracy to addict children and kill people. I do not intend sarcasm here. Decent, kind, patriotic, hardworking people do go off to work every day in corporations that create terrible consequences for the world, when allowed to do so. When we fail to keep corporations in their proper economic place and to protect our political space, we corrupt virtue in all of us.

The crimes of corporations, from trading with the enemy to stealing from children, as well as the political corruption caused by corporate power, happen because people make decisions on behalf of the corporation. Yet it is not because those people are evil. It is because government, crippled by corporate "rights" and corporate power, has abandoned its duty to control the powerful tool in which people find themselves working. When we, the people, cannot control corporations because of fabricated constitutional rights and dangerous imbalances in lobbying and election spending, people making corporate decisions are rewarded for not exercising virtue and they are punished for exercising it. Corporate decisions then overwhelmingly favor the private, not the public, interest, and the corporate, not the American, interest.

Not long after the BP disaster in the Gulf of Mexico exposed how deeply and corruptly the oil corporations had insinuated themselves into our government, Senator Sheldon Whitehouse, former attorney general of Rhode Island and a former US attorney, took to the Senate floor. He issued a warning and plea to the American people:

> Have we now learned what price must be paid when the stealthy tentacles of corporate influence are allowed to reach into and capture our agencies of government?
>
> I pray, let us have learned this; let us have learned that lesson. I sincerely pray we have learned our lesson, and that this will never happen again. But let's not just pray.
>
> In this troubled world God works through our human hands; grows a more perfect union through our human hearts; creates his beloved community through our human thoughts and ideas. So it is not enough to pray. We must act.
>
> We must act in defense of the integrity of this great government of ours, which has brought such light to the world, such freedom and equality to our country. We cannot allow this government—that is a model around the world, that inspires people to risk their lives and fortunes to come to our shores—we cannot allow any element of this government to become the tool of corporate power, the avenue of corporate influence, the puppet of corporate tentacles.[34]

We are people. We love. We pray. We act. We are all on the same side. So let's get to work.

Chapter Seven
Restoring Democracy and Republican Government

*[Political equality] is something that is so fundamental
that sooner or later it is going to be recognized.
Whether this will happen through a constitutional
amendment or through changes in Supreme Court
doctrine I do not know. But it will happen.*

—Judge Guido Calebresi[1]

*Great corporations exist only because they are created
and safeguarded by our institutions; and it is therefore
our right and duty to see that they work in harmony
with these institutions.*

—President Theodore Roosevelt[2]

Where we go from here is the same as it ever has been for Americans: toward a republic of self-governing citizens who have an equal voice, equal rights, and an equal vote. When we hear "keep your eyes on the prize," that's the prize. Modest adjustments and inside-Washington fixes will not get us there anymore. We have the tools, though, if we use them, to take us much further along the way.

First, we must restore our constitutional foundation of human liberty and balanced powers. We need to accelerate the work for a Twenty-Eighth Amendment to the Constitution to reverse *Citizens United* and corporate constitutional rights. For thirty years, we have been in a power struggle over the Constitution and Bill of Rights, but only one side—the side of organized big money and corporate power—has shown up to the fight. It is time for the people to take the field. Without ending the corporate rights veto over our laws and without reforming the domination of our government by the concentrated wealth of the few, elections will become more meaningless and representative democracy a fading memory.

Second, we must have fundamental, sweeping reform of elections, government ethics, and corporate law. Election and lobbying laws should punish, rather than reward, corrupt crony capitalism and bribe-based politics. If we intend to control rather than be controlled by corporate and money power, we must end the systemic corruption of government that we now quaintly call "lobbying" and "fundraising."

Third, we need a new era of corporate law reform and accountability to curb the misuse of amassed power in large corporations. These reforms will enable corporations do what they were intended to do: serve as effective tools for economic activity to benefit, rather than damage, society. We must insist, rather than beg, that corporations serve the public interest. "Socially responsible" businesses should not be alternative or optional approaches. Unreformed nineteenth-century corporate thinking and unfair, undemocratic dominance of Delaware corporate law no longer serve the nation or the world.

These three steps are not mutually exclusive. They do not require a particular order of accomplishment. Indeed, pushing all of the steps forward at the same time will best enhance the progress overall. Each step helps address the fundamental problem of the dominance of corporate power and concentrated wealth over our government, and together, they create the framework for effective, lasting democracy.

Already, this work is much further along than many people realize. In the rest of this chapter, I lay out more details and the state of progress or challenges in each category of reform. In the following chapter, you will find specific ways you can engage in the area that is of most interest to you.

We will win. And we will leave a chance to the next generations of Americans and free people around the globe to continue the work to ensure that government of the people "does not perish from the earth."

Step 1: The Constitutional Foundation

Citizens United calls the question: will our Constitution be turned into a tool for the powerful few to control who governs? Or will the Constitution do what it is intended to do: prevent powerful special interest factions from corrupting and ultimately destroying equal justice, government of the people, and the inherent rights of all?

Millions of Americans have responded to that question and have made astonishing progress to ensure that the answer is the correct one. The method, as before in our history, is the constitutional amendment process, combined with a determined response in the courts.

Why a Constitutional Amendment Effort?

The rapid growth since *Citizens United* of the national, cross-partisan campaign for the Twenty-Eighth Amendment reflects a growing consensus about the nature of the problem we face.

If that problem simply concerned a lack of disclosure about the source of funding for campaigns, we could fix that with better disclosure laws. If the problem were merely one of shareholders not having control over how corporations are spending their money in politics, securities laws and shareholder rules could fix that.

We know, however, that the problem goes much deeper. *Citizens United* frames core questions of what America is all about. That is why the constitutional amendment work is so important and why so many have engaged in that work.

In the few years since the *Citizens United* decision, millions of Americans have worked to do what constitutional amendment efforts have always done: forge a national consensus on basic principles that transcend partisan politics. They are taking those principles—here, the role of republican citizenship versus concentrations of wealth and global corporations in politics and governing—to the country by a resolution process. They are forcing the debate about the Twenty-Eighth Amendment in virtually every community in the land, whether politicians want that debate or not.

Congress cannot overrule the Supreme Court, nor can the states, but it is not true that the Supreme Court has the last word on what the Constitution means. Under our system of government, the Supreme Court has the second-to-last word; the people have always had the last word. When the Supreme Court gets it catastrophically wrong, as it has done before, the Amendment process is the correction; it is the rudder that Americans reach for to bring us back on course.

We know this because we have seen it again and again. Much that is right about our democracy, and much that we now take for granted, exists only because Americans before us did the seemingly impossible. They amended the Constitution;

they insisted on the people having the last word over the Court and other branches of government. With successful amendment campaigns, they guaranteed equal voting and participation for all races; they insisted on voting rights for women, after the Supreme Court ruled that the Constitution provided no such thing; they demanded that all people eighteen and older have the right to vote after the Supreme Court ruled otherwise; they insisted that equality in voting cannot exist if poll tax barriers are placed in front of those with less money, property, or power; they insisted on election of US senators by the people rather than by a corrupt appointment process; they rejected the Supreme Court's ruling that a fair federal income tax violated the Constitution; they made Congress accountable to the people when Congress raised its pay; they insisted that the states were not subservient to the federal judiciary when bondholders wanted to drag states into federal court. None of this happened without successful amendment campaigns by the American people.

Throughout our history, the people, using the constitutional amendment process, "rose up to say no to a Supreme Court decision that had favored propertied interests at the expense of other constitutional values."[3] At least six times, we have amended the Constitution to overturn erroneous Supreme Court decisions. *Citizens United* deserves the same fate.

Amendment campaigns, even campaigns such as the Equal Rights Amendment that fall short, spur overdue national conversations and progress in times of crisis, confusion, and doubt. They define our values and shape us as a people. They keep the Supreme Court honest and accountable to the people. They make government of and by the people real.

Seeking a constitutional amendment to reverse *Citizens United* and to re-empower the people ourselves may seem audacious. It is. Some who are discouraged or cynical claim that the Twenty-Eighth Amendment will never happen, that Americans cannot achieve dramatic constitutional reform anymore. Don't buy that. That admission of weakness, masquerading as sophisticated political analysis, has never worked when Americans faced a fundamental challenge to the vision of liberty and equality that is our birthright.

It would be one thing if the constitutional amendment path was novel or untested, but it is not. We have amended the Constitution twenty-seven times, seventeen times since adopting the Bill of Rights. Indeed, the Constitution itself might never have made it out of the Philadelphia Convention in 1787 and on to ratification by the people and states had Article V's procedure for amendment not been included.[4]

Nor is the amendment tool ancient history. The Twenty-Seventh Amendment (requiring an intervening election before any congressional pay hike takes effect) became part of the Constitution in 1992. The voting age amendment came in 1971. Indeed, going back to the Seventeenth Amendment in 1913, almost every decade in the twentieth century saw a new amendment become part of the Constitution. The only exceptions were the 1940s and the 1980s. We are overdue.

What's the Strategy and Where Do We Stand?

Article V of the Constitution spells out the amendment process: Congress must pass a resolution with a two-thirds vote, and the resolution must then be ratified in three-quarters of the states. Another method under Article V may be called for if Congress fails to act; amendments also may be enacted in a constitutional convention called by the states and then ratified by three-quarters of the states. All twenty-seven amendments to date have been passed by a two-thirds vote of Congress and ratified by three-quarters of the states.

The plan is not to ask Congress alone to do this. If we stand down and merely hope and wait for Congress to do the job, we will fail. Congress will not do it, not without a national movement forcing action.

The winning road map runs through our communities and the states, not via lobbyists or politicos in Washington, D.C. In the end, Congress will need to vote out an amendment bill (and several versions of the Twenty-Eighth Amendment are already pending in Congress). Constitutional amendments, however, are not won by narrow majorities or short-term, inside political games. They are won not by political calculation based on a broken status quo, but on a national strategy that changes that status quo forever.

Resolve to Succeed

From the earliest days of our republic, citizen resolutions have been one of the most effective means of organizing and expressing the will of the people. That remains the case today.

By early 2014, 600 cities and towns in every region of America had passed resolutions demanding the Twenty-Eighth Amendment: Brecksville, Ohio, and New York City; Charleston, West Virginia, and Los Angeles, California; Teton County, Idaho, and Chicago, Illinois; Savannah, Georgia, and Boston, Massachusetts; Springfield, Missouri, and Portland, Maine; and hundreds more.[5]

These resolutions have succeeded because people are willing to take a stand. In Greenbelt, Maryland, Jennifer Robinson helped get it done. She says, "I really had to work myself up to do it, but seeing all the other people there supporting this cause was so exciting. And the city council passed the resolution unanimously! They sent a letter to our state legislature supporting a constitutional amendment."[6]

What Jennifer Robinson did in her town rippled out into other communities, and to the state capitol, helping make Maryland one of sixteen states so far that have resolved to condemn *Citizens United* and call for enactment of the Twenty-Eighth Amendment. California, Colorado, Connecticut, Delaware, Hawaii, Illinois, Maine, Maryland, Massachusetts, Montana, New Jersey, New Mexico, Oregon, Rhode Island, Vermont, and West Virginia are all on record for the Twenty-Eighth Amendment. That's more than one-third of the number of states needed for ratification, and more are on the way.

These resolutions are not confined to states or municipalities. Americans have initiated resolutions and organized discussions of the implications of *Citizens United* and the state of our democracy, in town meetings, religious conventions, universities, business groups, labor unions, and anywhere else Americans assemble together.[7]

Now Congress is paying attention. By 2014, 30 senators and 130 representatives had signed onto Twenty-Eighth Amendment bills. That is more than one-third of the way to the necessary two-thirds of Congress needed.

This progress did not happen because of top-down, big-money mobilization. Just the opposite: the progress to date has come because millions of Americans started taking steps, individually and together, without a lot of resources, to stand up for our values and the future of democracy.

Look what happened in Montana. Until 1912, when Montana people used the initiative process to ban corporate election spending, "a war of corporate interests . . . drowned out the voices of Montanans."[8] As Governor Steve Bullock, who served as Montana attorney general at the time of the *Citizens United* decision, explains:

> *This was corruption as it was understood since the framing of the Constitution: not just bribery but harnessing government power to benefit a single corporate faction at the expense of the broader and more diverse interests represented by the people themselves.*[9]

After *Citizens United*, a corporate front group emerged in Montana, although it was incorporated in Colorado. The secretive entity called itself Western Tradition Partnership and initiated what its internal documents called an "election program." This "program" involved the raising and funneling of unlimited, *secret* money of corporations and wealthy donors into state elections. The Western Tradition Partnership documents promised donors that no one "will ever know you helped make this program possible" and "you can just sit back on election night and see what a difference you've made."[10]

Under Montana's century-old law, this plan was flat-out illegal. Western Tradition Partnership, however, pointed to the *Citizens United* decision, maintaining that the Supreme Court had stripped the people of Montana and every other state of the power to keep corporate money out of state elections. Western Tradition Partnership sued the attorney general to stop him from enforcing the century-old Montana law.

Western Tradition Partnership lost the case in the Montana Supreme Court. No matter; the front group changed its name to American Tradition Partnership and appealed to the US Supreme Court. There, four members of the Supreme Court declared that *Citizens United* was a mistake and should be overturned. That alone is a remarkable indictment so soon after a major decision.

Unfortunately, the five members of the Court who had supported the decision in the *Citizens United* decision refused to even consider the possibility that they were wrong. Instead, they summarily reversed the judgment of the Montana Supreme Court, struck down the law, and sent notice that every state, city, and town was fair game for front group "election programs" and that nothing could be done about it.[11]

People in Montana did not much like that. Within a few weeks, 40,000 Montana voters had signed petitions for a ballot initiative that condemned the Supreme Court's error and instructed Montana's representatives to ensure the passage of the Twenty-Eighth Amendment. The initiative called for a constitutional amendment that overturns *Citizens United*, "establishes that corporations are not human beings with constitutional rights," and "accomplishes the goals of Montanans in achieving a level playing field in election spending."[12]

Montana small business owners, ranchers, farmers, lawyers, teachers, and others from all walks of life signed on.[13] Dozens of faith leaders echoed the writing of Bishop Jessica Crist, of the Evangelical Lutheran Church in Montana: "[P]eople, not corporations and special interests, are made in the image of God. . . . This is a faith issue. This is a values issue. . . . This is not a partisan issue [but] a justice issue."[14]

Montana Governor Brian Schweitzer, a Democrat, stood side by side with Lieutenant Governor John Bohlinger, a Republican, in a video to support the ballot initiative and the Twenty-Eighth Amendment. "Corporations are not people and they should not control our government," they declared. A former secretary of state in Montana, also a Republican, rallied support as well: "I've lived here 94 years," said Verner Bertelsen, "and I've never seen a corporation I wanted to dance with yet."[15]

Some Montanans took a different view, of course, and the referendum offered the opportunity for debate. State Senator Dave Lewis called the initiative "a waste of time and effort" because a constitutional amendment "is something that will be approved when pigs fly."[16] Most Montanans, however, did not share the senator's cynicism.

On November 6, 2012, Montana voters chose Mitt Romney over Barack Obama, 55 to 45 percent. Then they approved I-166, the constitutional amendment ballot initiative, by a vote of 75 to 25 percent.[17] They also elected Steve Bullock, the attorney general who battled big corporate money all the way to the Supreme Court, as governor. The same day, in Colorado, where Western Tradition Partnership was incorporated, voters also approved a Twenty-Eighth Amendment ballot initiative by a nearly identical margin of 74 to 26 percent.[18]

Pigs are not yet flying, and much work remains to be done in Montana and elsewhere. But what Montana people did to push back against *Citizens United* and "corporate rights" shows the road map, and it shows how much ordinary Americans everywhere can do.

How Will the Amendment Be Worded?

Not long after the Montana vote, Jon Tester, a Montana farmer and a US senator, introduced the People's Rights Amendment in the Senate. The amendment reaffirms that our constitutional rights are human, not corporate, rights. He also joined dozens of senators in cosponsoring a parallel amendment bill that reaffirms the equality of every American citizen and our rights to free, fair elections. These two pieces—holding that the words *people* and *person* in our Constitution do not mean "corporation," and that we, the people, have the right to make fair election rules—are the two key pieces of effective amendment language to overturn *Citizens United*.

A constitutional amendment "to overturn *Citizens United*" should, in fact, overturn *Citizens United*. Two activist judicial errors work together in *Citizens United* to corrode and eventually destroy representative democracy and effective republican government: first, the twisting of the First Amendment speech rights to disregard the equality of every American, to force unlimited spending rules on all elections, and to lock in the domination of American government by a "wealth faction"; and second, the assignment to corporations of constitutional rights that are the rights of humanity, creating a "corporate veto" over the public interest.

Several of the amendment resolutions now pending in Congress address the first problem, that of unlimited election spending and contributions. One of the best examples, sometimes called the Political Equality Amendment, is included in the Resources section at the end of this book.[19]

Other pending amendment resolutions address the second problem, that of judicial fabrication of corporate constitutional rights. The bill that Montana Senator Jon Tester introduced is one such amendment bill.[20] Another bill, sometimes called the We, the People amendment, seeks to address both problems in a single amendment.[21] Each of these is included in the Resources section that follows Chapter Eight. In total, thirteen variations of amendment resolutions to overturn *Citizens United* were introduced in the 2012–2014 Congress. All of these amendment bills can be found in one place online at www.freespeechforpeople.org.[22]

The resolutions moving ahead in every state and community in the nation do not need to wait for final agreement on the exact language of the Twenty-Eighth Amendment. That will come. Discussion, debate, and work to ensure that we ultimately have the best Twenty-Eighth Amendment will continue, as it should. At this stage, the various amendment bills reflect the robust demand for reform, and are a healthy sign of progress. No part of our

Constitution ever got there without due consideration of language and alternatives, and the Twenty-Eighth Amendment will be no different. A consensus on amendment language will emerge soon enough. In the meantime, the community and state resolutions create the opportunity for the essential debate and the forging of consensus. A sample resolution is included in the Resources section and is available online.[23]

Step 2: Clean the Swamp:
Self-Government and Free, Fair Elections

Along with restoring our constitutional foundation, a second category of necessary reform might be called "cleaning the swamp." You should be able to run for office without groveling to corporations and the rich. You should be able to vote for someone who does not have to grovel and owe allegiance to corporations and the rich. And every American ought to have equal representation in a government that is accountable to its citizens. Little of that is true now.

Cleaning the swamp requires deep changes in how elections are funded and how politicians raise money. It requires transparency and disclosure. It requires severance of the link between special interest lobbying (which is natural and necessary in a democracy) and the role of lobbyists in raising money for the politicians they lobby (which is corruption). And it requires putting all citizens back into the election-funding process.

In elections and lawmaking—two of the most important public responsibilities of citizens in a republic—we now rely on a few rich people, unions, and the biggest global corporations to fund campaigns, candidates, and elections. They don't do this for nothing. Those who pay for campaigns and elections are those who get the representation. We should not be surprised to find that corporations and the rich are now very well represented and everyone else is not.

Some form of citizen funding, vouchers, or public financing of federal and state elections is among the most essential steps if we do not want elected representatives owing fealty only to corporations, unions, and the top sliver of American wealth. We expect and demand public financing of our roads, canals, airports, armed services, and schools because we want those to serve all of the people. Why should we not insist on public financing of our elections so that all of the people can participate and be represented?

In early 2014, the Government of the People Act was introduced in Congress. The act outlines what good reform looks like: Candidates could choose to raise a large number of small contributions from many people rather than from a class of big donors. The Government of the People Act would create an incentive for that choice and empower all Americans to participate. First, citizen contributions to a candidate of their choice of $1 to $150 would be amplified on a six-to-one basis by a newly created "Freedom from Influence Fund." No large contributions would be matched at all. Second, the first $25 people contribute would qualify for a "My Voice" refundable tax credit. This would be paid for by closing corporate tax loopholes.[24]

This model already has been tested in the laboratories of democracy—several of the states, such as Maine and Arizona—and it works. In Maine, for example, voters used the state ballot initiative process in 1996 to make politicians more accountable to the people, rather than special interests. The popular ballot initiative, which Mainers call "Clean Elections," created a system of matching small donations and public funding. Regardless of political party or viewpoint, anyone in Maine who wanted to run for office could choose not to participate in the pay-to-play, privatized election funding system. Instead, they could opt into the "Clean Elections" system, which used a combination of small donations matched by modest public funds. Everyone plays by the same rules and everyone is eligible, no matter their party (or nonparty).

The public cost stays reasonable because candidates do not receive anything until they qualify by raising a significant number of small donations. A candidate must collect at least 3,250 contributions of $5 or more from registered Maine voters. This "seed money" must amount to at least $40,000, and it must come from individuals only. No contribution can exceed $100.[25] The thresholds and funding are much less for state representative candidates.

Lo and behold, with the Clean Elections law in place, candidates and elected officials became very interested in the views of Maine voters who might have only $5 or $50 to pitch in.[26] Along with other reforms, such as term limits, Clean Elections work in Maine. Regular citizens can and do serve in the statehouse. They do not need to become "lifers" before serving their constituents well or taking leadership posts. Voters hear more diverse views, see more third party and independent candidates, and face less extremism and rancorous hyper-partisanship. Once the election is over, the views of ordinary citizens still matter to the elected representative because everyone, not just the few "heavy hitter" donors, plays a role in funding the elections.

With Clean Elections, candidates win (or lose) on the basis of their ideas and qualifications, rather than on their coziness with corporations, unions, and big donors. Once in office, representatives with independence from funders can consider arguments on the merits, rather than on how big a money haul a particular lobbyist can bring in.

With the post-*Citizens United* dramatic rise of big money dominance, people in Maine and Arizona relied a fair mechanism to allow the Clean Elections system to coexist with the big-money system. To prevent the destruction of the Clean Elections mechanisms by unlimited spending from corporations and special interests, the law included a trigger mechanism, so that public funding rose if millions of dollars of outside money came into a race. This way, a range of candidates could still make a reasonable choice to run under a workable Clean Elections system, and voters could still hear that range of ideas and views, even if other candidates chose to use the unlimited private donor approach. As a result of this common-sense approach to election funding, Maine and Arizona have the fewest elections where incumbents run uncontested, and turnout for elections runs high.[27]

Now that is all at risk. *Citizens United* and a more recent 5–4 decision, *American Free Enterprise Club PAC v. Bennett*, threaten to destroy this effective reform. A year and a half after *Citizens United*, the Supreme Court struck down Arizona's Clean Elections law because it created a trigger to increase funding if privately funded candidates, or outside groups, dumped additional millions into a race. The five *Citizens United* justices found that the funding trigger violated the free speech rights of the big donors and their chosen candidates.[28] Now "free speech" means the right to drown out all competing speech and all views except those of richest donors.

Despite the Supreme Court's extension of its *Citizens United* folly in the Arizona public funding case, Americans are not giving up on clean elections. In Maine, citizens convened a Clean Elections Convention in May 2014, and are moving a ballot initiative that not only will defend but will expand citizen-funded elections. New Yorkers are closing in on winning public funding in state elections, and across several states and at the federal level, the the movement to defend against privatization of what belongs to every American continues to grow nationally.

In addition to the campaign finance problem at election time, however, much of the corruption- and greed-driven decline for

America and the world happens between elections. Corporations spend billions of dollars on lobbying and the rest of us are more or less shut out.

Lobbying today is not "normal." Bribery is bribery. It should be a scandal, not a yawn, when politicians behave as Billy Tauzin (the congressman who delivered the Medicare law for the pharmaceutical companies) and Phil Gramm (the former senator who became UBS vice chairman after stripping America of protections against financial collapse) behaved. Politicians who do that, and the corporations that pay them to do that, should not only be shamed, they should be prosecuted.

To be clear, I am not calling Tauzin and Gramm criminals. Like anyone else, they are presumably innocent until proven guilty of a crime, and they have not been accused of committing any crime. That's the problem. What they did was only shameful, low, heedless, unpatriotic, and selfish, rather than illegal. We should, however, change the law so that it would be a criminal act for members of Congress to go on to work as lobbyists for companies or industries that benefited from the government during their term of service. Whatever happened to the model of politicians, from George Washington to Harry Truman and Dwight Eisenhower, who served their country and then returned, happily and quietly, home?

We should demand much stricter rules for disclosure but also for corporate lobbying spending itself. We should no longer allow government employees, including our representatives, to go back and forth, between government and corporate lobbying. We should have reporting and disclosure of every meeting our representatives have with lobbyists. We should ban the gift giving, wining and dining, and junket funding of our representatives by corporate lobbyists.

An excellent example of proposed legislation to this and more is the American Anti-Corruption Act.[29] Members of Congress would be prohibited from soliciting and receiving contributions from corporations, including the corporate lobbyists, that they regulate. The fraudulent "noncoordination" between Super PACs and campaigns would be curbed. Representatives and senior staff would not be permitted to bargain for job offers while in office and would be subject to a five-year restriction on lobbying after they leave office. All political contributions would be disclosed, and Americans would keep $100 of their money otherwise payable as a tax to be able to make able an equal contribution to the candidate of their choice.

Ideas like the American Anti-Corruption Act and the Government by the People Act are ambitious. As with the Constitutional amendment efforts, these reforms reflect what most Americans know: we are beyond small adjustments to a corrupted system. We need to go to the root of the problem and only "big" solutions will do the job.

Naturally, Congress is not in a hurry to act because so much of what has become acceptable, even embraced, in Washington, would change. Increasingly, though, Americans are working together to build the organized will to force Congress to change. You can plug into these efforts through the "portals" described in the next chapter.

Step 3: Reforming the Corporation

Who says corporations are accountable only to shareholders? Why should we not expect that those who take the government-created privilege of incorporation balance that privilege with standards for the livelihood of employees, our economy, and the health of the environment and of the communities in which they do business? Should not the size and complexity of a corporation at some point warrant a federal charter rather than a state charter from the most corporate-friendly state that transnational corporations can find (or can pressure)? Why should not all American citizens have a say in deciding what standards we expect from global corporations that choose to do business here? Should the corporate status be perpetual, without some ability of the people to evaluate whether the corporation has complied with the law and served the public interest as intended?

In America, we are free, or should be, to answer these questions in the democratic way: we can debate and then vote to make whatever answers best serve the country. The rules of corporations come from us (see Chapter Three).[30] If we do not like how the corporate rules are working out, we need to change them. We need to dust off and use some of the rules that already exist, such as revocation of corporate status when corporations repeatedly violate the law.

At least two principles should guide corporate law reform to restore balance between large corporations and human beings and our government. First, incorporation is a privilege. Second, transnational corporations should not be able to use the corporate law of a single state, such as Delaware, without proper national corporate standards and safeguards.

Principle 1: Incorporation Is a Privilege

The corporate charter is a privilege from the public; we should expect public accountability and benefit. Corporate law is a public matter, not a private one. Corporate law defines parameters of corporate conduct and shapes our world, our families, and our communities in profound ways. We cannot afford to leave it to corporate lawyers to decide what they think corporate duties and responsibilities should be. Corporate law may seem boring at first, but we need to care about corporate law as much as we care about any other law or issue, from the environment to the economy, from healthy communities to strong families, from energy to foreign policy and war.

The consequences of corporate law, for better or worse, have as big an impact on those issues and others as any other law, and perhaps more.

Professor Kent Greenfield at Boston College Law School has laid out the kind of clear standard that we should expect our public incorporation laws to have at their core:

> No corporation, even one making money for its core constituents, should be allowed to continue unchallenged and unchanged if its operation harms society. . . . The corporation is an instrument whose purpose is to serve the collective good, broadly defined, and if it ceases to serve the collective good, it should not be allowed to continue its operation, at least not in the same way. If we all knew that all corporations, or corporations of a certain type, or even an individual corporation created more social harm than good, no society in its right mind would grant incorporation to those firms.[31]

This commonsense standard is not new. It is rooted in traditional reasons why states allowed business corporations in the first place. Americans have always been suspicious of government-created advantages built into those corporations. We used to do a much better job at making sure that the public benefits of a corporate charter outweighed the public harms. Current corporate law still reflects remnants of this approach, and at a minimum we should insist that our public officials start enforcing that law again.

Charter revocation is one example of existing law that too often is ignored. As described in Chapter Six, in every state, even Delaware, the ability to operate as a corporation, or the corporate charter, is "subject to dissolution or the revocation or forfeiture of the corporate charter."[32] An example of a charter revocation request filed by Free Speech For People and Appalachian Voices concerning Massey Energy is included in the Resources at the back of this book. The Resources section also contains links to more information about charter revocation.

Remnants of nineteenth- and twentieth-century corporate law, though, are not enough. We need to modernize the corporation to serve our present needs. After *Citizens United*, for example, people like Paul Spencer, a high school history and government teacher in Arkansas, have started the work to reform corporate charter laws to make clear that no corporation is authorized to spend corporate money to influence elections.[33] Others go further and propose that corporations be mandated to have a public purpose.[34]

Increasing numbers of states, including Virginia, Maryland, New Jersey, and Vermont, have recently enacted incorporation laws for "benefit corporations" or "B corporations." Under these laws, benefit corporations "must create a material positive impact on society and the environment, consider how decisions affect workers, community, and the environment, and publicly report their social and environmental performance according to third-party standards."[35] These and many other reforms would make corporations work well for their owners and employees, the public, the economy, and the earth. That is the least that we should expect when we grant the public privilege of incorporation.

Principle 2: Incorporation Is a National or International Matter

No single state, be it Delaware or any other, should make the rules for multinational corporations. With Delaware making the rules for most global corporations, a few legislators and judges representing 900,000 people set the course for the lives of 310 million Americans and the rest of the world's people who bear the consequences of corporate power. That's not democratic, fair, or wise. When some states try to improve corporate law, large corporations play the states off one another to get the most corporate-friendly law. If Delaware decides that its corporate law requires managers to consider not only profit but also workers, community, the environment, or other criteria, corporations can reincorporate in another state with lower standards. The corporation does not even have to move its headquarters or offices; its lawyers simply file some paperwork.[36]

Once corporations reach a certain size and operate in countries around the world, why should we leave the rules of the road for the corporation to one state? Uncontrolled corporate power is methodically taking national and international treasures away from all of us: our government, our wealth, the Gulf of Mexico, the Appalachian Mountains, water in the ground from New York to California, the air, the land, and more. We should have national standards and corporate laws for large multinational corporations. This could be done either by way of a federal incorporation law or by federal law that sets minimum (but not maximum) standards for state incorporation laws used by corporations operating in interstate commerce.[37]

At least with publicly traded corporations, the Securities and Exchange Commission (SEC) now provides some federal oversight of corporate affairs. This limited oversight, however, is focused on protecting shareholders rather than all people or society. Still, providing shareholders with information and a say with respect to corporate political influence would help. Socially responsible investment firms and other shareholders are increasingly active as shareholders to demand disclosure of policies and accountability for corporations. This shareholder consciousness about the consequences of corporate conduct and active involvement in improving that conduct is essential.

"Shareholder democracy" has been difficult as a practical matter because of the control of large corporations by its executives and frequently too-cozy boards of directors. After *Citizens United*, some members of Congress proposed a shareholder approval requirement for any political expenditure by corporations. And the SEC recently developed a rule requiring publicly traded corporations to give shareholders a say in the nomination of board members, rather than being presented with a slate to rubber stamp.[38] You may not be surprised by now to hear that this reform is going the way of so many others in our country. The US Chamber of Commerce sued the SEC to block the rule, claiming that any requirement that corporations include shareholder-nominated directors in the corporations' proxy statement violates the corporations' First Amendment rights. The corporations won again, and a federal court in Washington, D.C., struck down this reform.

So long as the rules for corporations are quietly made by corporate lawyers in Delaware, in arcane SEC rulemaking, or by overzealous judges imposing their own corporate policy preferences, necessary reform for the kind of sustainable economy that we need in the twenty-first century will be difficult to achieve. More businesses and people, however, are determined to change the rules to ensure that corporations, our economy, and our democracy work for everyone, "for ourselves and our posterity." In the next chapter, you can find the resources to join this work.

Chapter 8
Do Something

*"It is not 'can any of us imagine better?' but, 'can
we all do better?' . . . The occasion is piled high with
difficulty, and we must rise with the occasion. As our
case is new, so we must think anew, and act anew. We
must disenthrall ourselves, and then we shall save our
country."*
—Abraham Lincoln[1]

"It is always impossible until it is done."
—Nelson Mandela[2]

I t is not enough to complain, or even to
imagine better, though both of those
steps may be necessary. We also must "all do better." What you do
is up to you, but do not wait for someone else or for the politicians
to get the job done. Bring whatever you have: bring your experience,
expertise, and energy to this work. The progress so far has happened
only because many people started taking one step at a time.

You do not have to be Michael McCarthy, who returned from
military service in Afghanistan to walk across the length of New
Hampshire to protest crony capitalism and corruption, nor can we

all be Doris Haddock, who walked 3,200 miles across the country at the age of eighty-nine to fight for election spending law reform.[3] Many modest but effective steps are available for all of us.

Peter Pease lives in Lincoln, Massachusetts, which, as with many New England towns, is governed by an annual town meeting of all citizens. He decided to put together a presentation on *Citizens United* and the Twenty-Eighth Amendment, and dozens of his neighbors collected petitions to put an amendment resolution onto the town meeting agenda. This gave their community an opportunity to learn, to debate, and to act. In a vote, Twenty-Eighth Amendment resolution passed by a very wide margin. People in hundreds of towns and cities across New England and the country have followed this model.

In Chester, Montana, Margaret Novak and her husband, Mike, signed themselves and their twenty-year-old grocery business onto the fight for the right of Montanans to keep corporate money out of Montana elections. They joined Free Speech For People's brief all the way to the Supreme Court and helped show business support for the winning Montana ballot initiative that followed.[4]

Rose Petsche lives in Brooksville, Ohio, a community that politicos would call "deep red," by which they mean conservative. Inspired by a local resolution idea from Move to Amend, she worked with her neighbors to form Brecksville Citizens for Transparent Politics. They put a local initiative on the ballot that created "Democracy Day" in the town, bringing people in the community together to debate the call for the Twenty-Eighth Amendment to reverse *Citizens United*. Some city officials unsuccessfully sought to keep the initiative off the ballot, but Brecksville voters approved the measure. The first Democracy Day was held in February 2013.[5]

Others are helping to clean the swamp of corrupt politics. Elizabeth Lindquist is a pharmacist who lives in Roscoe, Illinois, with her husband and two children. She also is a citizen cosponsor of the American Anti-Corruption Act, bringing together people of widely different political views in her community to force Congress to act. Using citizen tools from Represent.US,[6] Lindquist has organized people of various political viewpoints in two congressional districts in Illinois. They meet together, organize public events, educate and provide information to others their communities, and push their elected representatives to enact fundamental reforms to end corruption and cronyism in government. Lindquist is leading the way to a model that would work in every congressional district in the country, bringing Americans together regardless of party or politics to win the anticorruption reform we need.

Thousands of these examples are happening all across the country, even with what some might think of as arcane areas of corporate law reform. Remember Betty Harrah, who insisted that the attorney general of Delaware not ignore the corporate charter revocation law after Massey Energy, a Delaware corporation, killed her brother in the coalmine explosion? She is another so-called "ordinary" citizen who did the extraordinary; she traveled to Wilmington, Delaware, to personally tell her story to the powerful, and she spoke for many others in West Virginia. Thirty thousand Americans stood with her in signing the "De-Charter Massey" petition; hundreds of people in Wilmington, Delaware, took an evening to hear her and learn why we need corporate law reform; and still more helped spread the word, raise money, and keep the corporate charter revocation and accountability work moving.[7]

Other people are no longer willing to do business as usual. They are organizing their business activities into employee- or customer-owned cooperatives (co-ops) or incorporating their businesses as "benefit corporations." Many Americans are bypassing the global corporations that extract wealth from their communities, and instead buying from locally owned businesses.

In Lansing, New York, Jason Salfi's business, Comet Skateboards, employs twenty-nine people in the manufacture and sale of high-performance skateboards. The Comet Skateboards corporation is one of the founding "certified benefit corporations," or B corporations. Salfi and his colleagues are "hardwiring" into the corporation and their business a public purpose and a series of practices that not only serve their business and shareholders but also serve the community, the environment, and employees. They seek to "B the Change" by modeling a different, better kind of corporation.[8] And they are not alone. By the beginning of 2014, more than 900 businesses had become certified benefit corporations, and twenty states had enacted new corporate laws facilitating the creation of benefit corporations.[9]

The cynics and the big-money politicos think Americans do not care enough or lack the will to win a Twenty-Eighth Amendment, to demand a citizen-funded, small-donor election funding, or to make the rules for corporations rather than the other way around; in short, to govern ourselves.

But we can and we are. And you can start simply. Here are five things anyone can do right now:

- Sign the online petitions of the groups identified in the following charts.
- Share the fact that you did so online and offline in your social networks.
- Write a letter to the editor of your local paper.
- Write a letter to your elected representatives.
- Contribute money to the groups of your choice.

Now here are five more:

- Find out if your town, city, or state has enacted a resolution calling for a constitutional amendment to overturn *Citizens United.*

- If so, ask your congressional representatives if they've followed your community's resolve by cosponsoring a constitutional amendment.

- If not, use the form resolutions and petitions online (see organizations following) and start one.

- Ask your neighbors, family, and friends how they feel about this. Listen, engage, and inform.

- Ask your representatives exactly what they are doing to help. Check out their funders at http://www.opensecrets.org and ask (in writing, in a town hall meeting, or on social network sites) why they are collecting this money instead of working to end corruption. Do not vote for those who are not helping.

I could go on with this, listing numerous actions you can take right now. Instead, check out the following charts and explore the information and specific steps that you feel comfortable taking. Consider these groups and links as starting point "portals" for you to access good work and effective projects. I have arranged these into sections covering the three main areas of reform—protecting the Constitution, cleaning up campaign finance and elections, and reforming corporations. Additional organizations and links are included in the Resources section, and no doubt you may find many other organizations—local, state, national—that do good work as well.

Do not be turned off by the number of groups or different strategies. That is a good thing. Throughout our history, we have seen waves of organizations and advocacy groups forming "in major bursts . . . in periods of national cultural and political debate."[10] That is how Americans have national conversations and move the country closer to our best ideals. Americans once again are coming together into a wide array of groups to meet the need of an overdue cultural and political debate. That shows the growing energy and commitment of so many people to overturn *Citizens United* and fix our country. This is America: Not everyone has to do the same thing, or join the same group. Different strategies are not mutually exclusive but strengthen the effort.

The national organizations listed in the next section work together and with regional and local groups to improve coordination, support, and cooperation, so there is not a lot of duplication. A lot of other national as well as state and local groups are not included here but may interest you as well. You can find them in the Resources section after this chapter, in the endnotes, or online. Finally, you do not need to wait for an organization to tell you what to do, and none of us should sit back and wait until everything is perfectly arranged to deliver the winning strategy. We can all do something, now. We can do even more working with friends, neighbors, fellow citizens, even with those with whom we do not agree on much else.

More resources follow this chapter and in the endnotes. Check out these resources, share them, bring this book and the other resources to clubs or local discussion groups, and use them. Together, we can imagine better. And we can do better.

We, the People:
The Constitutional Foundation

I'm interested in overturning *Citizens United*, restoring the Constitution for equal, free people and winning the Twenty-Eighth Amendment. Where do I start and what can I do?

Table 3
Correcting the Court:
Restoring Our Constitutional Rights and the Republic

Organizations, mission statements, resources, and tools

Common Cause
www.commoncause.org

Common Cause is a nonpartisan, nonprofit advocacy organization founded in 1970 as a vehicle for citizens to make their voices heard in the political process and to hold their elected leaders accountable to the public interest.

Common Cause and its state chapters are helping to lead a national campaign for a constitutional amendment to reverse the Supreme Court's *Citizens United* decision.

Free Speech For People
www.freespeechforpeople.org

Launched on the day of the Supreme Court's *Citizens United* ruling, Free Speech For People is a national nonpartisan organization that catalyzes and leads the growing movement across the country for a constitutional amendment to overturn the ruling and reclaim our democracy. Join our campaign and follow us on Facebook and Twitter. Through our organizer's toolkit, you can access resources on the amendment movement, hold a house party with your friends and neighbors and show a video on why we must act, help generate public support for the movement, and get your community to pass a resolution calling for an amendment.

Resolutions, letter to the editor tool, petition/signature collection, contacting legislators, brochures, stickers, organizing tools, and more at
www.freespeechforpeople.org/get-involved

Amendment language, Q&A, state updates at
www.freespeechforpeople.org/amendments

Table 3 (continued)
Correcting the Court:
Restoring Our Constitutional Rights and the Republic

Organizations, mission statements, resources, and tools

Money Out, Voters In Coalition
www.moneyoutvotersin.org

Money Out / Voters In (MOVI) is an organization of grassroots volunteers seeking to educate, energize and mobilize ourselves and those who join with us in the movement to establish within the US Constitution the truths that money does not equal (free) speech and corporations are not entitled to the constitutional rights and protections intended solely for the benefit of individuals.

Move to Amend
www.movetoamend.org

Formed in 2009 in preparation for the *Citizens United* ruling, Move to Amend is a coalition of hundreds of organizations and hundreds of thousands of individuals committed to social and economic justice, ending corporate rule, and building a vibrant democracy that is genuinely accountable to the people, not corporate interests.

We are calling for an amendment to the US Constitution to unequivocally state that inalienable rights belong to human beings only and that money is not a form of protected free speech under the First Amendment and can be regulated in political campaigns.

Resolutions, petition/signature collection, social media, brochures, stickers, and more at **www.movetoamend.org/action**

Also, a "take action toolkit" at **www.movetoamend.org/toolkit**

To get involved go to **www.movetoamend.org/action** or call 707-269-0984.

People for the American Way
www.pfaw.org

Through its Government By the People campaign, People for the American Way (PFAW) advocates for a constitutional amendment to overturn cases like *Citizens United v. FEC* and *Buckley v. Valeo* to restore the ability of Congress and the states to fully regulate the raising and spending of money on elections. PFAW's website has a rich set of materials for activists, including toolkits to help pass resolutions and ballot initiatives in communities, lobby members of Congress to cosponsor resolutions, and raise awareness through letters to the editor and social media. PFAW plays a key coordinating role among the amendment advocacy groups, including tracking at United4ThePeople.org, the growing support around the country for amending the Constitution to restore government of, by, and for the people.

Resolutions, letter to the editor tool, petition/signature collection, contacting legislators, brochures, stickers, and more at **www.pfaw.org/issues/government-people/amending-constitution-government-and-people**

For more information, visit us at **www.pfaw.org/GovernmentByThePeople.**

Public Citizen
www.democracyisforpeople.org

Public Citizen's Democracy Is for People project is building a movement to counteract the US Supreme Court's ruling in *Citizens United v. Federal Election Commission*, take democracy off the auction block, and preserve constitutional rights for people—not corporations. Our big push is for a constitutional amendment to overturn the decision.
www.democracyisforpeople.org/page.cfm?id=9

Resolutions, letter to the editor tool, petition/signature collection, letter to legislators, brochures, stickers, and more at
www.democracyisforpeople.org/page.cfm?id=21

StampStampede
www.stampstampede.org

"The system isn't broken, it's fixed. Amend the Constitution." Ben Cohen of Ben & Jerry's fame is leading a "stampede" to stamp dollar bills and to give Americans a voice. The Stamp Stampede is a petition on steroids. It is a way for you to raise your voice and make it heard for two and a half years. It provides a concrete way for people to take action that will have a lasting and growing impact. It is the constant and growing drumbeat that will not be silenced.

Building the Stampede community and how to spread the word at
www.stampstampede.org/pages/build-the-movement

Twenty-Eighth Amendment resources at
www.stampstampede.org/pages/money-in-politics

United for the People
www.united4thepeople.org

A website from the aforementioned groups and more than 150 others that stand together for the work of overturning *Citizens United*. The website contains updated information about local and state resolutions, state and national legislator support for the Twenty-Eighth Amendment, and various amendment resolutions pending in Congress.

Resources and links at **www.united4thepeople.org/resources.html**

US PIRG
www.uspirg.org

Access the Reclaim Democracy campaign
www.uspirg.org/issues/usp/reclaiming-our-democracy

US PIRG, the federation of state public interest research groups, is working town by town and state by state to pass local resolutions to build the grassroots power necessary to pass a constitutional amendment to overturn *Citizens United* and allow for limits on big money in elections to protect political equality for all Americans. You can get started by working in your town to pass a city or state resolution. If you are in a state that has already passed a resolution, there is still more work to be done to hold Congress accountable. Go to our website to sign up to get involved at **www.uspirg.org/issues/usp/reclaiming-our-democracy**

Table 3 (*continued*)
Correcting the Court:
Restoring Our Constitutional Rights and the Republic

Organizations, mission statements, resources, and tools

Wolf PAC
www.wolf-pac.com

Wolf PAC seeks to restore true democracy in the United States by pressuring our *state* representatives to pass a Twenty-Eighth Amendment to our Constitution to end corporate personhood and enable publicly financed all elections.

WolfPAC supports a constitutional amendment that embodies the following principles: Corporations have none of the constitutional rights of human beings. Corporations should not be allowed to give money to any politician, directly or indirectly. No politician should be able to raise $100 (in today's dollars) from any person or entity.

All elections should be publicly financed. **www.wolf-pac.com/28th**

Citizen action for WolfPAC focuses on getting state legislatures to call for an Article V Convention at **www.wolf-pac.com/the_plan**

99Rise – Demand Democracy
www.99rise.org

99Rise is a network of activists and organizers dedicated to building a mass movement to reclaim our democracy from the domination of big money.

We believe that only by getting big money out of politics—by winning a democracy that responds to the real needs of "the 99 percent"—will we open the door to finally realizing the promise of the American Dream.

We thus seek a constitutional amendment and supplemental federal legislation that would guarantee the principle of political equality, as well as ensure that neither private wealth nor corporate privilege could be used to exercise undue influence over elections and policymaking. To this end, we are committed to deploying the most powerful tool of social and political change: strategic nonviolent resistance.

Take action with 99Rise at **www.99rise.org/action**

The amendment campaign is great, but what about work in the courts to overturn Citizen United?

Table 4
Restoring Fair Courts and Legal Advocacy

Organizations, mission statements, resources, and tools

American Constitution Society
www.acslaw.org

The American Constitution Society (ACS) is a nationwide network of lawyers, law students, judges, and policymakers who believe that law should be a force to improve the lives of all people. ACS addresses the aftermath of *Citizens United* and counters the activist legal movement that has sought to erode our enduring constitutional values through live programming in more than 200 lawyer and student chapters throughout the country; opportunities for members to engage on the issues by connecting with key leaders; timely and accessible publications; the widely read ACSBlog; and member projects like *Justice at Risk*, an empirical examination of the impact of business donations on decisions in the state courts, and the Voting Rights Institute, a collaboration with the Campaign Legal Center to train the next generation of voting rights litigators.

Join ACS at **https://www.acslaw.org/membership**

To connect with ACS lawyers and law students and educate and activate citizens in your community, support ACS or email ACS staff at **info@acslaw.org.**

Brennan Center
www.brennancenter.org

The Brennan Center for Justice at NYU School of Law is a nonpartisan public policy and law institute that brings scholarship, legislative and legal advocacy, and communications to bear on fundamental issues of democracy and justice. *Citizens United* and other court rulings obliterated a century of campaign finance laws. Now a handful of special interests threaten to dominate political funding, often through Super PACs and shadowy nonprofits. We seek to advance a new system of small donor public financing that would provide multiple matching funds for small gifts and give ordinary voters a far louder voice in presidential and congressional elections. We also seek a new legal context for money in politics: a long-term drive to overturn *Citizens United* so that the Constitution is once again a charter for a self-governing democracy.

Learn more at **www.brennancenter.org/money-politics**

Sign up at **www.brennancenter.org/signup**

Table 4 (*continued*)
Restoring Fair Courts and Legal Advocacy

Organizations, mission statements, resources, and tools

The Campaign Legal Center
www.campaignlegalcenter.org

The Campaign Legal Center is a nonpartisan, nonprofit organization that works in the areas of campaign finance and elections, political communication, and government ethics. The Campaign Legal Center also participates in generating and shaping our nation's policy debates about money in politics, disclosure, political advertising, and enforcement issues.

Sign up at
www.campaignlegalcenter.org/index.php?option=com_forme&fid=1&Itemid=63

Constitution Accountability Center (CAC)
www.theusconstitution.org

Constitutional Accountability Center, a think tank, public interest law firm, and action center, defends our Constitution's vision of a democracy of, by, and for "we, the people." In legal briefs in landmark campaign finance cases and extensive reports on the Constitution's text and history, CAC has shown that *Citizens United* has no basis in the Constitution. The ruling flouts our Constitution's text and history and perverts our Constitution's promise of democracy for all. "We, the people," must take our Constitution back and overturn the grievous error of *Citizens United*.

To keep up to date and involved, join at **www.constitutionalprogressives.org**
and follow CAC's blog, **www.theusconstitution.org/text-history**

Demos
www.demos.org

Demos works for an America where we all have an equal say in our democracy and an equal chance in our economy. Demos combines research, advocacy, and strategic communications. Demos seeks to end the domination of government by the economic elite by empowering small donors with public financing; ensuring transparency of all political spending; and transforming the constitutional paradigm for the First Amendment from one that privileges money over people to one that puts people back at the center of our democracy.

Learn more and take action at
www.demos.org/issue/campaign-finance-reform

Free Speech For People
www.freespeechforpeople.org

Free Speech For People's Legal Advocacy Program (**www.freespeechforpeople. org/initiatives**) engages in legal advocacy in the courts to ensure correction of the Supreme Court's rulings in *Citizens United v. FEC* and *Buckley v. Valeo*. The program also advances corporate charter reform in the states and serves as a critical resource for the growing movement for a Twenty-Eighth Amendment to reclaim our democracy. With a legal advisory committee of scholars, former judges, and lawyers (**www.freespeechforpeople.org/node/597**) and a network of pro bono attorneys and other supporters, the Free Speech For People files briefs in the Supreme Court and other courts, initiates reforms, and convenes debate to chart a path to jurisprudence that supports rather than undermines American government of the people.

Links and background to legal initiatives at
www.freespeechforpeople.org/initiatives

Cleaning the Swamp: Elections and Government for People

I want to believe in election and government integrity again and make government of the people real. What can I do?

Table 5
Reform Organizations Helping to Clean the Swamp

Organizations, mission statements, resources, and tools

Americans for Campaign Reform
www.acrreform.org

Americans for Campaign Reform is a community of citizens who believe that public funding is the most critical long-term public policy issue our nation faces. What's at stake are nothing less than the health of our democracy, the quality of our leadership, and our government's ability to tackle the serious problems that affect us all: health care, energy policy, education, the environment, and the economy.

See "Get Involved" at **www.acrreform.org**

Center for Responsive Politics
www.opensecrets.org

The Center for Responsive Politics informs citizens about how money in politics affects their lives; empowers voters and activists by providing unbiased information; and advocates for a transparent and responsive government.

The CRP website Open Secrets is an indispensable tool for Americans reclaiming our democracy. Check it out at **www.opensecrets.org**

Table 5 (*continued*)
Reform Organizations Helping to Clean the Swamp

Organizations, mission statements, resources, and tools

Center for Media and Democracy (CMD)
www.prwatch.org/cmd/index.html

The Center for Media and Democracy investigates and exposes the undue influence of corporations and front groups on public policy, including PR campaigns, lobbying, and electioneering. CMD's original reporting helps educate the public and aid grassroots action about policies affecting people's lives—their rights and the health of our democracy.

Take action and links at **www.sourcewatch.org/index.php/SourceWatch**

National Institute on Money in State Politics
www.followthemoney.org

The National Institute on Money in State Politics is a nonpartisan, nonprofit organization revealing the influence of campaign money on state-level elections and public policy in all fifty states. We encourage transparency and promote independent investigation of state-level campaign contributions by journalists, academic researchers, public-interest groups, government agencies, policymakers, students and the public at large.

An excellent state-level counterpart to Open Secrets at **www.followthemoney.org**

Justice at Stake
www.justiceatstake.org

Justice at Stake is a national organization focused on keeping courts fair and impartial. *Citizens United* raised the threat facing elected courts to an unprecedented level. Where there is public support, states may need to consider the appointment of judges or public financing of judicial elections as possible ways to protect courts from campaign cash.

Learn more and get involved at
www.justiceatstake.org/issues/state_court_issues/justice-at-stake-and-judicial-elections/

Public Campaign
www.publiccampaign.org

Public Campaign fights for proposals and mobilizes the public behind solutions that allow everyday Americans to have their voice heard and count in elections and policymaking. Public Campaign educates the public, policymakers, and nonprofit leaders alike on the importance of small dollar public financing systems and how these proposals would make elections more fair and a government "of, by, and for the people."

Sign up at **www.publiccampaign.org**

Public Campaign Action Fund: **www.campaignmoney.org**

188

Represent US
www.represent.us

Represent Us supports the American Anti-Corruption Act to overhaul campaign finance, impose strict lobbying and conflict of interest laws, and end secret political money. They mobilize millions of Americans—conservatives and progressives, young and old, every issue group fighting K Street, online and offline—to join this campaign.

Read the plan and take action at **www.represent.us/#takeaction**

Rootstrikers
www.rootstrikers.org

Working to end the system of corruption in Washington, D.C., pushing for constitutional amendment, citizen funding of elections, the New Hampshire Rebellion, and more.

Take Action Options at **www.rootstrikers.org**

Note: Virtually all of the organizations identified above that are working on the Twenty-Eighth Amendment and to overturn *Citizens United* in the courts also work on the "clean the swamp" effort.

Making Corporations Better and Accountable

How do I get involved in the effort to make corporations more effective and more accountable to all of us?

Table 6
Better Business

Organizations, mission statements, resources, and tools

American Independent Business Alliance
www.amiba.net

The American Independent Business Alliance helps communities launch and operate an Independent Business Alliance® (IBA), "buy independent, buy local" campaigns, forward prolocal policies, and other initiatives to support local entrepreneurs and vibrant local economies.

Join, start an IBA, check out resources, and more at **www.amiba.net**

American Sustainable Business Council
www.asbcouncil.org

The American Sustainable Business Council (ASBC) is a coalition of business organizations and businesses creating a vibrant, just, and sustainable economy. ASBC and its members represent 200,000 businesses and 325,000 business leaders. From issues advocating for a strong democracy, fair elections, against

Table 6 (*continued*)
Better Business

Organizations, mission statements, resources, and tools

American Sustainable Business Council (continued)

Citizens United, for a fair tax system, to safer chemicals and addressing climate change, ASBC is raising up the voice, presence, and power of business to create jobs, grow business, and build a sustainable economy.

Reverse *Citizens United*, strengthen democracy:
www.asbcouncil.org/campaigns/election-integrity

B Corporations

B Corps are a new type of company that uses the power of business to solve social and environmental problems.

bcorporation.net is a hub for certified B corporations, including information on how and why to become a B corp, profiles and B Impact reports for every company in the community, and an overview of B Lab, the nonprofit behind the certification.

benefitcorp.net has information on benefit corporations, a new voluntary corporate form that allows companies to meet higher standards of corporate purpose accountability and transparency. The site provides information to businesses, lawyers, directors, and legislators interested in registering as benefit corporations or passing legislation.

b-analytics.net provides information on the B Analytics Platform, which houses the largest database of social and environmental performance data for private companies. It is also the exclusive source of data on certified B corporations and GIIRS-rated companies and funds. The website is used by investors, fund managers, entrepreneurs, and business associations to learn about the various data collection, measurement, benchmarking, and reporting options available through the customizable platform.

Check out the B the Change campaign, reachable at **www.bcorporation.net/b-the-change**, where individuals can join a movement of people using business as a force for good.

BALLE
www.bealocalist.org

Fostering the emergence of a new economics that will move our society in a more positive direction is at the core of our work. Localism seeks to gradually displace failing structures and systems with economic structures that benefit. The BALLE community is changing how we think about the purpose of business and the economy. Together, we are changing mindsets from "every-man-for-himself" to an understanding that real security comes from community—from sharing, not hoarding, from partnership, not domination.

Get connected: at **www.bealocalist.org/get-connected**

Capital Institute
http://www.capitalinstitute.org

Capital Institute is a nonpartisan, transdisciplinary collaborative launched in 2010 by John Fullerton, a former JPMorgan managing director. Its mission is to explore and effect economic transition to a more just, regenerative, and sustainable way of living on this earth through the transformation of finance. Capital Institute's *Field Guide to Investing in a Regenerative Economy* is about sharing an alternative, hopeful vision of the regenerative economy and building a movement around it through collaborative storytelling.

Share your own regenerative economy business or project stories at **www.fieldguide.capitalinstitute.org/share-your-story.html**

Center for the Advancement of the Steady State Economy
www.steadystate.org

The mission of CASSE is to advance the steady state economy, with stabilized population and consumption, as a policy goal with widespread public support. CASSE educates citizens, organizations, and policymakers on the conflict between economic growth and (1) environmental protection, (2) ecological and economic sustainability, and (3) national security and international stability. CASSE promotes the steady state economy as a desirable alternative to economic growth and explores the transition to a steady state economy.

Take action at **www.steadystate.org/act**

Ethical Markets
www.ethicalmarkets.com

Ethical Markets fosters the evolution of capitalism beyond models based on materialism, maximizing self-interest and profit, competition, and fear of scarcity. Knowledge is not scarce, and our economic models can move toward sharing, cooperating, and a new abundance. We believe capitalism combined with humanity's growing knowledge of the interdependence of all life on planet earth can evolve to serve today's new needs and our common future—beyond maximizing profits for shareholders and management to benefiting all stakeholders.

Explore at **www.ethicalmarkets.com**

Free Speech For People
www.freespeechforpeople.org

Free Speech For People works to challenge the misuse of corporate power and restore republican democracy to the people. In addition to constitutional amendment and legal advocacy work, Free Speech For People works to renew and reform corporate charter laws and other tools to make corporations responsible and accountable to the public.

Help enforce charter revocation laws for corporations that engage in repeated criminal conduct at **www.freespeechforpeople.org/corporatecharterreform**

Table 6 (continued)
Better Business

Organizations, mission statements, resources, and tools

The New Economy Coalition
www.neweconomy.net

The mission of the New Economy Coalition (NEC) is to convene and support all those who might contribute to an economy that is restorative to people, place, and planet and that operates according to principles of democracy, justice, and appropriate scale. Faced with interconnected ecological and economic crises, we believe that shared prosperity, sustainability, and an equitable society require deep, systemic changes to both our economy and our politics. We support a just transition to a new economy that enables both thriving communities and ecological health.

Explore at **www.neweconomy.net**

Slow Money
www.slowmoney.org

Slow Money is focused on democratizing finance and helping people to invest in their communities, starting with food.

Look for a local group or investment club near you at **www.slowmoney.org** or engage with Slow Money entrepreneurs via the event and funding platform at **www.gatheround.org**.

❖   ❖   ❖

Inscribed high on the walls of the Jefferson Memorial in Washington is a more moderate version of Jefferson's "water the tree of liberty with blood" recognition of the need to preserve a revolutionary spirit among the free people of America. "I am not an advocate for frequent changes in laws and constitutions," wrote Jefferson. "But laws and institutions must go hand in hand with the progress of the human mind. . . . We might as well require a man to wear still the coat which fitted him when a boy as civilized society to remain ever under the regimen of their barbarous ancestors."[11]

We know, having seen the successful execution of the Powell-Chamber plan for a long corporate drive for power, that current interpretation of the Constitution does not simply reflect "the progress of the human mind." The creation of corporate rights and the transfer of power from the people to large corporations did not happen because we, the people, now have a more enlightened view of free speech and the Constitution. Rather, we, the people, are on the receiving end of that well-funded, well-organized, years-long corporatist campaign to twist our Constitution and subvert our government of people.

Accordingly, this is not a mere policy debate. We face a constitutional struggle, a national struggle. If that struggle is to be won, the Constitution must be returned to a charter of rights of sovereign people, determined to govern ourselves. If we do the necessary work now for the Twenty-Eighth Amendment, for reform of our election and campaign spending laws, and for better corporate rules, we will preserve government, a republic, of the people. In so doing, we will have defended in our time what the founders' generation called the rights of man and what we, after two centuries of hard work and improbable successes by generations of Americans, can proudly call the rights of people.

Resources

Presented here are the following resources:

Citizens' Rights Amendment

Political Equality Amendment

We, the People Amendment

Sample Amendment Resolution

Questions and Answers about the Twenty-Eighth Amendment

Free Speech for People and Appalachian Voices' Request for
Revocation of Massey Energy Company Charters

Sources and Recommended Reading

You will find a great deal of additional resources by accessing the "portals" identified in Chapter 8.

People's Rights Amendment

Amendment XXVIII

SECTION I. We the people who ordain and establish this Constitution intend the rights protected by this Constitution to be the rights of natural persons.

SECTION II. The words *people, person,* or *citizen* as used in this Constitution do not include corporations, limited liability companies, or other corporate entities established by the laws of any state, the United States, or any foreign state. Such corporate entities are subject to any regulation as the people, through their elected state and federal representatives, deem reasonable and as are otherwise consistent with the powers of Congress and the States under this Constitution.

SECTION III. Nothing contained herein shall be construed to limit the people's rights of freedom of speech, freedom of the press, free exercise of religion, and all such other rights of the people, which rights are inalienable.

Citizens' Equality Amendment

Amendment XXVIII

SECTION 1. To advance the fundamental principle of political equality for all, and to protect the integrity of the legislative and electoral processes, Congress shall have power to regulate the raising and spending of money and in-kind equivalents with respect to federal elections, including through setting limits on—

(1) the amount of contributions to candidates for nomination for election to, or for election to, federal office; and

(2) the amount of funds that may be spent by, in support of, or in opposition to such candidates.

SECTION 2. To advance the fundamental principle of political equality for all, and to protect the integrity of the legislative and electoral processes, each state shall have power to regulate the raising and spending of money and in-kind equivalents with respect to state elections, including through setting limits on—

(1) the amount of contributions to candidates for nomination for election to, or for election to, state office; and

(2) the amount of funds that may be spent by, in support of, or in opposition to such candidates.

SECTION 3. Nothing in this article shall be construed to grant Congress the power to abridge the freedom of the press.

SECTION 4. Congress and the states shall have power to implement and enforce this article by appropriate legislation.

We, the People Amendment

Amendment XXVIII

SECTION 1. [Artificial Entities Such as Corporations Do Not Have Constitutional Rights]

The rights protected by the Constitution of the United States are the rights of natural persons only.

Artificial entities established by the laws of any state, the United States, or any foreign state shall have no rights under this Constitution and are subject to regulation by the people, through federal, state, or local law.

The privileges of artificial entities shall be determined by the people, through federal, state, or local law, and shall not be construed to be inherent or inalienable.

SECTION 2. [Money is Not Free Speech]

Federal, state, and local government shall regulate, limit, or prohibit contributions and expenditures, including a candidate's own contributions and expenditures, to ensure that all citizens, regardless of their economic status, have access to the political process, and that no person gains, as a result of their money, substantially more access or ability to influence in any way the election of any candidate for public office or any ballot measure.

Federal, state, and local government shall require that any permissible contributions and expenditures be publicly disclosed.

The judiciary shall not construe the spending of money to influence elections to be speech under the First Amendment.

Sample Amendment Resolution

WHEREAS,

We, the people adopted and ratified the United States Constitution to protect the free speech and other inherent rights of people, not corporations, and to ensure the survival of liberty and preserve self-government of equal citizens;

Free and fair elections are essential to democracy and effective self-governance;

Corporations are not people; they are entities created by the law of states and nations;

For the past three decades, the Supreme Court has wrongly transformed the First Amendment and Constitution into a powerful tool for corporations seeking to evade and invalidate the people's laws;

This corporate misuse of the Constitution reached an extreme conclusion in the United States Supreme Court's ruling in *Citizens United v. Federal Election Commission*;

Citizens United v. Federal Election Commission overturned long-standing precedent prohibiting corporations from spending corporate general treasury funds in our elections;

Citizens United v. Federal Election Commission unleashed a torrent of corporate money in our political process unmatched by any campaign expenditure totals in United States history;

Citizens United v. Federal Election Commission purports to invalidate state laws and even state constitutional provisions separating corporate money from elections;

Citizens United v. the Federal Election Commission and related decisions purport to (1) deprive the people of the ability to enact even-handed, legal limits on spending in the electoral process, (2) impose unequal playing fields by mandating unregulated and unlimited spending by wealthy individuals, corporations, and other entities to influence elections, candidate selection, policy decisions, and sway votes and elections, and (3) empower those with the most money to have an unfair advantage and create systemic corruption in our Republic;

Citizens United v. Federal Election Commission presents a serious and direct threat to our republican democracy;

Article V of the United States Constitution empowers and obligates the people and states of the United States of America to use the constitutional amendment process to correct those egregiously wrong decisions of the United States Supreme Court that go to the heart of our democracy and republican self-government;

and

The people and states of the United States of America have strengthened the nation and preserved liberty and equality for all by using the amendment process throughout our history, including in seven of the ten decades of the twentieth century, and reversing seven erroneous Supreme Court decisions;

NOW THEREFORE BE IT RESOLVED THAT WE CALL ON THE UNITED STATES CONGRESS TO PASS AND SEND TO THE STATES FOR RATIFICATION A CONSTITUTIONAL AMENDMENT TO REVERSE *CITIZENS UNITED V. FEDERAL ELECTION COMMISSION* AND TO RESTORE CONSTITUTIONAL RIGHTS AND FAIR ELECTIONS TO THE PEOPLE.

By the people of _____ on _____.
                                  [place]   [date]

Questions and Answers about the Twenty-Eighth Amendment

Why do we need a constitutional amendment? Can't Congress fix this?

Congress could begin to address some of the problems of *Citizens United*. Congress could enact laws requiring disclosure of political spending by corporations, for example. It is telling, though, that even that limited measure failed to pass in a vote on the Senate floor after *Citizens United*.

Short of disregarding the Supreme Court's decision—which would drastically undermine the Court's legitimacy and threaten the rule of law—Congress cannot overrule the Supreme Court's interpretation of the Constitution.

That is why constitutional amendments have always been necessary to correct egregiously wrong Supreme Court decisions, from the 1856 ruling that African Americans, "whether emancipated or not," are not citizens and "had no rights which the white man is bound to respect"[1] to the 1874 decision that even if women were citizens, they had no right to vote because the Constitution did not guarantee the right to vote as among the fundamental rights, privileges, or immunities of citizenship.[2]

Congress and the states can and should take many steps to make elections more fair and to improve the likelihood that legislatures will reflect the will of the people, from approving public funding mechanisms to eliminating barriers to registration and voting. None of these will be sufficient, however, without the Twenty-Eighth Amendment.

What will be the impact of the amendment on day-to-day business operations? Don't corporations have to be "persons" in order to function in our economy?

The Twenty-Eighth Amendment will have no impact on day-to-day or other operations of corporations. No activity of a business corporation requires the fabrication of corporate constitutional rights. The rights of individual people (doing business in a corporation or otherwise) are unchanged by the Twenty-Eighth Amendment.

The features that make corporations useful tools for economic activity come from state and federal legislation, not the Constitution. For two centuries, corporations were able to carry out their business purposes without the fabrication of constitutional rights, and the concept of "corporate speech rights" did not exist before 1978. Until the *Citizens United* ruling in 2010, we were free to use federal law to control corporate spending in elections and did so for more than a century.

The Twenty-Eighth Amendment will restore core democratic rights to citizens without changing the productive role of corporations in our economy. State and federal laws define corporations and set the rules for the use of the corporate form. These laws are unaffected by the amendment, and people in the states will be free to enact corporate laws that they determine are best.

Doesn't the law say corporations are "persons"?

Under state and federal law, corporations are "persons" for the purposes of contracting, suing, being sued, transacting business, and continuity of operations as employees come and go. Under state and federal law, corporations are "persons" for numerous purposes, from trademark protection to criminal prosecution. That kind of legal definition of corporations is a prudent policy choice made by legislation in the democratic process. That is not the same as defining our Constitution and Bill of Rights.

The Twenty-Eighth Amendment has no effect whatsoever on those state and federal laws. The amendment will stop the radical and improper application of the corporate "person" concept to the rights of real people under the Constitution and Bill of Rights.

What effect will the Twenty-Eighth Amendment have on our ability to use corporate entities in our business dealings?

None. The amendment does not limit in any fashion the many ways in which people and the states can design and use corporate or other economic legal entities.

The amendment simply states a fundamental truth: whatever corporate entities the state or federal governments create do not have constitutional rights. Instead, their rights and obligations are set out in state or federal corporate laws and other laws.

The corporate form has huge advantages, and we support state policies that encourage easy incorporation. We just shouldn't confuse those policy advantages with constitutional rights.

Does that mean people will lose their rights when they do business in the corporate form?

No. The Twenty-Eighth Amendment protects all rights of all people, whether or not they own, run, work for, or buy from corporations.

Whether the rights at issue are speech, due process, or any other human right, the people involved in a corporation—the CEO and executives, employees, shareholders, or other people in a corporation—retain all of their rights as people.

The amendment simply means that we will not allow courts to pretend that corporations are people when it comes to the Constitution and Bill of Rights.

What about property rights? Will this change shareholder rights? Rights to due process?

The Twenty-Eighth Amendment will protect all constitutional rights of people, be they property rights or other rights.

Take an egregious hypothetical example, just to illustrate: Say the government decides it needs computer technology for some reason and enacts a law requiring that Apple deliver all of its intellectual property to the US government. Apple sues to block the law, claiming that the government is taking private property without due process in violation of the Fifth Amendment (or the Fourteenth Amendment, if a state government tries this). Does Apple have constitutional rights not to have its property taken without due process?

The due process clause says that "no person" can be deprived of life, liberty, or property without due process. Apple is not a "person" under the Constitution's due process clause, but there are plenty of real people involved in this hypothetical who do have due process rights not to have the value of their Apple shares turned over to the government without due process. Nothing about the amendment would prevent those real people from protecting their rights.

The claim could be brought directly by the corporation using statutes such as the federal Tort Claims Act. The claim could also be brought by the corporation, if it is deemed to have standing by the Court to raise the rights of its shareholders. The claim could be brought by the shareholders as a class.

Another possibility to litigate the question may include challenges to the constitutional power of the federal government to take such action, an approach taken when the Supreme Court invalidated the Truman administration's nationalization of the American steel industry in 1952. The Twenty-Eighth Amendment does not empower the government to seize property or do anything in violation of our liberties.

The Constitution protects against deprivations of private property without due process and just compensation, and nothing about the Twenty-Eighth Amendment changes that. The specific approach for protecting property rights in the context of corporations after the Twenty-Eighth Amendment would depend on the circumstances and on the jurisprudence developed by the Court after ratification. On top of all of this, people, businesses, and legislators are extremely unlikely to sit idly by while government seizes property. The best guarantee of the liberties of the people and guard against government over-reach is not the unconstitutional fabrication of corporate rights but rather a healthy Constitution of checks and balances, liberties of the people, and an active, engaged citizenry. The Twenty-Eighth Amendment protects and enhances exactly that.

What about freedom of the press and media? Aren't they all corporations?

The Twenty-Eighth Amendment will not limit freedom of the press in any way, and explicitly guarantees freedom of press and other rights. The First Amendment protects freedom of speech and freedom of the press, as well as freedom of religion, assembly, and petition. All of these are rights of the people. The Twenty-Eighth Amendment does not change the First Amendment; it strengthens it. As Supreme Court Justice John Paul Stevens declared so clearly, *Citizens United* is "a radical departure from what has been settled First Amendment law."

It has never been necessary or advisable to have activist judges create new "corporate rights" in the Constitution simply because owners of large press and media operations tend to use the privilege of incorporation for their operations. People may engage in press activity using a corporation for the activity's business operations, but the right at stake remains a right of human beings. The press machines, computers, and buildings used by people in the media do not have constitutional rights. We understand that those "things" are tools that help people carry out the press activity. The corporation also is a tool to help people carry out the press activity, and it makes no more sense to insist on "corporate rights" because the *New York Times* operates in a corporate form as to insist on "building rights" because they operate in a building.

The freedom of press applies to press/media functions regardless of whether a corporation owns and operates those functions. That has always been true and will continue to be true after the People's Rights Amendment is ratified. Indeed, the *New York Times* in an editorial calling for the reversal of *Citizens United* makes this very point:

> It is not the corporate structure of media companies that makes them deserving of constitutional protection. It is their function—the vital role that the press plays in American democracy—that sets them apart.

More information is available at: www.freespeechforpeople.org/sites/default/files/FSFP%20on%20freedom%20of%20the%20press.pdf.

Will an amendment affect the ability of nonprofit associations and unions to give in elections as well? Will it affect my religious institution's status as a corporation? What about nonprofit corporations?

The Twenty-Eighth Amendment will have no impact on people's rights to associate freely or worship as they wish. Freedoms such as religion, speech, and assembly are not predicated on the creation by the state of corporate entities that are granted tax deductions and other state-based advantages.

The federal law (the Bipartisan Campaign Reform Act of 2002) struck down by *Citizens United* equally applied to unions, nonprofits, and for-profit corporations.

If union activity, charitable activity, or advocacy activity is done by a corporate entity, the corporation is expected to comply with laws applicable to corporations.

Whatever corporate form and rules government comes up with must be evenhanded and apply equally to all religions and all points of view. Government cannot say Protestants but not Unitarians can organize their church as a nonprofit corporation. Government cannot say that a synagogue but not a church can give tax-deductible contributions to its nonprofit corporate entity. Government cannot do that because the rights of people would be violated. That has nothing to do with whether those people use a corporation to organize the institution.

There's no reason to be afraid of a fair rule for all that says anyone who wants to organize a church using a corporate form can do so, but it must comply with corporate (and other) laws. It has always worked that way, and the Twenty-Eighth Amendment doesn't change that.

More on the "associational standing" doctrine that enables nonprofit corporations to defend the rights of their human members is contained in a 2014 Supreme Court brief of Free Speech For People, the Auburn Theological Seminary, and Hollander Sustainable Brands, LLC, available at www.freespeechforpeople.org/sites/default/files/13-356%20tsac%20 Free%20Speech%20for%20People.pdf.

What about freedom to associate? Aren't corporations just like any other association?

A corporation is not just like any other association of people. A corporation is a specific creation of state or federal statute that may be used only for purposes defined by the statute that permitted its creation. "Those who feel that the essence of the corporation rests in the contract among its members rather than in the government decree . . . fail to distinguish, as [those in] the eighteenth century did, between the corporation and the voluntary association."[3] That distinction has always been true and is true now. A corporation is a government-created structure for doing business and is available only by statute.

We, as people, have the right to associate. We have a choice to incorporate, if we like the balance of benefits and burdens that the corporate laws provide.

Could there be unintended consequences for our economy? Corporations seem essential now. Could this amendment upend the complex workings of corporations in our economy?

The Twenty-Eighth Amendment does nothing to change the role of corporations in our economy. The responsibility for defining the economic role of corporations would remain where it had always been before the Court fabricated corporate rights: with the people and our elected representatives. The corporate entity will continue to be a very useful economic tool. Ending "corporate person" rights in the Constitution has nothing to do with federal and state laws that make corporations like "persons" who may enter into contracts, sue and be sued, and so on.

In fact, the amendment, although not intended as an economic reform, will probably help the economy. Corporate "rights" (which are really about global corporate power) are harming the American economy. The vast majority of businesspeople and corporations do not need or want "rights" to defy democratically enacted laws or to be pushed into buying more and more political ads. The amendment would not upend anything about corporations in our economy except the abuse of the Bill of Rights by transnational corporations seeking to attack our laws.

Won't this lead to big government? Government telling us how much we can spend and so on?

This amendment is not regulation. It is about liberty for us as people to debate and decide for ourselves what size government should be or what regulations make sense. Regulatory policy now is driven by the billions of dollars in lobbying spending, with the biggest, most global corporations and spenders writing the rules.

You can find more details and a lot more information via the constitutional amendment portals in Chapter 8.

Free Speech For People and Appalachian Voices' Request for Revocation of Massey Energy Company Charters

June 8, 2011

By Electronic and First Class Mail

(Attorney.General@State.DE.US)

The Honorable Beau Biden
Attorney General, State of Delaware
Carvel State Office Building
820 N. French Street
Wilmington, DE 19801

  Re: Request to Investigate Revocation of Massey
     Energy Company Corporate Charters

Dear Attorney General Biden:

We write today, on behalf of Free Speech For People and Appalachian Voices, to request investigation by your office into a Delaware corporation that has engaged in repeated and sustained violations of law, contributing to the deaths of people in central Appalachia and to the destruction and devastation of our environment and communities. We request that you investigate and consider bringing proceedings to revoke the charter of the Massey Energy Company corporation and its Delaware corporate subsidiaries ("Massey"). As Massey became a wholly-owned subsidiary corporation of another Delaware corporation, Alpha Natural Resources, Inc. ("Alpha"), on June 1, 2011, we request that you take appropriate steps to ensure Alpha's cooperation in your inquiry.[1]

  Free Speech for People is a national campaign to combat unconstitutional doctrines of "corporate rights" that threaten our republican democracy and government of, for and by the American people. Hundreds of thousands of Americans have joined Free Speech for People's call for a constitutional amendment to restore the United States Constitution and fair elections to the people in response to the US Supreme Court's recent ruling in *Citizens United v. FEC*. Responsible oversight of state-created corporations is an essential obligation of citizenship and self-government, and Free Speech for People works for

---

[1] US Securities and Exchange Commission, Alpha Rule 424 prospectus, May 19, 2011 ("On January 28, 2011, Alpha, Mountain Merger Sub and Massey entered into an agreement and plan of merger pursuant to which Mountain Merger Sub will merge with and into Massey, which will be the surviving corporation of the Merger and a wholly owned subsidiary of Alpha.")

accountability with respect to the privileges and conditions that apply to corporate charters granted by the people and our states.

Appalachian Voices is an award-winning, environmental organization committed to protecting the land, air and water of the central and southern Appalachian region. Since the impacts of coal threaten Appalachia more than any other single source of pollution, Appalachian Voices is committed to reducing coal's impact on the region and to advancing its vision for a cleaner energy future.

Massey Energy Company is the 4th largest coal company in the country, with revenues estimated for 2011 at more than $4 billion. The corporation keeps its headquarters in Richmond, VA and maintains substantial mine operations in central Appalachia. Although Massey avails itself of Delaware corporate charter laws, the company has virtually no business in Delaware. Following the Massey-Alpha merger, the combined company will be the second largest coal company, with estimated earnings for 2011 at more than $8 billion. Alpha also avails itself of Delaware corporate charter laws but maintains virtually no business in Delaware.

On April 5, 2010 an explosion in Massey's Upper Big Branch Mine in southern West Virginia killed 29 men working in the mine. We have attached the May 19, 2011 Report of the Governor's Independent Investigation Panel, which has determined that the explosion was preventable, and was caused by Massey's pattern of disregarding safety laws and undermining law enforcement. As discussed further herein, the Report chronicles Massey's repeated violations of law and its "normalization of deviancy."

I. The Corporate Charter in Delaware and Elsewhere Is A Privilege Subject to Revocation in Cases of Repeated Unlawful Conduct

As you know, many of the world's largest corporations, including Massey, have chosen to use corporate charters granted by the people and General Assembly of Delaware. While Delaware has welcomed the widespread use of Delaware corporate charters even for business conducted well beyond Delaware's borders, the people of Delaware and the General Assembly have always insisted that the corporate charter is a privilege, not a right. Delaware, like other states, reserves the right to revoke or forfeit state corporate charters when they are abused or misused, as in cases of repeated unlawful conduct. In Delaware and elsewhere, corporate charters are only granted "subject to dissolution or the revocation or forfeiture of the corporate charter." See 8 Del. Code § 284. See also 5 Del. Code §§ 732, 1520, 1631 (credit card and bank corporate charters subject to revocation).

The Delaware Constitution (Article IX, §1) requires that the General Assembly "shall, by general law, provide for the revocation or forfeiture of the charters or franchises." The General Assembly has followed this mandate of the people by enacting Title 8, Section 284 of the General Corporations Law entitled "Revocation or Forfeiture of Charter; Proceedings." That section provides:

(a) The Court of Chancery shall have jurisdiction to revoke or forfeit the charter of any corporation for abuse, misuse or nonuse of its corporate powers, privileges or franchises. The Attorney General shall, upon the Attorney General's own motion or upon the relation of a proper party, proceed for this purpose by complaint in the county in which the registered office of the corporation is located.

(b) The Court of Chancery shall have power, by appointment of receivers or otherwise, to administer and wind up the affairs of any corporation whose charter shall be revoked or forfeited by any court under any section of this title or otherwise, and to make such orders and decrees with respect thereto as shall be just and equitable respecting its affairs and assets and the rights of its stockholders and creditors.

In Young v. the National Association for the Advancement of White People, 35 Del.Ch. 10, 109 A.2d 29 (1954) the Chancery Court stated, "there is no question but that this Court will forfeit a corporate charter where the abuse of its privileges and franchises is clear." 109 A.2d at 31. The Court added that such revocation of a corporate charter is appropriate in cases of "a sustained course of fraud, immorality or violations of statutory law . . . ." Id. In a subsequent action brought by the Attorney General to revoke a corporate charter, the Chancery Court affirmed again that "continued serious criminal violations by corporate agents in the course of the discharge of their duties could very well constitute the misuse of a charter." Craven v. Fifth Ward Republican Club, 37 Del.Ch. 524, 528, 146 A.2d 400, 402 (1958) (granting preliminary injunction).

II. "The Normalization of Deviance"—The Report of the Governor's Independent Investigation Panel, May 19, 2011.

On April 5, 2010 an explosion in Massey's Upper Big Branch Mine in southern West Virginia killed 29 men working in the mine. The Governor of West Virginia appointed an independent investigation panel to determine the cause of the explosion, and to impartially find facts that would help prevent similar disasters in the future. Numerous Massey executives refused to cooperate with the investigation. A Massey official was indicted in March 2011, charged with lying to the Federal Bureau of Investigation.[2]

The Report of the Governor's Independent Investigation Panel (the "Report") concerning the explosion and deaths describes in more than 100 pages how Massey repeatedly placed profits ahead of worker safety and compliance with the law, and has a long history of criminal and civil violations of law. Describing a shocking corporate culture of illegality, "enemies lists", "codes of silence," and a "too big to be regulated" attitude, the Report states, "Massey exhibited a corporate mentality that placed the drive to produce above worker safety."[3]

The Report concludes that the fatal explosion at the Massey mine was caused by Massey's systemic failure to comply with basic, existing standards, such as maintaining adequate ventilation systems, complying with standards for applying rock dust and water spraying. Massey did not record many safety hazards, and when recorded, did not correct them.

The Report identifies a longstanding "culture" at Massey that is "causing incalculable damage to mountains, streams, and air in the coalfields; creating health risks for coalfield residents by polluting streams, injecting slurry into the ground and failing to control coal waste dams and dust emissions from processing plants; using vast amounts of money to

---

[2] http://blogs.findlaw.com/blotter/2011/03/security-chief-from-massey-mines-explosion-charged-with-lying-to-fbi-and-obstructing-the-investigati.html

[3] Report at 99–100.

influence the political system; and battling government regulation regarding safety in the coalmines and environmental safeguards for communities."[4]

As alarming as the corporate violations that caused the death of scores of men, the independent panel identified failures of the government agencies that should have been enforcing the law to protect the lives of the people working in Massey's mines. As the report says, "merely having laws on the books has never been enough to ensure worker safety. The ability of the government to rigorously enforce those laws is a hard-earned right paid for with the blood of coalminers."[5]

The West Virginia Independent Investigation Panel linked the failure of government's law enforcement directly to the corruption of government caused by the campaign spending and political influence of Massey and its CEO. The Report describes how, after a West Virginia Court concluded that Massey had intentionally and wrongfully acted in disregard of the rights of another business and destroyed the business, the CEO, Don Blankenship, spent $3 million to fund a vicious judicial election campaign accusing the incumbent judge of being "soft on sex offenders." That judge lost the election to "a virtually unknown lawyer" who was a "personal friend" of Blankenship and was "more sympathetic to Massey's interests."[6]

The Report provides "a graphic illustration of the intertwining of coal and government that works to the detriment of those dedicated to creating an atmosphere in which miners are assured safe working conditions."[7]

Massey "relish[ed] the opportunity to challenge inspectors' enforcement actions by disputing findings and arguing about what the law requires." The Vice-President for safety at Massey openly said, "don't worry, we'll litigate it away" about a violation found by an inspector. Still, in 2009 alone, federal inspectors wrote 515 citations and orders for safety violations and 48 "withdrawal orders" for significant and substantial violations.[8] Massey CEO's message in the Annual Report for 2009 says, "we are proud of our safety record." The CEO's message goes on to label climate change science a "misinformation scandal" and to express "concern" with "environmental extremism" and "ill-considered regulations."[9]

III. Other Violations of Law By Massey

According to the Report, in one ten-year period, Massey was cited for 62,923 federal violations including more than 25,000 considered "significant and substantial." Fifty-nine men who worked in Massey's mines were killed in accidents during that time.[10]

In January 2006, a fire at Massey's Aracoma Alma mine killed two men. Federal investigators determined that the fatal fire was caused by Massey's "reckless disregard"

---

[4] Report at 92.

[5] Report at 76.

[6] Report at 85.

[7] Report at 85.

[8] Report at 77.

[9] 2009 Annual Report at 16–17.

[10] Report at 93.

for safety rules at the Aracoma mine.[11] On December 23, 2009, Massey's subsidiary, the Aracoma Coal Company pleaded guilty to ten criminal violations of mine safety laws, including a felony conviction for a willful violation causing death, and agreed to pay a $2.5 million criminal fine. According to the Independent Investigation Report, Massey CEO Don Blankenship may have been aware of the violations before the fire occurred.

In January 2008 Massey Energy Company, Inc. paid a $20 million fine for Clean Water Act violations in West Virginia and Kentucky. The United States Department of Justice and the Environmental Protection Agency described the fine as the largest civil penalty in the history of the EPA.[12]

Under the Delaware Constitution and revocation law, the "Court will forfeit a corporate charter where the abuse of its privileges and franchises is clear." Young v. the National Association for the Advancement of White People, 35 Del.Ch. 10, 109 A.2d 29 (1954). We respectfully urge you to investigate whether, as seems clear, Massey Energy Company and its subsidiary corporations have forfeited the privilege of their corporate charters, and to initiate forfeiture proceedings using your authority under Title 8.

Thank you for your consideration. We are available to discuss this referral with you further at your convenience, and we look forward to hearing from you.

Sincerely,

Jeffrey D. Clements
General Counsel
Free Speech For People
9 Damonmill Square, Suite 4B
Concord, Massachusetts 01742

Phone: (978) 287-4901
Fax: (978) 287-4900
jclements@freespeechforpeople.org

Willa Coffey Mays
Executive Director
Appalachian Voices
191 Howard Street
Boone, North Carolina 28607

Phone: (828) 262-1500
Fax: (828) 262-1540
willa@appvoices.org

---

[11] Report at 92.

[12] January 17, 2008 announcement, Massey Energy to Pay Largest Civil Penalty Ever for Water Permit Violations, available at http://yosemite.epa.gov/opa/admpress.nsf/b1ab9f485b098972852562e7004 dc686/6944ea38b888dd03852573d3005074ba!OpenDocument

Sources and Recommended Reading

The following list is by no means exhaustive. Also check out the sources in the endnotes as well.

The Constitution

Declaration of Independence

United States Constitution

Amar, Akhil Reed. *America's Constitution: A Biography*. New York: Random House, 2005.

Cogan, Neil H., ed. *The Complete Bill of Rights: The Drafts, Debates, Sources and Origins*. New York: Oxford University Press, 1997.

Frohnen, Bruce, ed. *The American Republic: Primary Sources*. Indianapolis, Ind.: Liberty Fund, 2002.

Hamilton, Alexander, James Madison, and John Jay. *The Federalist*. New York: Cambridge University Press, 2003. (Originally published 1788.)

Handlin, Oscar, and Mary Flug Handlin. *Commonwealth: A Study of the Role of Government in the American Economy, Massachusetts, 1774–1861*. Cambridge, Mass.: Belknap Press of Harvard University Press, 1947.

Horwitz, Morton J. *The Transformation of American Law, 1870–1960*. New York: Oxford University Press, 1992.

Horwitz, Morton J. *The Transformation of American Law, 1780–1860*. Cambridge. Mass.: Harvard University Press, 1997.

Kammen, Michael, ed. *The Origins of the American Constitution: A Documentary History*. New York: Viking Penguin, 1986.

Kyvig, David E. *Explicit and Authentic Acts: Amending the Constitution, 1776–1995*. Lawrence: University Press of Kansas, 1996.

Schwartz, Bernard. *The Bill of Rights: A Documentary History*. New York: Chelsea House/McGraw Hill, 1971.

Corporations and the Constitution

Hartmann, Thom. *Unequal Protection: How Corporations Became "People" and How You Can Fight Back* (2nd ed.). San Francisco: Berrett-Koehler, 2010.

Kerr, Robert L. *The Corporate Free Speech Movement: Cognitive Feudalism and the Endangered Marketplace of Ideas*. New York: LFB, 2008.

Nace, Ted. *Gangs of America: The Rise of Corporate Power and the Disabling of Democracy*. San Francisco: Berrett-Koehler, 2003.

Corporate Power and Human Life

Bakan, Joel. *The Corporation: The Pathological Pursuit of Profit and Power.* New York: Free Press, 2004.

Coll, Steve. *Private Empire: ExxonMobil and American Power.* New York: Penguin Press, 2012.

Hauter, Wenonah. *Foodopoly: The Battle over the Future of Food and Farming in America.* New York: The New Press, 2012.

Kelley, Marjorie. *The Divine Right of Capital: Dethroning the Corporate Aristocracy.* San Francisco: Berrett-Koehler, 2001, 2003.

Klein, Naomi. *No Logo.* New York: Picador, 2002.

Korten, David C. *When Corporations Rule the World* (2nd ed.). Bloomfield, Conn.: Kumarian Press/San Francisco: Berrett-Koehler, 2001.

Linn, Susan. *Consuming Kids: Protecting Our Children from the Onslaught of Marketing and Advertising.* New York: Anchor Books, 2005.

Monks, Robert A. G. *Citizens Dis-United: Passive Investors, Drone CEOs, and the Corporate Capture of the American Dream.* Cape Elizabeth, Maine: Lens Foundation for Corporate Excellence, 2013.

Potter, Wendell. *Deadly Spin: An Insurance Company Insider Speaks Out on How Corporate PR Is Killing Health Care and Deceiving Americans.* New York: Bloomsbury Press, 2010.

Rothkopf, David. *Power, Inc.: The Epic Rivalry Between Big Business and Government—and the Reckoning That Lies Ahead.* New York: Farrar, Straus, and Giroux, 2012.

Schor, Juliet. *Born to Buy: The Commercialized Child and the New Consumer Culture.* New York: Scribner, 2004.

Schwartz, Ellen, and Suzanne Stoddard. *Taking Back Our Lives in the Age of Corporate Dominance.* San Francisco: Berrett-Koehler, 2000.

Wallach, Lori. *The Rise and Fall of Fast Track Authority.* Washington, D.C.: Public Citizen, 2013.

Corporate Law

Greenfield, Kent. *The Failure of Corporate Law.* Chicago: University of Chicago Press, 2006.

Henn, Harry, and John R. Alexander. *Law of Corporations* (3rd ed.). Saint Paul, Minn.: West, 2002. (Originally published 1983.)

Stout, Lynn. *The Shareholder Value Myth: How Putting Shareholders First Harms Investors, Corporations, and the Public.* San Francisco, Berrett-Kohler, 2012.

Cleaning the Swamp

Edwards, Mickey. *The Parties Versus the People: How to Turn Republicans and Democrats into Americans*. New Haven: Yale University Press, 2012.

Hacker, Jacob S., and Paul Pierson. *Winner-Take-All Politics: How Washington Made the Rich Richer—and Turned Its Back on the Middle Class*. New York: Simon & Schuster, 2010.

Kaiser, Robert G. *So Damn Much Money*. New York: Vintage Books, 2009.

Lessig, Lawrence. *Republic, Lost: How Money Corrupts Congress—and a Plan to Stop It*. New York: Twelve, 2011.

Nichols, John, and Robert McChesney. *Dollarocracy: How the Money and Media Election Complex Is Destroying America*. New York: Nation Books, 2013.

Schweizer, Peter. *Extortion: How Politicians Extract Your Money, Buy Votes, and Line Their Own Pockets*. Boston: Houghton Mifflin Harcourt, 2013.

Stiglitz, Joseph E. *Freefall: America, Free Markets, and the Sinking of the World Economy*. New York: W.W. Norton, 2010.

Other Works

Chute, Carolyn. *The School on Heart's Content Road*. New York: Atlantic Monthly Press, 2008.

Diamond, Jared. *Collapse: How Societies Choose to Fail or Succeed*. New York: Viking, 2004.

Notes

Introduction: What's at Stake

1. *Sebelius v. Hobby Lobby Stores, Inc.*, http://www.scotusblog.com/case-files/cases/sebelius-v-hobby-lobby-stores-inc/. See also Amicus Brief of Free Speech For People, Auburn Theological Seminary and Hollender Sustainable Brands LLC, http://www.freespeechforpeople.org/sites/default/files/13-356%20tsac%20Free%20Speech%20for%20People.pdf

Chapter One: American Democracy Works, and Corporations Fight Back

1. Bruce Frohnen, ed. *The American Republic: Primary Sources* (Indianapolis: Liberty Fund, 2002), http://oll.libertyfund.org/title/669/206314 (accessed April 6, 2011).
2. Center for Responsive Politics, http://www.opensecrets.org/bigpicture/ (accessed December 12, 2013) ($7 billion estimate); Robert McChesney and John Nichols, *Dollarocracy: How the Money and Media Election Complex Is Destroying America* (Nation Books, 2013) ($10 billion estimate).
3. Wealthy donors, Super PACs, corporations, unions, and other interests spent at least $2.8 billion in state elections in 2012. National Institute on Money in State Politics, http://www.followthemoney.org/database/nationalview.phtml (accessed December 18, 2013).
4. Center for Public Integrity, May 30, 2013, http://www.publicintegrity.org/2013/05/30/12740/tobacco-giant-funded-conservative-nonprofits (accessed December 31, 2013).
5. Lee Fang, *The Nation*, October 11, 2012, http://www.thenation.com/blog/170496/loophole-allows-saudi-arabian-businesses-spend-freely-our-election (accessed December 13, 2013).
6. Blair Bowie and Adam Lioz, *Billion Dollar Democracy: The Unprecedented Role of Money in the 2012 Election*, Demos & US PIRG (January 2013) at 8–11.
7. Blair Bowie and Adam Lioz, *Billion Dollar Democracy: The Unprecedented Role of Money in the 2012 Election*, Demos & US PIRG (January 2013) at 10.
8. Americans for Campaign Reform, *Money in Politics: Who Gives?*, http://www.acrreform.org/research/money-in-politics-who-gives/ (accessed December 19, 2013); Sunlight Foundation, *The Political One Percent of the One Percent*, December 13, 2011, http://sunlightfoundation.com/blog/2011/12/13/the-political-one-percent-of-the-one-percent/ (accessed December 19, 2013).
9. Debates in the Massachusetts Constitutional Convention of 1917–1918, at 22.
10. Ibid.
11. *Washington Post*, November 8, 2012, http://www.washingtonpost.com/blogs/govbeat/wp/2013/11/08/initiative-spending-booms-past-1-billion-as-corporations-sponsor-their-own-proposals/ (accessed December 18, 2013); *New York Times*, October 12, 2012, http://www.nytimes.com/2012/10/17/us/politics/california-ballot-initiatives-dominated-by-the-very-rich.html (accessed December 18, 2013).

12. *Washington Post*, January 6, 2013, http://www.washingtonpost.com/blogs/govbeat/wp/2013/11/06/big-corporate-spending-pays-off-in-washingtons-genetically-modified-food-fight/ (accessed January 2, 2014).

13. *New York Times*, January 2013, http://www.nytimes.com/2013/01/03/us/chevron-hits-rough-patch-in-richmond-calif.html?pagewanted=2&_r=0&ref=us (accessed December 18, 2013).

14. The Tillman Act, 34 Stat. 864 (1907), now a part of 18 US Sec. 610. The Taft Hartley Act, 61 Stat. 136 (1947), now 29 US § 401–531, added unions.

15. The First Amendment states: "Congress shall make no law respecting an establishment of religion, or prohibiting the free exercise thereof; or abridging the freedom of speech, or of the press; or the right of the people peaceably to assemble, and to petition the government for a redress of grievances."

16. Free Speech For People, *Across The Aisle: The Growing Trans-Partisan Opposition to Citizens United*, June 10, 2013, http://freespeechforpeople.org/sites/default/files/AcrossTheAisle-6-10-2013.pdf.

17. Dale Robertson, quoted in "The SCOTUS 'Corporate Cash for Candidates' Decision: Left, Right, and Tea," *Reid Report*, January 10, 2010, http://blog.reidreport.com/2010/01/supco-campaign-cash-decision-reactions/ (accessed July 21, 2011).

18. Hart Research Associates, December 2010, http://freespeechforpeople.org/sites/default/files/FSFP%20Nationwide%20Voter%20Survey-1.pdf.

19. Free Speech For People, *1/3 of the Way There*, September 2013, http://www.freespeechforpeople.com/node/601.

20. Senator John McCain on PBS NewsHour, June 14, 2012, http://www.pbs.org/newshour/bb/politics/jan-june12/mccain_06-14.html at 9:56.

21. Robert L. Kerr, *The Corporate Free Speech Movement: Cognitive Feudalism and the Endangered Marketplace of Ideas* (New York: LFB, 2008).

22. James Madison, "To J. K. Paulding," March 10, 1827, in Gaillard Hunt, ed., *The Writings of James Madison* (New York: Putnam, 1900), Vol. 9.

23. Thomas Jefferson, "To George Logan," November 12, 1816, in *The Works of Thomas Jefferson* (New York: Putnam, 1904–1905), Vol. 12, http://oll.libertyfund.org/title/808/88352 (accessed July 21, 2011).

24. Andrew Jackson, "Fifth Annual Message to Congress (December 3, 1833)," Miller Center, http://millercenter.org/scripps/archive/speeches/detail/3640 (accessed July 21, 2011).

25. Martin Van Buren, "First Annual Message to Congress (December 5, 1837)," Miller Center, http://millercenter.org/scripps/archive/speeches/detail/3589 (accessed July 21, 2011).

26. The Powell memorandum, "Attack on American Free Enterprise System," dated August 23, 1971, is among his papers archived at Washington and Lee University Law School and can be viewed online at http://law.wlu.edu/powellarchives/. Powell's visit to the US Chamber of Commerce in Washington, D.C., on August 24, 1971, is confirmed by his correspondence with Eugene Snydor, which also is among his papers. The Powell memorandum and its implications have been widely examined. See, for example, Jerry Landay, "The Powell Manifesto: How a Prominent Lawyer's Attack Memo Changed America," August 20, 2002, *Media Transparency*; William K. Black, "My Class, Right or Wrong: The Powell Memorandum's 40th Anniversary," *New Economic Perspectives*, April 25, 2011.

27. Linda Greenhouse, "The Legacy of Lewis F. Powell, Jr.," *New York Times*, December 4, 2002, http://www.nytimes.com/2002/12/04/politics/04SCOT.html (accessed June 22, 2011); Gerald Gunther, "Lewis F. Powell, Jr.: A Fine Judge, a Remarkable Human Being," *Columbia Law Review*, April 1999; and Gerald Gunther, "A Tribute to Justice Lewis F. Powell, Jr.," *Harvard Law Review*, December 1987.

28. Sandra Day O'Connor, *The Majesty of the Law: Reflections of a Supreme Court Justice* (New York: Random House, 2003), p. 150.

29. John Conyers Jr., may be an exception. At Powell's confirmation hearings in November 1971, Conyers, then the president of the Old Dominion Bar Association, asserted that Powell "for much of his life waged war on the Constitution," referring to his role as a member of the Richmond, Virginia, school board during the years of resistance to *Brown v. Board of Education*. Conyers testified against Powell's nomination, pointing to alleged discrimination at Powell's law firm, at Philip Morris, and in Powell's private clubs, which banned African Americans (except that one allowed members to bring "colored servants with them to the club only if they are dressed in appropriate attire"). Conyers also cited Powell's "close association with a variety of corporate giants." US Senate, Committee on the Judiciary, "Hearings on the Nominations of William H. Rehnquist, of Arizona, and Lewis F. Powell, Jr., of Virginia, to Be Associate Justices of the Supreme Court of the United States," November 3–10, 1971, http://www.gpoaccess.gov/congress/senate/judiciary/sh92-69-267/browse.html (accessed June 21, 2011).

30. Judge Gladys Kessler, the federal judge who oversaw the 2006 racketeering trial of the cigarette corporations, documented the role of each corporate participant, including the Tobacco Institute, in the decades-long illegal cigarette corporation RICO conspiracy. Her conclusions, affirmed by the US Court of Appeals for the District of Columbia, are set out in her final opinion of more than 1,600 pages in *United States v. Philip Morris USA, Inc., et. al.*, Civil Action 99-2496 (GK), August 17, 2006, http://www.justice.gov/civil/cases/tobacco2/amended%20opinion.pdf (accessed June 22, 2011).

31. The documents include a May 1970 letter from Powell to Philip Morris chief executive officer Joseph Cullman concerning what the cigarette corporations collectively called an "attack" to discredit the American Cancer Society. The coordinated attack on the Cancer Society in April 1970 was among the specific "racketeering" acts identified by the Department of Justice in the federal complaint. Powell had "long thought that" the cigarette corporations should challenge the "extremism" of the American Cancer Society. He congratulated Cullman on the "recent moves" that Powell called "constructive" and likely to "restrain" the American Cancer Society. Legacy Tobacco Documents Library, http://legacy.library.ucsf.edu/action/document/page?tid=luc98e00 (accessed January 4, 2014).

32. Ibid.

33. *Laurus & Brother Company v. Federal Communications Commission*, 447 F.2d 876 (1971).

34. Transcript, Philip Morris–Lewis Powell, December 1972, http://tobaccodocuments.org/pm/2010030023-0048.html.

35. Powell's memorandum to the Chamber came to public attention only after Powell was on the Court. A nationally syndicated columnist disclosed the existence of the Powell memo late in 1972 and questioned whether Powell could be an impartial judge in cases involving large corporations. The Chamber executive who had requested Powell's memorandum, Eugene Snydor, privately told Powell, "I regret exceedingly" the "slip up" of a Chamber staff person that resulted in the "unauthorized disclosure of your now famous memo." Correspondence, October 3, 1972, Papers of Lewis Powell, Washington & Lee University Law School.

36. See *First National Bank of Boston v. Bellotti*, 435 US 765 (1978); *FEC v. Wisconsin Right to Life*, 551 US 449 (2007); *Thompson v. Western States Medical Center*, 535 US 357 (2002) (federal restriction on drug advertising invalidated); *Lorillard v. Reilly*, 533 US 525 (2001) (tobacco advertising law invalidated); *Greater New Orleans Broadcasting Association v. United States*, 527 US 173 (1999) (federal advertising of gambling and casinos struck down); *44 LiquorMart v. Rhode Island*, 517 US 484 (1996) (alcohol price advertising invalidated); *Rubin v. Coors Brewing Co.*, 514 US 476 (1995) (restriction on promotion of alcohol level invalidated); *City of Cincinnati v. Discovery Network*, 507 US 410 (1993) (city street restriction on news racks for advertising held unconstitutional); *Pacific Gas & Electric Co. v. Public Utilities Commission of California*, 475 US 1 (1986) (law requiring utilities to make bill envelopes, which are property of rate payers, available to other points of view than corporate interests corporation struck down); *Central Hudson Gas & Electric Corp. v. Public Service Commission of New York*, 447 US 557 (1980)

(advertising limit on promotion of energy consumption invalidated); *Bellsouth Telecomm. v. Farris*, 542 F.3d 499 (6th Cir. 2008) (states may not limit corporations from misinforming customers that shareholders charge law was a "tax"); *Allstate Insurance Co. v. Abbott*, 495 F.3d 151 (5th Cir. 2007) (law regarding advertising of auto body shops tied to auto insurers invalidated); *This That & the Other Gift & Tobacco v. Cobb County, Georgia*, 439 F.3d 1275 (11th Cir. 2006) (ban on advertisements of sexual devices invalidated); *Passions Video v. Nixon*, 458 F.3d 887 (8th Cir. 2006) (restriction on advertisements of sexually explicit businesses invalidated); *Bad Frog Brewery v. New York State Liquor Authority*, 134 F.3d 87 (2d Cir. 1998); *International Dairy Foods Association v. Amestoy*, 92 F.3d 67 (2d Cir. 1996) (Vermont GMO label law invalidated); *New York State Association of Realtors v. Shaffer*, 27 F.3d 834 (2d Cir. 1994) (invalidating "nonsolicitation" zones for real estate brokers); *Sambo's Restaurants v. City of Ann Arbor*, 663 F.2d 686 (6th Cir. 1981) (corporation violation of agreement with city to not use prejudicial name protected by First Amendment); *John Donnelly & Sons v. Campbell*, 639 F.2d 6 (1st Cir. 1980) (invalidating billboard pollution law); *Washington Legal Foundation v. Friedman*, 13 F. Supp. 2d 51 (D.D.C. 1998) (invalidating off-label marketing law); and *Equifax Services v. Cohen*, 420 A.2d. 189 (Me. 1980) (Maine credit reporting statute violates First Amendment).

37. See *First National Bank of Boston v. Bellotti*, 435 US 765, 826 and n. 6 (1978) (Rehnquist, dissenting) ("The free flow of information is in no way diminished by the Commonwealth's decision to permit the operation of business corporations with limited rights of political expression. All natural persons, who owe their existence to a higher sovereign than the Commonwealth, remain as free as before to engage in political activity. . . . The Fourteenth Amendment does not require a State to endow a business corporation with the power of political speech."); *Central Hudson Gas & Electric Corp. v. Public Service Commission of New York*, 447 US 557 (1980) (Rehnquist, dissenting) ("I disagree with the Court's conclusion that the speech of a state-created monopoly, which is the subject of a comprehensive regulatory scheme, is entitled to protection under the First Amendment."); and *Pacific Gas & Electric Co. v. Public Utilities Commission of California*, 475 US 1, 26, 24 (1986) (Rehnquist, dissenting) ("Nor do I believe that negative free speech rights, applicable to individuals and perhaps the print media, should be extended to corporations generally. . . . PG&E is not an individual or a newspaper publisher; it is a regulated utility. The insistence on treating identically for constitutional purposes entities that are demonstrably different is as great a jurisprudential sin as treating differently those entities which are the same."). See also *Virginia Board of Pharmacy v. Virginia Citizens Consumer Council*, 425 US 748, 784 (1976) (Rehnquist, dissenting) ("The Court speaks of the importance in a 'predominantly free enterprise economy' of intelligent and well-informed decisions as to allocation of resources. . . . While there is again much to be said for the Court's observation as a matter of desirable public policy, there is certainly nothing in the United States Constitution which requires the Virginia Legislature to hew to the teachings of Adam Smith in its legislative decisions regulating the pharmacy profession.").

38. Alliance for Justice, *Justice for Sale: Shortchanging the Public Interest for Private Gain* (Washington, D.C.: Alliance for Justice, 1993).

39. Amicus brief of the US Chamber of Commerce, *First National Bank of Boston v. Bellotti*, US Supreme Court, 1977 WL 189653 (1977).

40. *First National Bank of Boston v. Bellotti*, 435 US 765 (1978).

41. *Central Hudson Gas & Electric Corp. v. Public Service Commission of New York*, 447 US 557 (1980).

42. National Chamber Litigation Center, "Business Is Our ONLY Client" and "Celebrating Thirty Years of Advocacy in the Courts," *Business Advocate*, Spring 2007.

43. Center for Responsive Politics, Lobbying: Top Spenders, 1998–2013, http://www.opensecrets.org/lobby/top.php (accessed January 4, 2014).

44. Center for Responsive Politics, Lobbying: Ranked Sectors, 1998–2013, http://www.opensecrets.org/lobby/top.php?indexType=c&showYear=a (accessed January 4, 2013).

45. Center for Responsive Politics, Lobbying: Top Spenders, 1998–2013, http://www.opensecrets.org/lobby/top.php (accessed January 4, 2014).

46. The Center for Media and Democracy has revealed extensive information about ALEC and SPN, http://www.alecexposed.org/wiki/ALEC_Exposed (accessed January 4, 2013).

47. Erwin Chemerinsky, *The Roberts Court at Age Three*, 54 Wayne Law Review 947, 962 (2008). ("[T]he Roberts Court is the most pro-business Court of any since the mid-1930s."); Lee Epstein, William M. Landes, and Richard A. Posner, *How Business Fares in the Supreme Court*, 97 Minnesota Law Review 1145, 1184 (2013) ("[T]he Roberts Court is much friendlier to business than either the Burger or Rehnquist Courts, which preceded it, were.") Constitutional Accountability Center, *Not So Risky Business: The Chamber of Commerce's Quiet Success Before the Roberts Court*, May 1, 2013, http://theusconstitution.org/text-history/1966/not-so-risky-business-chamber-commerces-quiet-success-roberts-court-early-report (accessed January 4, 2013).

48. Brennan Center for Justice, National Institute on Money in State Politics, Justice at Stake, *The New Politics of Judicial Elections, 2011–2012*, http://newpoliticsreport.org (accessed December 30, 2013); American Constitution Society, *Justice at Risk*, June 2013.

49. Andrew Cohen, *An Elected Judge Speaks Out Against Judicial Elections*, The Atlantic, September 3, 2013, citing American Constitution Society, *Justice at Risk*, June 2013.

50. *Scientific American*, December 23, 2013, http://www.scientificamerican.com/article.cfm?id=dark-money-funds-climate-change-denial-effort; Poll data, Gallup Poll, Environment, http://www.gallup.com/poll/1615/environment.aspx#1 (accessed January 4, 2014).

Chapter Two: Corporations Are Not People—and They Make Lousy Parents

1. Kessler, Final Opinion, 974.

2. *Bad Frog Brewery v. New York State Liquor Authority*, 134 F.3d 87, 91 and n. 1 (2d Cir. 1998).

3. *Laurus & Brother Company v. Federal Communications Commission*, 447 F.2d 876 (1971).

4. *United States v. Philip Morris USA, Inc., et. al.*, Civil Action 99-2496 (GK), August 17, 2006, http://www.justice.gov/civil/cases/tobacco2/amended%20opinion.pdf (accessed June 22, 2011).

5. Kessler, Final Opinion, 1207–1208.

6. Ibid., 1008–1115.

7. Ibid., 972.

8. Ibid., 1207

9. Ibid., 977–978.

10. *Lorillard Corp. v. Reilly*, 533 US 525 (2001), citing studies by the FDA that "72% of 6 year olds and 52% of children ages 3 to 6 recognized 'Joe Camel,' the cartoon anthropomorphic symbol of R. J. Reynolds' Camel brand cigarettes." After the introduction of Joe Camel, Camel cigarettes' share of the youth market rose from 4 percent to 13 percent.

11. Ibid., 534–535.

12. Ibid., §1.

13. *Lorillard Tobacco Co. v. Reilly*, 2001 WL 193609 (US), 20 (US amicus brief, 2001). Tom Reilly had succeeded Harshbarger as attorney general of Massachusetts.

14. See Brief of the Washington Legal Foundation in *Lorillard Tobacco Co. v. Reilly*, and *Altadis USA. v. Reilly*, 2001 WL 34135253 (US): The importance of advertising in our free-market economy cannot easily be overstated.

15. *Lorillard Corp. v. Reilly*, 533 US 525 (2001).

16. *R.J. Reynolds Tobacco Co. v. Food & Drug Admin.*, 696 F.3d 1205, 1211 (D.C. Cir. 2012). When the cigarette corporations tried similar litigation in Australia, the Australian court rejected

the arguments entirely. Australia does not recognize a corporate right "not to speak." The Australian highest court called the companies' arguments about an unconstitutional taking of property "delusive," "synthetic," and "unreal." High Court of Australia, Reasons for Decision, October 2012 http://www.austlii.edu.au/au/cases/cth/HCA/2012/43.html (accessed December 20, 2013).

17. *New York Times* poll, July 28, 2013, http://www.nytimes.com/2013/07/28/science/strong-support-for-labeling-modified-foods.html (accessed December 17, 2013).

18. No On 37: Stop the Deceptive Food Labeling Scheme, http://www.noprop37.com/facts/. For spending, see Maplight, Prop 37: Genetically Engineered Food, http://votersedge.org/california/ballot-measures/2012/november/prop37/funding#.Usmr9KVOEds.

19. *Washington Post*, November 6, 2013, http://www.washingtonpost.com/blogs/govbeat/wp/2013/11/06/big-corporate-spending-pays-off-in-washingtons-genetically-modified-food-fight/ (accessed December 21, 2013).

20. Michael Pollan, "Playing God in the Garden," *New York Times*, October 25, 1998, http://www.nytimes.com/1998/10/25/magazine/playing-god-in-the-garden.html (accessed July 21, 2011).

21. Parliament of Canada, Standing Senate Committee on Agriculture and Forestry, "rBST and the Drug Approval Process," Interim Report, March 1999, http://www.parl.gc.ca/Content/SEN/Committee/361/agri/rep/repintermar99-e.htm#C.%20Conclusions%20Reached (accessed April 28, 2011).

22. Personal communication, March 8, 2011.

23. Vermont's proposed findings of fact no. 9, George Aff. 45, Ex. N (FDA letter, July 27, 1994), in *International Dairy Foods Association v. Amestoy*, 92 F.3d 67 (2nd Circ. 1996).

24. *International Dairy Foods Association v. Amestoy*, 6 V.S.A. (1996), §2754(c).

25. Affidavit of Donald George, acting commissioner and director of the Animal and Dairy Industries Division of the Vermont Department of Agriculture filed in *International Dairy Foods*.

26. Ibid.

27. Kessler, final order, 4–5, 97.

28. The commissioner described the industry tactics as an attempt to "subvert the process." George affidavit, *International Dairy Foods*.

29. *International Dairy Foods*, Surreply brief of State of Vermont, 8; Groves affidavit; Buckley affidavit.

30. *Monsanto Company v. Oakhurst Dairy*, US District Court for the District of Massachusetts, Case 1:03-cv-11273-RCL, Answer of Oakhurst Dairy.

31. *International Dairy Foods*, memorandum in support of plaintiffs' renewed motion for preliminary injunction, 2, 16.

32. *International Dairy Foods Association v. Amestoy*, 898 F.Supp.246, 250 (D. Vt. 1995).

33. *International Dairy Foods Association v. Amestoy*, 92 F.3d 67 (2nd Cir. 1996).

34. Personal communication, March 8, 2011.

35. Powell, "Attack."

36. Thomas Jefferson, *Notes on Virginia* (1782).

37. *Wisconsin v. Yoder*, 406 US 205, 213, 225 (1972).

38. Susan Linn and Courtney L. Novosat, "Calories for Sale: Food Marketing to Children in the 21st Century," *Annals of the American Academy of Political and Social Science*, 615 (2008): 133–155.

39. Campaign for a Commercial-Free Childhood, "Ronald McDonald Report Card Ads Expelled from Seminole County; CCFC Campaign Ends Controversial In-School Marketing Program," January 17, 2008, http://commercialfreechildhood.org/pressreleases/ronaldmcdonald.htm (accessed July 22, 2011).

40. Channel One, "Terms and Conditions of Network Participation," http://help.channelone.com/pdfs/12-07-07/2008-Link-LeftNav&Contact-Terms.pdf (accessed September 4, 2011), p. 4.

41. Juliet B. Schor, *Born to Buy: The Commercialized Child and the New Consumer Culture* (New York: Scribner, 2004), p. 21.

42. In 2006, 82 percent of schools had corporate advertisements. Alex Molnar, David R. Garcia, Faith Boninger, and Bruce Merrill, *A National Survey of the Types and Extent of the Marketing of Foods of Minimal Nutritional Value in Schools* (Tempe: Commercialism in Education Research Unit, Arizona State University, 2006).

43. Jennifer Medina, "Los Angeles Schools to Seek Sponsors," *New York Times*, December 15, 2010.

44. Alex Molnar, Faith Boninger, Gary Wilkinson, Joseph Fogarty, and Sean Geary, *Effectively Embedded: Schools and the Machinery of Modern Marketing: The Thirteenth Annual Report on Schoolhouse Commercializing Trends, 2009–2010* (Boulder, Colo.: National Education Policy Center, 2010), http://nepc.colorado.edu/publication/Schoolhouse-commercialism-2010 (accessed March 15, 2011).

45. Catey Hill, "10 Things Snack Food Companies Won't Say," *Smart Money*, November 15, 2010, http://www.smartmoney.com/spending/for-the-home/10-things-snack-food-companies-wont-say/?page=3 (accessed July 22, 2011).

46. California Pan-Ethnic Health Network and Consumers Union, *Out of Balance: Marketing of Soda, Candy, Snacks and Fast Foods Drowns Out Healthful Messages*, September 2005, http://nepc.colorado.edu/files/CERU-0509-140-OWI.pdf (accessed July 22, 2011).

47. Linn and Golin, "Beyond Commercials," pp. 13–14.

48. Federal Trade Commission, *Marketing Food to Children and Adolescents: A Review of Industry Expenditures, Activities, and Self-Regulation* (Washington, D.C.: Federal Trade Commission, 2008), http://www.ftc.gov/os/2008/07/P064504foodmktingreport.pdf (accessed July 22, 2011).

49. FTC Improvements Act of 1980, Pub. L. No. 96-252, Sections 11(a)(1), 11(a)(3), 94 Stat. 374 (1980), codified in part at 15 US §57a(i).

50. Molnar et al., *Effectively Embedded*.

51. Allen D. Kanner, "Today's Class Brought to You by . . . ," *Tikkun*, January–February 2009, pp. 25–26, http://www.commercialfreechildhood.org/articles/featured/todaysclass.pdf (accessed July 22, 2011).

52. American Petroleum Institute, "Progress Through Petroleum," http://www.classroom-energy.org/oil_natural_gas/progress_through_petroleum/index.html# (accessed August 17, 2011).

53. Ibid.

54. Center for Science in the Public Interest, "Corporate-School Partnerships Good for Profits, Not Kids," September 25, 2002, http://www.cspinet.org/new/200209252.html (accessed July 22, 2011); Coca-Cola Company, "Mission, Vision & Values," 2010, http://www.thecoca-colacompany.com/ourcompany/mission_vision_values.html (accessed July 22, 2011).

55. US Government Accountability Office, "For-Profit Colleges: Undercover Testing Finds Colleges Encouraged Fraud and Engaged in Deceptive and Questionable Marketing Practices," August 4, 2010, http://www.gao.gov/products/GAO-10-948T (accessed July 22, 2011).

56. US Senate Health, Education, Labor and Pensions Committee, *For Profit Higher Education: The Failure to Safeguard the Federal Investment and Ensure Student Success*, July 30, 2012.

57. US Senate Health, Education, Labor and Pensions Committee, *For Profit Higher Education: The Failure to Safeguard the Federal Investment and Ensure Student Success*, July 30, 2012 ($32 billion annually).

58. US Government Accountability Office, "For-Profit Colleges: Undercover Testing Finds Colleges Encouraged Fraud and Engaged in Deceptive and Questionable Marketing Practices," August 4, 2010, http://www.gao.gov/products/GAO-10-948T (accessed July 22, 2011).

59. Tom Harkin, "For-Profit College Investigation," *Tom Harkin, Iowa's Senator* (newsletter), n.d., http://harkin.senate.gov/forprofitcolleges.cfm (accessed July 22, 2011).

60. Ibid.

61. Statement of Senator Tom Harkin, chairman of the Senate Committee on Health, Education, Labor, and Pensions, March 10, 2011.

62. Tamar Lewin, "Hearing Sees Financial Success and Education Failures of For-Profit College," *New York Times*, March 10, 2011, http://www.nytimes.com/2011/03/11/education/11college.html (accessed August 17, 2011).

63. Tamar Lewin, "Flurry of Data as Rules Near for Commercial Colleges," *New York Times*, February 4, 2011, http://www.nytimes.com/2011/02/04/education/04colleges.html (accessed July 23, 2011). Complaint, *Coal. for Educ. Success v. United States*, No. 1:11-cv-00287 (D.D.C. February 2, 2011).

Chapter Three: If Corporations Are Not People, What Are They?

1. Victor Hugo, *Les Miserables: A Novel*, trans. Charles Wilbour (New York: Carleton, 1862), p. 95.

2. *Western Tradition Partnership v. Bullock*, Montana Supreme Ct. No. DA-11-0081, at 79 (Nelson, J. dissenting).

3. *Citizens United*, 24.

4. *First National Bank of Boston v. Bellotti*, 435 US 765, 777 (1978).

5. *Consolidated Edison Co. of New York v. Public Service Commission of New York*, 447 US 530, 540 (1980). Justice Rehnquist joined Justice Blackmun in dissent.

6. *Central Hudson Gas & Electric Corp. v. Public Service Commission of New York*, 447 US 557, 570 (1980). Only Justice Rehnquist in dissent pointed out that a "public utility is a state-created monopoly," and that the state law was an economic regulation," not a "speech" restriction.

7. *Lorillard v. Reilly*, 53 US 525 (2001) (Thomas, concurring).

8. Not long after the 1971 Powell memo, Joseph Coors, the Coors Charitable Foundation, and eighty-seven corporations helped start and fund the Heritage Foundation.

9. *Rubin v. Coors Brewing Co.*, 514 US 476, 479 (1995). "Respondent" refers to the party that won the case in the federal court below the Supreme Court and is "responding" to the other party's appeal.

10. David Ciepley 1 *Journal of Law and Courts* 221–245, Fall 2013.

11. "A corporation is a legal entity created through the laws of its state of incorporation." Cornell University Law School, Legal Information Institute, "Corporations: An Overview," n.d., http://topics.law.cornell.edu/wex/Corporations (accessed July 23, 2011).

12. Harry G. Henn and John R. Alexander, *Law of Corporations*, 3rd ed. (Saint Paul, Minn.: West, 1991).

13. Kent Greenfield, *The Failure of Corporate Law* (Chicago: University of Chicago Press, 2006), pp. 30–33.

14. "Those who feel that the essence of the corporation rests in the contract among its members rather than in the government decree . . . fail to distinguish, as the eighteenth century did, between the corporation and the voluntary association." [Oscar Handlin and Mary Flug Handlin, *Commonwealth: A Study of the Role of Government in the American Economy: Massachusetts, 1774–1861* (Cambridge, Mass.: Belknap Press, 1961; originally published 1947), p. 92 and n. 18.]

15. See, for example, Virginia Statutes, §13.1-812 ("unlawful for any person to transact business in the Commonwealth as a corporation or to offer or advertise to transact business in the Commonwealth as a corporation unless the alleged corporation is either a domestic corporation or a foreign corporation authorized to transact business in the Commonwealth. Any person who violates this section shall be guilty of a Class 1 misdemeanor."

16. "More than 50% of all publicly-traded companies in the United States including 63% of the *Fortune* 500 have chosen Delaware as their legal home." http://www.corp.delaware.gov/aboutagency.shtml. See also Greenfield, *Failure of Corporate Law*, pp. 107–108.

17. Greenfield, *Failure of Corporate Law*, pp. 107–108.
18. Daniel R. Fischel, The "Race to the Bottom" Revisited: Reflections on Recent Developments in Delaware's Corporation Law, 76 *Northwestern University Law Review* 913 (1982);
19. Delaware Code, Annotated title 8, §102.
20. See Henry Hansmann Reinier Kraakman, "Toward Unlimited Shareholder Liability for Corporate Torts," 100 *Yale Law Journal* 1879, 1880 (1991).
21. Delaware Code, Annotated title 8, §102.
22. See e.g., Handlin and Handlin, *Commonwealth*; Horowitz, Morton. *The Transformation of American Law*, Vol. 1. (Cambridge: Harvard University Press, 1979).
23. In attributing the "corporate person" to legislatures, I recognize the role of common law courts in developing the metaphor. Ultimately, however, the common law is subject to legislative choice. Legislatures may keep, modify or, as often is the case, abolish common law. Where and when the "person" metaphor is appropriate for corporations, then, depends on legislative choice, not Constitutional mandate. See, e.g. *FCC v. AT & T Inc.*, 131 S. Ct. 1177, 1185 (2011). (interpreting Congressional intent in statutory meaning in FOIA of "person" and "personal privacy," concluding that corporations were not capable of asserting "personal privacy" under statute).
24. *Marshall v. Baltimore and Ohio Railroad Co.*, 57 US 314 (1853).
25. *First National Bank of Boston v. Bellotti*, 435 US 765 (1978) (Rehnquist, dissenting).
26. *Santa Clara County v. Southern Pacific Railroad Co.*, 118 US 394 (1886) ("As the judgment can be sustained upon this [state law] ground it is not necessary to consider any other questions raised by the pleadings and the facts found by the court"; 416.)
27. Thom Hartmann, *Unequal Protection: How Corporations Became "People" and How You Can Fight Back*, 2nd ed. (San Francisco: Berrett-Koehler, 2010); Ted Nace, *Gangs of America: The Rise of Corporate Power and the Disabling of Democracy* (San Francisco: Berrett-Koehler, 2003).
28. *Pembina Consolidated Silver Mining and Milling Co. v. Commonwealth of Pennsylvania*, 125 US 81, 188–189 (1888); *Missouri Pacific Railway Co. v. Mackey*, 127 US 205 (1888); *Minneapolis & Saint Louis Railway Co. v. Herrick*, 127 US 210 (1888); *Minneapolis & Saint Louis Railway Co. v. Beckwith*, 129 US 26 (1889); *Charlotte, Columbia and Augusta Railroad Co. v. Gibbes*, 142 US 386 (1892); *Covington and Lexington Turnpike Road Co. v. Sandford*, 164 US 578 (1896); *Gulf, Colorado and Santa Fe Railway Co. v. Ellis*, 165 US 150 (1897); and *Kentucky Finance Corp. v. Paramount Auto Exchange Corp.*, 262 US 544 (1923).
29. Henn and Alexander, *Law of Corporations*, p. 24 and n. 2, citing Edwin Merrick Dodd, *American Business Corporations Until 1860* (1954); Joseph Stancliffe Davis, *Essays in the Earlier History of American Corporations* (1917); Simeon E. Baldwin, "American Business Corporations Before 1789," in *Annual Report of the American Historical Association*, pp. 253–274 (1902). See also Handlin and Handlin, *Commonwealth*, pp. 99, 162.
30. Handlin and Handlin, *Commonwealth*, pp. 106–133; *Louis K. Liggett Co. v. Lee*, 288 US 517, 548–560 (1933) (Brandeis, dissenting).
31. Restrictions on corporate purposes were the norm. See ibid. See also *Head and Amory v. Providence Insurance Co.*, 6 US (2 Cranch) 127, 166–167 (1804) ("a corporation can only act in the manner prescribed by law").
32. James Wilson, "Of Corporations," in ed. Kermit L. Hall and Mark David Hall, *Collected Works of James Wilson*, (Indianapolis, Ind.: Liberty Fund, 2007), vol. 2, ch. 10, http://oll.libertyfund.org/title/2074/166648/2957866 (accessed July 22, 2009).
33. *Trustees of Dartmouth College v. Woodward*, 17 US 518, 636 (1819).
34. *Hope Insurance Co. v. Boardman*, 9 US (5 Cranch) 57, 58 (1809).
35. *Bank of Augusta v. Earle*, 38 US 519, 587 (1839).
36. *Pembina Consolidated Silver Mining and Milling Co. v. Commonwealth of Pennsylvania*, 125 US 181, 188–189 (1888).
37. Grover Cleveland, "Fourth Annual Message to Congress (December 3, 1888)," Miller Center, http://millercenter.org/scripps/archive/speeches/detail/3758 (accessed July 24, 2011).

38. Theodore Roosevelt, *Theodore Roosevelt: An Autobiography* (New York: Scribner, 1929) (originally published 1913), p. 423; Theodore Roosevelt, "Sixth Annual Message to Congress (December 3, 1906)," Miller Center, http://millercenter.org/scripps/archive/speeches/detail/3778 (accessed July 24, 2011).

39. Roosevelt, *Roosevelt*, p. 425. And he went further, writing supportively of the Progressive reformers: "They realized that the Government must now interfere to protect labor, to subordinate the big corporation to the public welfare, and to shackle cunning and fraud exactly as centuries before it had interfered to shackle the physical force which does wrong by violence" (p. 425).

40. Theodore Roosevelt, speech delivered August 31, 1910, cited in Hartmann, *Unequal Protection*, p. 161.

41. US Constitution, Amend. XVI and Amend. XVII.

42. *Connecticut General Life Insurance Co. v. Johnson*, 303 US 77, 85–87 (1938).

43. *United States v. Morton Salt Co.*, 338 US 632, 651–652 (1950).

44. Kentucky Constitution, §150 (1891).

45. *First National Bank of Boston v. Bellotti*, 435 US 765, 826 and n.6 (Rehnquist, dissenting).

46. Ibid., 822–823.

47. *Austin v. Michigan Chamber of Commerce*, 494 US 652 (1990).

48. Ibid., 658–659 (1990), quoting *Federal Election Commission v. Massachusetts Citizens for Life*, 479 US 238, 257 (1986).

49. *McConnell v. Federal Election Commission*, 540 US93, 205 (2002).

50. The Commonwealth of Virginia provides an on-line guide to the steps to forming a non-profit corporation at http://vdba.virginia.gov/non_profit.shtml.

51. Charlie Cray, "Using Charters to Redesign Corporations in the Public Interest," in William H. Wist, ed., *The Bottom Line or Public Health* (Oxford: Oxford University Press, 2010), http://www.corporatepolicy.org/pdf/CrayCharters2010.pdf (accessed June 13, 2011).

Chapter Four: Corporations Don't Vote; They Don't Have To

1. Murray Hill Inc., "Supreme Court Ruling Spurs Corporation Run for Congress; First Test of 'Corporate Personhood' in Politics," January 25, 2010, http://www.murrayhillweb.com/pr-012510.html (accessed March 24, 2011).

2. Ibid.

3. 2011 poll, Hart Research Associates and Free Speech for People: 7 percent of respondents thought that the American people were on a "fair and level" playing field with corporations in our political system; 61 percent worried "a great deal" or "quite a bit" that corporations have too much influence over government; 80 percent support a constitutional amendment to overturn *Citizens United* and make clear that corporations do not have the same rights as people.

4. Jim Leach, "Citizens United: Robbing America of Its Idealism," 142 *Dædalus: Journal of the American Academy of Arts & Sciences* 95 (Spring 2013).

5. The Chamber's 2012 Form 990 tax filing describes $53.8 million in political spending in 2012 alone, while its filing with the FEC describes $35.7 million and $33 million in the 2012 and 2010 elections. http://www.citizensforethics.org/pages/dark-money-disclosure-990-tax-returns (accessed January 10, 2014); Public Citizen, *Disclosed Corporate Contributions to the US Chamber*, October 28, 2013.

6. Chamber 990 Tax filing.

7. *Wall Street Journal*, September 11, 2001, http://online.wsj.com/article/SB1000015411979219346.html.

8. *New York Times*, January 8, 2014, http://thecaucus.blogs.nytimes.com/2014/01/08/chamber-to-split-with-tea-party-in-g-o-p-primaries/; Heritage Foundation, November 10, 2013, http://blog.heritage.org/2013/11/10/why-conservatives-and-the-business-lobby-cant-just-get-along/.

9. Tom Hamburger, "Chamber of Commerce Vows to Punish Anti-Business Candidates," *Los Angeles Times*, January 8, 2008, http://www.latimes.com/entertainment/la-na-chamber8jan08,0,454295.story (accessed April 14, 2011).

10. US Chamber Watch, Public Citizen, http://www.fixtheuschamber.org/issues/local-chambers-vs-us-chamber (accessed January 10, 2014).

11. US Chamber Watch, "The US Chamber: A Multimillion-Dollar Shell Game," 2011, http://www.fixtheuschamber.org/news/news/inside-chambers-million-dollar-shell-game (accessed April 14, 2011); US Chamber Watch, "Beyond the $86 Million Buyout: What Else We Found in the Chamber's 990s," November 17, 2010, http://www.fixtheuschamber.org/tracking-the-chamber/beyond-86-million-buyout-what-else-we-found-chambers-990s (accessed April 14, 2011).

12. Ibid.

13. Trevor Potter, quoted in Drew Armstrong, "Insurers Gave US Chamber $86 Million Used to Oppose Obama's Health Law," *Bloomberg News*, November 17, 2010, http://www.bloomberg.com/news/2010-11-17/insurers-gave-u-s-chamber-86-million-used-to-oppose-obama-s-health-law.html (accessed April 4, 2011).

14. Health Care for America Now, "Breaking the Bank: CEOs from 10 Health Insurers Took Nearly $1 Billion in Compensation, Stock from 2000 to 2009," August 2010, http://hcfan.3cdn.net/684f3fa81c1e757518_01m6bxg6s.pdf (accessed March 28, 2011).

15. Payday for Payers, August 11, 2012, http://www.modernhealthcare.com/article/20120811/MAGAZINE/308119967 (accessed January 10, 2014).

16. Forbes highest paid executives, http://www.forbes.com/lists/2012/12/ceo-compensation-12_rank.html.

17. Wendell Potter, *Deadly Spin: An Insurance Company Insider Speaks Out on How Corporate PR Is Killing Health Care and Deceiving Americans* (New York: Bloomsbury Press, 2010), pp. 136–141.

18. Keith Johnson, "Exodus: Apple Leaves Chamber of Commerce over Climate Spat," *Wall Street Journal*, October 5, 2009, http://blogs.wsj.com/environmentalcapital/2009/10/05/exodus-apple-leaves-chamber-of-commerce-over-climate-spat/ (accessed April 14, 2011).

19. *Boston Globe*, December 28, 2013, http://www.bostonglobe.com/metro/2013/12/28/american-federation-teachers-revealed-funder-behind-mysterious-pro-walsh-pac-during-mayoral-campaign/g58NRCxjp3OMZLtoBQE0yN/story.html?s_campaign=8315 (accessed December 28, 2013).

20. Glenn Spencer, "*Citizens United*, Election Spending, and the DISCLOSE Act," *Chamberpost*, July 8, 2010, http://www.chamberpost.com/2010/07/citizens-united-election-spending-and-the-disclose-act/ (accessed April 14, 2011).

21. Ryan J. Reilly, "Citizens United President Enjoys 'Bitching and Moaning' over Supreme Court Case," *TPMMuckraker*, December 1, 2010, http://tpmmuckraker.talkingpointsmemo.com/2010/12/citizens_united_president_enjoys_bitching_and_moan.php (accessed April 14, 2011).

22. Gerald Mayer, "Union Membership Trends in the United States," *Federal Publications*, paper no. 174, August 31, 2004, http://digitalcommons.ilr.cornell.edu/cgi/viewcontent.cgi?article=1176&context=key_workplace (accessed April 15, 2011). See also Bureau of Labor Statistics, Union Members Summary, 2013, http://www.bls.gov/news.release/union2.nr0.htm (accessed January 27, 2014).

23. Bureau of Labor Statistics, Union Members Summary, 2013, http://www.bls.gov/news.release/union2.nr0.htm (accessed January 27, 2014).

24. Public Integrity, November 14, 2013, http://www.publicintegrity.org/2013/11/14/13691/citizens-united-ruling-helped-unions-win-state-elections (accessed January 10, 2014)

25. Jon Youngdahl, "No Secrets Surrounding SEIU's Political Contributions" (letter), *Washington Post*, October 21, 2010, http://www.washingtonpost.com/wp-dyn/content/article/2010/10/20/AR2010102004912.html (accessed April 15, 2011). SEIU contributed $18 million and engaged in $23 million in "independent" spending in 2012. Center for Responsive Politics, http://www.opensecrets.org/orgs/summary.php?id=d000000077 (accessed January 10, 2014).

26. *National Association of Manufacturers (NAM) v. NLRB* No. 12-5068 (D.C. Cir. 2013), http://www.cadc.uscourts.gov/internet/opinions.nsf/E16F1375FA672CCE85257B64004E8BB2/$file/12-5068-1434608.pdf (accessed November 14, 2013).

27. Michael J. Carden, "National Debt Poses Security Threat, Mullen Says," US Department of Defense, *News*, August 27, 2010, http://www.defense.gov/news/newsarticle.aspx?id=60621 (accessed April 28, 2011).

28. US Treasury Daily Report, http://www.treasurydirect.gov/NP/debt/current (accessed January 10, 2014).

29. Report, Federal Reserve Bank, St. Louis, http://research.stlouisfed.org/publications/review/12/11/Thornton.pdf (accessed December 27, 2013); Congressional Budget Office, Choices for Deficit Reduction, December 20, 2013.

30. Bilmes, Linda J. "The Financial Legacy of Iraq and Afghanistan: How Wartime Spending Decisions Will Constrain Future National Security Budgets." HKS Faculty Research Working Paper Series RWP13-006, March 2013.

31. Pew Charitable Trusts, "The Great Debt Shift: Drivers of Federal Debt Since 2001," April 2011, http://www.pewtrusts.org/uploadedFiles/wwwpewtrustsorg/Fact_Sheets/Economic_Policy/drivers_federal_debt_since_2001.pdf (accessed June 13, 2011); See also Kathy A. Ruffing and Joel A. Friedman, *Center on Budget and Policy Priorities*, *Update*, February 2013, http://www.cbpp.org/files/10-10-12bud.pdf (accessed January 11, 2014).

32. Congressional Budget Office, May 14, 2013, http://www.cbo.gov/publication/44176 (accessed January 10, 2014).

33. Bipartisan Policy Center Debt Reduction Task Force, "Restoring America's Future: Executive Summary," November 2010, http://bipartisanpolicy.org/sites/default/files/FINAL%20DRTF%20EXECUTIVE%20SUMMARY_0.pdf (accessed March 29, 2011); Center on Budget and Poly Priorities, *Where Do Our Federal Tax Dollars Go?*, April 12, 2013, http://www.cbpp.org/cms/?fa=view&id=1258 (accessed January 10, 2014).

34. Chris Hellman, National Priorities Project, "$1.2 Trillion for National Security," March 1, 2011, http://nationalpriorities.org/en/pressroom/articles/2011/03/01/tomgram-chris-hellman-12-trillion-for-national-sec/ (accessed August 28, 2011).

35. Tax revenues came to 15 percent of GDP in 2009. National Commission on Fiscal Responsibility and Reform, "The Moment of Truth," December 2010, http://www.fiscalcommission.gov/sites/fiscalcommission.gov/files/documents/TheMomentofTruth12_1_2010.pdf (accessed July 25, 2011).

36. Cato Institute, *Cato Handbook for Policymakers*, 7th ed. (Washington, D.C.: Cato Institute, 2010), p. 279, http://www.cato.org/pubs/handbook/hb111/hb111-26.pdf (accessed April 15, 2011); Public Citizen, "Corporate Welfare," http://www.citizen.org/congress/welfare/index.cfm (accessed April 15, 2011).

37. Chris Edwards, "Agriculture Subsidies," Cato Institute, June 2009, http://www.downsizinggovernment.org/agriculture/subsidies (accessed March 31, 2011).

38. Environmental Working Group, *Farm Subsidies*, http://farm.ewg.org/region.php?fips=00000 (accessed January 11, 2014).

39. US Comptroller, Defense Budget ("Green Book"), March 2012, http://comptroller.defense.gov/defbudget/fy2013/FY13_Green_Book.pdf.

40. This "zombie" program has finally died. http://abcnews.go.com/Blotter/zombie-35-stealth-fighter-alternate-engine-finally-dies/story?id=15074110.

41. As many as 30 million Americans will remain uninsured after the Affordable Care Act is implemented. See Physicians for a National Health Program, http://www.pnhp.org/news/2013/june/30-million-to-remain-uninsured-under-obamacare-new-state-by-state-estimates-at-health.

42. National Research Council. *US Health in International Perspective: Shorter Lives, Poorer Health.* Washington, D.C.: The National Academies Press, 2013.

43. Central Intelligence Agency, *2013 World Factbook*, https://www.cia.gov/library/publications/the-world-factbook/rankorder/2102rank.html (accessed January 12, 2014).

44. *Wall Street Journal*, "Obamacare's Secret History," June 13, 2012, http://online.wsj.com/news/articles/SB10001424052702303830204577446470015843822 (accessed January 12, 2014).

45. CBS News and *New York Times*, "American Public Opinion: Today vs. 30 Years Ago," February 1, 2009, http://www.cbsnews.com/htdocs/pdf/SunMo_poll_0209.pdf (59% favor government health insurance); Henry J. Kaiser Family Foundation, "Public Opinion on Health Care Issues," July 2009, http://www.kff.org/kaiserpolls/upload/7945.pdf (single-payer government plan favored by 50%); Ricardo Alonso-Zaldivar and Janet Hook, "Times/Bloomberg Poll: Obama Healthcare Ideas Favored," October 25, 2007, http://articles.latimes.com/2007/oct/25/nation/na-poll25/2 (53 percent want "government-run, government-financed health insurance program that would cover all Americans"); Physicians for a National Health Program, "Where Are We on Reform?" December 31, 2007, http://www.pnhp.org/news/2007/december/where_are_we_on_refo.php (54 percent support a "single-payer health care system that is a national health plan financed by taxpayers in which all Americans would get their insurance from a single government plan"). All sites accessed July 25, 2011.

46. Olga Pierce, "Medicare Drug Planners Now Lobbyists, with Billions at Stake," ProPublica, October 20, 2009, http://www.propublica.org/article/medicare-drug-planners-now-lobbyists-with-billions-at-stake-1020 (accessed March 29, 2011).

47. Robert G. Kaiser, *So Damn Much Money* (New York: Vintage Books, 2009), p. 309.

48. Robert Pear, "House's Author of Drug Benefit Joins Lobbyists," *New York Times*, December 14, 2011, http://query.nytimes.com/gst/fullpage.html?res=9C00E2DF1430F935A25751C1A9629C8B63&pagewanted=all (accessed April 28, 2011).

49. Pierce, "Medicare Drug Planners Now Lobbyists."

50. *Wall Street Journal*, "Obamacare's Secret History," June 13, 2012, http://online.wsj.com/news/articles/SB10001424052702303830204577446470015843822 (accessed January 12, 2014).

51. Kaiser, *So Damn Much Money*, p. 366.

52. Robert Reich, "The White House Deal with Big Pharma Undermines Democracy, Healthcare Reform," *Salon*, August 10, 2009, http://www.salon.com/news/opinion/feature/2009/08/10/pharma (accessed March 23, 2010).

53. CIGNA Annual report, 2012.

54. CIGNA 2012 Political Activity Report, http://www.cigna.com/assets/docs/corporate-governance/politicalContribution.pdf.

55. Wendell Potter, "Public Integrity," April 29, 2013, http://www.publicintegrity.org/2013/04/29/12581/opinion-insurers-hiding-political-spending.

56. Potter, *Deadly Spin*, pp. 68–72.

57. Jared Diamond, *Collapse: How Societies Choose to Fail or Succeed*, Viking Press, 2005.

58. Subsidies, see Price of Oil and reports referenced therein, http://priceofoil.org/fossil-fuel-subsidies/; Political spending, see Center for Responsive Politics data, http://www.opensecrets.org/industries/indus.php?ind=E01 (accessed January 12, 2014).

59. Environmental Law Institute, "Estimating US Government Subsidies to Energy Sources, 2002–2008," September 2009, http://www.elistore.org/Data/products/d19_07.pdf (accessed April 20, 2011).

60. George W. Bush, "President Addresses the American Society of Newspaper Editors Convention," April 14, 2005, http://georgewbush-whitehouse.archives.gov/news/releases/2005/04/20050414-4.html (accessed April 1, 2011).

61. US Energy Information Administration, What Is the Role of Coal in the US?, August 2013, http://www.eia.gov/energy_in_brief/article/role_coal_us.cfm (accessed December 30, 2013).

62. Paul R. Epstein and others, "Full Cost Accounting for the Life Cycle of Coal," *Annals of the New York Academy of Sciences* 1291 (February 17, 2011): 73–98, http://onlinelibrary.wiley.com/doi/10.1111/j.1749-6632.2010.05890.x/full (accessed March 27, 2011).

63. Ibid.

64. Environmental Protection Agency, "Mercury Maps: Linking Air Deposition and Fish Contamination on a National Scale," January 2005, http://water.epa.gov/type/watersheds/datait/maps/fs.cfm (accessed April 21, 2011). "As of December 2003, 45 states had issued fish advisories for mercury covering more than 13,000,000 lake acres and over 750,000 river miles, due to emissions from coal-fired power plants, waste incinerators, mercury cell chlorine manufacturing facilities, and other sources."

65. Matthew L. Wald, "Stimulus Money Puts Clean Coal Projects on a Faster Track," *New York Times*, March 16, 2009, http://www.nytimes.com/2009/03/17/business/energy-environment/17coal.html (accessed August 30, 2011). Also see Taxpayers for Common Sense, "Clean Coal Gets Boost in House and Senate Stimulus Bills," January 30, 2009, http://www.taxpayer.net/search_by_tag.php?action=view&proj_id=1842&tag=coal%20subsidies&type=Project (accessed August 18, 2011).

66. Epstein and others, "Full Cost Accounting."

67. Pew Center on Global Climate Change, "Climate Change 101: Understanding and Responding to Global Climate Change," January 2011, http://www.pewclimate.org/docUploads/climate101-fullbook_0.pdf (accessed April 4, 2011).

68. Center for Public Integrity, "No Robust, Sustained Alternative Energy Policy," n.d., http://www.publicintegrity.org/investigations/broken_government/articles/entry/no_robust_sustained_alternative_energy_policy/ (accessed April 2, 2011); US Energy Information Administration *What Are the Major Sources and Users of Energy in the United States?* August 1, 2013, http://www.eia.gov/energy_in_brief/article/major_energy_sources_and_users.cfm.

69. Oil drilling in the Gulf given a "categorical exclusion" from the National Environmental Policy Act. http://www.eoearth.org/article/Deepwater_Horizon_oil_spill?topic=50364#gen34

70. http://www.nytimes.com/2012/03/05/business/deepwater-oil-drilling-accelerates-as-bp-disaster-fades.html?

71. Center for Responsive Politics, Energy Sector, 2013, https://www.opensecrets.org/industries/lobbying.php?cycle=2014&ind=E (accessed January 13, 2014).

72. Center for Responsive Politics, "Alternative Energy," http://www.opensecrets.org/industries./indus.php?ind=E1500 (accessed January 13, 2014).

73. Jim Snyder, "Oil Group Starts Political Giving as Congress Weighs Repeal of Tax Breaks," *Bloomberg*, February 24, 2011, http://www.bloomberg.com/news/2011-02-24/oil-group-starts-political-giving-as-congress-eyes-subsidies.html (accessed April 20, 2011).

74. *Washington Post*, January 5, 2014, http://www.washingtonpost.com/politics/koch-backed-political-network-built-to-shield-donors-raised-400-million-in-2012-elections/2014/01/05/9e7cfd9a-719b-11e3-9389-09ef9944065e_story.html (accessed January 13, 2014).

75. Colorado Ethics Watch, *Spend, Baby, Spend: How the Oil and Gas Controls Colorado*, May 2013, http://www.coloradoforethics.org/co-pages/spend-baby-spend (accessed December 31, 2013).

76. Paul de Barros, "Robert Kennedy Jr. Says West Virginia Coal Industry out of Control in Documentary," *Seattle Times*, July 21, 2011, http://www.dfw.com/2011/07/21/484290/robert-kennedy-jr-says-west-virginia.html (accessed July 27, 2011).

77. Epstein and others, "Full Cost Accounting": More than 500 mountains have been obliterated, the adjacent valleys filled, in Kentucky, Virginia, West Virginia, and Tennessee, completely altering some 1.4 million acres, burying 2,000 miles of streams. In Kentucky alone, there are 293 MTR [mountain top removal] sites, over 1,400 miles of streams damaged or destroyed, and 2,500 miles of streams polluted. Valley fill and other surface mining practices associated

with MTR bury headwater streams and contaminate surface and groundwater with carcinogens and heavy metals and are associated with reports of cancer clusters, a finding that requires further study.

78. I Love Mountains, http://www.ilovemountains.org; Appalachian Voices, http://www.appvoices.org; Kentucky Riverkeeper, http://www.appalachianstudies.eku.edu/kyriverkeeper/; Waterkeeper Alliance, http://www.waterkeeper.org.

79. Robert Kennedy Jr., "RFK Jr. on *Citizens United*" (video), June 11, 2011, http://www.freespeechforpeople.org; also available at http://www.youtube.com/watch?v=1k-DxVzq (accessed June 22, 2011).

80. "Harlan County, Kentucky: What Happened to Elmer's Fish Pond?" September 8, 2009, http://www.youtube.com/watch?v=VuPyevfufCE (accessed June 22, 2011).

81. Mark Baller and Leor Joseph Pantilat, "Defenders of Appalachia: The Campaign to Eliminate Mountaintop Removal Coal Mining and the Role of Public Justice," 37 *Environmental Law* 629, 640 (2007), http://legacy.lclark.edu/org/envtl/objects/37-3_Pantilat.pdf (accessed July 27, 2011).

82. *Bragg v. Robertson et al.*, Civil Action No. 2:98-0636 (US D. Ct. S.D. W.Va.), memorandum opinion and order granting preliminary injunction, March 3, 1999.

83. *Bragg v. West Virginia Coal Association*, 248 F.3d 275, 285 (4th Cir. 2001).

84. Francis X. Clines, "Judge Takes on Bush on Mountaintop Mining," *New York Times*, May 19, 2002, http://www.nytimes.com/2002/05/19/national/19STRI.html (accessed April 21, 2011); *Kentuckians for the Commonwealth v. Rivenburgh* (KFTC I), 204 F. Supp. 2d 927, 946 (S.D. W.Va. 2002). When the longstanding practice was challenged, the agencies undertook to change the rule so streams could be filled as immense waste dumps if the disposal had the "effect" of filling the waters of the United States. . . . Regulators were pushing ahead rapidly to change the rules, without regard for the purposes, policy, history, or language of Act itself [vacated, 317 F.3d 425 (4th Cir. 2003)].

85. Kennedy, "RFK Jr. on *Citizens United*."

86. John Cheves, "Coal Execs Hope to Spend Big under New Rules to Defeat Conway and Chandler," *Bluegrass Politics*, July 28, 2010, http://bluegrasspolitics.bloginky.com/2010/07/27/coal-execs-hope-to-spend-big-under-new-rules-to-defeat-conway-and-chandler/ (accessed April 21, 2011).

Chapter Five: Did Political Inequality and Corporate Power Destroy the Working American Economy?

1. Stephen Haber, "Introduction: The Political Economy of Crony Capitalism," in ed. Stephen Haber, *Crony Capitalism and Economic Growth in Latin America: Theory and Evidence*, (Stanford, Calif.: Hoover Institution Press, 2002), pp. xii–xv.

2. Robert A. G. Monks, *Citizens Dis-United: Passive Investors, Drone CEOs, and the Corporate Capture of the American Dream* (Lens Foundation for Corporate Excellence 2013).

3. For a full list of signatories, see http://asbcouncil.org/business-democracy-signatories (accessed January 15, 2014).

4. American Business Leaders on Campaign Reform, June 2013, Hart-American Viewpoint, for Committee for Economic Development, http://www.ced.org/pdf/Campaign_Finance%2C_Hart_and_AmView.pdf (accessed November 12, 2013).

5. James Roberts, "Cronyism: Undermining Economic Freedom and Prosperity around the World," Heritage Foundation, August 9, 2010, http://origin.heritage.org/Research/Reports/2010/08/Cronyism-Undermining-Economic-Freedom-and-Prosperity-Around-the-World (accessed July 28, 2011).

6. Robert Monks, quoted in Joel Bakan, *The Corporation: The Pathological Pursuit of Profit and Power* (New York: Free Press, 2004), p. 70.

7. Roosevelt, *Roosevelt*, p. 425.

8. Jim Leach, "Citizens United: Robbing America of Its Idealism," 142 *Dædalus: Journal of the American Academy of Arts & Sciences* 95 (Spring 2013).

9. Hacker and Pierson, *Winner-Take-All Politics*; Robert Kuttner, *The Squandering of America* (New York: Knopf, 2007); Paul Krugman, *Conscience of a Liberal* (New York, Norton, 2007); and Joseph E. Stiglitz, *Freefall* (New York: Norton, 2010).

10. US Census Bureau, US QuickFacts, January 7, 2014, http://quickfacts.census.gov/qfd/states/00000.html (accessed January 15, 2014).

11. Hacker and Pierson, *Winner-Take-All Politics*, p. 3.

12. Annie Lowrey, "The Rich Get Richer," *New York Times*, September 10, 2013, http://economix.blogs.nytimes.com/2013/09/10/the-rich-get-richer-through-the-recovery/; Pew Research Center, December 5, 2013, http://www.pewresearch.org/fact-tank/2013/12/05/u-s-income-inequality-on-rise-for-decades-is-now-highest-since-1928/ (accessed January 15, 2014).

13. Kurt Greenfield, *The Failure of Corporate Law* (Chicago: University of Chicago Press, 2006), p. 155.

14. Jared Bernstein and Karen Kornbluh, *Running Faster to Stay in Place: The Growth of Family Work Hours and Income* (Washington, D.C.: New America Foundation, June 2005, http://www.newamerica.net/files/nafmigration/archive/Doc_File_2437_1.pdf (accessed July 29, 2011): "Between 1970 and 2000, the percentage of mothers in the workforce rose from 38% to 67%."

15. US Census Bureau, *Income, Poverty and Health Insurance in the United States—2012*, September 2013, http://www.census.gov/prod/2013pubs/p60-245.pdf (accessed January 15, 2014).

16. Greenfield, *Failure of Corporate Law*, p. 156.

17. Gregory Leo Nagel, "The Effect of Labor Market Demand on US CEO Pay Since 1980," *Financial Review*, August 19, 2009, http://papers.ssrn.com/sol3/papers.cfm?abstract_id=1095690 (accessed August 17, 2011).

18. Richard McCormack, "The Plight of American Manufacturing," *American Prospect*, December 21, 2009, http://prospect.org/cs/articles?article=the_plight_of_american_manufacturing (accessed April 3, 2011).

19. Ibid.

20. Bernstein and Kornbluh, *Running Faster*.

21. Ron Rittenmeyer, chair of Electronic Data Systems, quoted in Brian Jackson, "EDS Says Offshoring Great for Profitability, Promises to Continue," *ITBusiness.ca* (Canada), April 23, 2008, http://www.itbusiness.ca/it/client/en/home/News.asp?id=48091 (accessed July 29, 2011).

22. Bernstein and Kornbluh, *Running Faster*.

23. Martin Gilens, *Affluence and Influence* (Princeton University Press 2012); Benjamin I. Page, Larry M. Bartels, and Jason Seawright, "Democracy and the Policy Preferences of Wealthy Americans," 11 *Perspectives on Politics* 51, 57 (March 2013); Adam Lioz, "Breaking the Vicious Cycle: How the Supreme Court Helped Create the Inequality Era and Why a New Jurisprudence Must Lead Us Out," 43 *Seton Hall Law Review* Article 4 (2013).

24. Stephen Haber, "Introduction: The Political Economy of Crony Capitalism," in ed. Stephen Haber, *Crony Capitalism and Economic Growth in Latin America: Theory and Evidence* (Stanford, Calif.: Hoover Institution Press, 2002), pp. xii–xv.

25. See Robert Frank on the relationship between income disparities and financial distress, http://www.robert-h-frank.com/ (accessed April 12, 2011).

26. Massachusetts is one of only eight states with a flat income tax rate. Urban Institute and Brookings Center, *Tax Policy Center Report*, March 2007, http://www.taxpolicycenter.org/publications/url.cfm?ID=1001064 (accessed April 2, 2011).

27. John Chesto, "Procter & Gamble Unveils Plans to Cut 215 Jobs from Its Gillette Factory in South Boston over Five Years," *Patriot Ledger*, August 7, 2008, http://www.patriotledger.com/

business/x1280301726/Procter-Gamble-unveils-plans-to-cut-215-jobs-from-its-Gillette-factory-in-South-Boston-over-five-years (accessed June 15, 2011).

28. "Fat Merger Payouts for CEOs," *Business Week*, December 12, 2005, http://www.businessweek.com/magazine/content/05_50/b3963106.htm (accessed June 15, 2001).

29. United for a Fair Economy, "Shareholders Press BankBoston on CEO Pay, Golden Parachutes, Layoffs After Fleet Merger," April 20, 1999, http://www.faireconomy.org/press_room/1999/shareholders_press_bankboston_on_ceo_pay_after_fleet_merger (accessed June 15, 2011); "13,000 Job Cuts Loom in Merger; FleetBoston, BofA Shareholders OK Giant Bank Deal," *San Francisco Chronicle*, March 18, 2004, http://articles.sfgate.com/2004-03-18/business/17417500_1_banking-resources-america-spokeswoman-eloise-hale-job-cuts (accessed June 15, 2011); Report of Trillium Asset Management available at http://trilliuminvest.com/resolutions/lending-4/ (accessed June 15, 2011).

30. "Digital May Fire 15,000; Major Restructuring If Buyout by Compaq Ok'd," *San Francisco Chronicle*, May 7, 1998, http://articles.sfgate.com/1998-05-07/business/17722530_1_chief-executive-robert-palmer-digital-compaq (accessed June 15, 2011).

31. Kerr, *Corporate Free Speech Movement*.

32. Robert A. G. Monks, *Citizens Dis-United: Passive Investors, Drone CEOs, and the Corporate Capture of the American Dream* (Lens Foundation for Corporate Excellence 2013).

33. AFL-CIO, Executive Pay-Watch, http://www.aflcio.org/Corporate-Watch/CEO-Pay-and-You/CEO-to-Worker-Pay-Gap-in-the-United-States/Pay-Gaps-in-the-World (accessed January 15, 2014).

34. AFL-CIO, "Trends in CEO Pay," 2011, http://www.aflcio.org/corporatewatch/paywatch/pay/ (accessed March 30, 2011).

35. The rare exceptions are those affiliated with national lobbying groups such as Emily's List.

36. Brief of Shaun McCutcheon at 39. See also Brief of the Republican National Committee, at 4, 50.

37. *McCutcheon v. Federal Election Commission*, 572 U.S. __ (2014).

38. *New York Times*, April 22, 2014 (http://www.nytimes.com/roomfordebate/2014/04/21/do-the-rich-call-the-shots-13/policy-differences-between-classes-are-actually-few); *See also* Sunlight Foundation, Influence Explorer, Private Equity & Investment Firms, http://influenceexplorer.com/industry/private-equity-investment-firms/2c322e47396548a59918b7bb64a5629e?cycle=-1 (covers through Q3 2013).

39. Tax Foundation, http://taxfoundation.org/blog/2013-tax-brackets (accessed January 15, 2014).

40. Thomas Edsall, "Obama Seeks to Kill Hedge Fund Tax Break," *Huffington Post*, February 26, 2009, http://www.huffingtonpost.com/2009/02/26/will-the-taxman-cometh_n_170082.html (accessed March 30, 2011). *See also* Sunlight Foundation, Influence Explorer, Private Equity & Investment Firms, http://influenceexplorer.com/industry/private-equity-investment-firms/2c322e47396548a59918b7bb64a5629e?cycle=-1 (covers through Q3 2013).

41. Ibid.

42. http://nypost.com/2013/12/29/hedge-fund-titan-to-pocket-3b-for-2013/.

43. Charles Ferguson's film *Inside Job* portrays the Citigroup story.

44. Del Jones and Edward Iwata, "CEO Pay Takes a Hit in Bailout Plan," *USA Today*, September 9, 2008, http://www.usatoday.com/money/companies/management/2008-09-28-executive-pay-ceo_N.htm (accessed June 15, 2011).

45. Strategic Management, "As Citigroup Increases Its High-Skilled Headcount in India, Will Others Follow?" http://knowledge.wharton.upenn.edu/india/article.cfm?articleid=4187 (accessed April 11, 2011).

46. Mitchell Martin, "Citicorp and Travelers Plan to Merge in Record $70 Billion Deal: A New No. 1: Financial Giants Unite," April 7, 1998, http://www.nytimes.com/1998/04/07/news/07iht-citi.t.html (accessed April 11, 2011).

47. "The Long Demise of Glass-Steagall," *Wall Street Fix*, PBS, May 8, 2003, http://www.pbs.org/wgbh/pages/frontline/shows/wallstreet/weill/demise.html (accessed April 11, 2011).

48. Martin, "Citicorp and Travelers."

49. Eric Dash and Louise Story, "Rubin Leaving Citigroup; Smith Barney for Sale," January 9, 2009, http://www.nytimes.com/2009/01/10/business/10rubin.html (accessed April 11, 2011).

50. Ibid.

51. Hacker and Pierson, *Winner-Take-All Politics*, p. 69.

52. Stiglitz, *Freefall*, p. 162

53. Ibid.

54. Robert B. Ekelund and Mark Thornton, "More Awful Truths About Republicans," Ludwig von Mises Institute, September 4, 2008, http://mises.org/daily/3098 (accessed June 15, 2011).

55. David Corn, "Foreclosure Phil," *Mother Jones*, Spring 2008, http://motherjones.com/politics/2008/05/foreclosure-phil (accessed April 11, 2011).

56. UBS admits that it "participated in a scheme to defraud the United States and its agency, the IRS, by actively assisting" rich customers to conceal assets to avoid taxes. See *United States v. UBS*, US S.D. Fla., 09-60033-CR, Deferred Prosecution Agreement.

57. Corn, "Foreclosure Phil."

58. Patrice Hill, "McCain Adviser Talks of 'Mental Recession,'" *Washington Times*, July 9, 2008, http://www.washingtontimes.com/news/2008/jul/09/mccain-adviser-addresses-mental-recession/ (accessed April 11, 2011).

Chapter Six: Corporations Can't Love

1. *The Writings of Benjamin Franklin*, Jared Sparks, editor (Boston: Tappan, Whittemore and Mason, 1840), Vol. X, p. 297, April 17, 1787.

2. Farewell Address, March 4, 1837, available at University of California/Santa Barbara American Presidency Project, http://www.presidency.ucsb.edu/ws/?pid=67087

3. See William Damon, *The Core of Civic Virtue*, The Hoover Digest, July 13, 2011 (http://www.hoover.org/publications/hoover-digest/article/84221), excerpted from Failing Liberty 101: *How We Are Leaving Young Americans Unprepared for Citizenship in a Free Society*, by William Damon (Hoover Institution Press, 2011). © 2011 by the Board of Trustees of the Leland Stanford Junior University.

4. James Madison, Virginia Ratifying Convention, June 20, 1788, http://press-pubs.uchicago.edu/founders/documents/v1ch13s36.html (accessed April 28, 2011).

5. *First National Bank of Boston v. Bellotti*, 435 US 765 (1978).

6. *Bank of America* (admitted to illegal bid rigging in municipal bond market); *United States v. General Motors*, 186 F.2d 562 (1951) (convicted of conspiracy to destroy public transportation); *United States v. General Motors Corp.*, 121 F.2d 376 (1941), cert. denied 314 US 618 (1941), rehearing denied, 314 US 710 (1941) (criminal antitrust conviction upheld); *United States v. Credit Suisse* (2009) ("admits that it committed crimes and systematically violated both US and New York State laws by moving hundreds of millions of dollars illegally through the US financial system on behalf of entities subject to US economic sanctions"); *United States v. UBS* (2009) (conspiracy to "defraud the United States by impeding the Internal Revenue Service"); *United States v. Deutsche Bank* (2010) ("unlawfully, willingly and knowingly participated in . . . $29 billion in bogus tax benefit" scheme); *United States v. WellCare Health Plans* (2009) ("knowingly and willingly" conspired to execute "a scheme to defraud two health care benefit programs"); *United States v. Volvo* (2008) ("kickbacks to the Iraqi government in order to obtain contracts for the sale of trucks and heavy commercial equipment"). BP's crimes are too numerous to include here and are identified in the text.

7. Greenfield, *Failure of Corporate Law*, p. 76.

8. 8 Del. Code § 284.

9. Delaware Constitution, Article IX, §1.

10. *Young v. the National Association for the Advancement of White People*, 35 Del.Ch. 10, 109 A.2d 29 (1954); *Craven v. Fifth Ward Republican Club*, 37 Del.Ch. 524, 528, 146 A.2d 400, 402 (1958).

11. Report of the Governor's Independent Investigation Panel, Upper Big Branch, May 2011 ("Report") at 92–93.

12. Report, United Mineworkers of America, October 11, 2010, http://www.umwa.org/?q=news/umwa-ubb-disaster-was-"industrial-homicide"; Robert F. Kennedy Jr. Joins Free Speech For People Call, http://www.freespeechforpeople.org/corporatecharterreform.

13. Report, *passim*.

14. Report at 85.

15. Report at 76.

16. Report at 97.

17. National Public Radio, May 24, 2011, http://www.npr.org/blogs/thetwo-way/2011/05/24/136619832/massey-mine-execs-reap-millions-in-takeover. Despite Alpha's acquisition of Massey, the Massey corporation still exists: its shareholders have simply been paid to transfer their shares to the Alpha corporation. Both Massey and Alpha have Delaware corporate charters and privileges subject to revocation.

18. *United States of America v. BP Exploration and Production, Inc.*, Guilty Plea Agreement, No. 2:12-cr-00292-SSV-DEK, November 2012, conviction entered January 29, 2013 ("BP Guilty Plea").

19. BP Guilty Plea Exhibit A.

20. http://content.usatoday.com/communities/greenhouse/post/2010/06/bp-tony-hayward-apology/1

21. *United States of America v. BP America, Inc.*, Deferred Prosecution Agreement (N.D. Illinois, No. 01-CR-683) (October 25, 2007).

22. U.S. Department of Justice Press Release, September 23, 1999.

23. South Coast Air Quality Management District Press Release, March 17, 2005.

24. EPA News Release, October 5, 2006.

25. US Department of Labor News Release, October 30, 2009.

26. US Department of Labor News Release, March 8, 2010.

27. Washington Department of Labor News Release, May 5, 2010.

28. Center For Public Integrity.

29. Correspondence, Gary Ruskin, Green Change to Attorney General Beau Biden, http://www.greenchange.org/article.php?id=5947 (accessed April 23, 2011); details BP's criminal violations.

30. Amicus brief, *Nike v. Kasky*, 2003 WL 835523 (2003).

31. Ibid.

32. Charles de Secondat Montesquieu, *The Spirit of Laws: A Compendium of the First English Edition* (Los Angeles: University of California Press, 1977), p. 130.

33. Daniel J. H. Greenwood, "Enronitis: Why Good Corporations Go Bad," *Columbia Business Law Review*, Vol. 2004, no 3 (2004), pp. 773–848.

34. Sheldon Whitehouse, speech to the US Senate, "Whitehouse Slams Corporate Influence at MMS, Proposes Legislation to Defend Integrity of Government," June 17, 2010, http://whitehouse.senate.gov/newsroom/press/release/?id=90941d79-ae11-496c-b541-34dbb0969848 (accessed July 30, 2011).

Chapter Seven: Restoring Democracy and Republican Government

1. *Ognibene v. Parkes*, 671 F.3d 174,199 (2d Cir. 2012).

2. Theodore Roosevelt, First Annual Address, December 1, 1901.

3. Akhil Reed Amar, *America's Constitution: A Biography* (New York: Random House, 2005), p. 405.

4. Amar, *America's Constitution*; David E. Kyvig, *Explicit and Authentic Acts: Amending the Constitution, 1776–1995* (Lawrence: University Press of Kansas, 1996).

5. For an updated tally of resolutions, see http://www.united4thepeople.org.

6. Sarah Byrnes, "In Small Groups and Small Towns, Opposition to Citizens United Spreads," *Yes Magazine*, March 22, 2012, http://www.yesmagazine.org/blogs/common-security-clubs/overturning-citizens-united-one-city-at-a-time.

7. See Colorado Faith Leaders Resolution, http://www.groundswell-movement.org/over-40-colorado-faith-leaders-voice-support-for-critical-campaign-finance-reform/; Resolution, Convention of the Unitarian Universalist Association, Charlotte, North Carolina, June 2011, http://www.uua.org/statements/statements/185343.shtml; ABC News, Universities Join Effort to Overturn Citizens United; http://abcnews.go.com/blogs/politics/2013/04/universities-join-effort-to-overturn-citizens-united-decision/; Business groups resolution, Business for Democracy, http://asbcouncil.org/node/19; Labor, AFL-CIO, http://www.aflcio.org/About/Exec-Council/EC-Statements/Restoring-Democracy, Communications Workers of America, http://www.cwa-union.org/issues/entry/c/money-in-politics/#.UuQrgqX0Bwc.

8. Testimony of Attorney General Steve Bullock, US Senate Committee on Rules and Administration, February 2, 2010.

9. Ibid.

10. *W. Tradition P'ship, Inc. v. Attorney Gen. of State*, 363 Mont. 220, 222, 271 P.3d 1, 3 cert. granted, judgment rev'd sub nom. *Am. Tradition P'ship, Inc. v. Bullock*, 132 S. Ct. 2490 (US 2012).

11. *Am. Tradition P'ship, Inc. v. Bullock*, 132 S. Ct. 2490 (US 2012).

12. Initiative 166, available at http://www.standwithmontanans.org/initiative_language (accessed January 21, 2014).

13. http://www.standwithmontanans.org/small_business_owners_for_i_166 and http://www.standwithmontanans.org/endorse.

14. Jessica Crist, "Safeguarding Democracy Is a Faith, Values, Non-Partisan Issue," *The Missoulian*, October 24, 2012, http://missoulian.com/news/opinion/columnists/safeguarding-democracy-is-a-faith-values-nonpartisan-issue/article_039c7d40-1de7-11e2-b606-0019bb2963f4.html (accessed December 20, 2013); Auburn Seminary, http://www.auburnseminary.org/whatshappening/faith-money-politics-and-citizens-united-way-forward?view=print (accessed December 20, 2013).

15. http://www.standwithmontanans.org.

16. Dave Lewis, Letter to the Editor, *Helena Independent Record*, http://helenair.com/news/opinion/readers_alley/explaining-opposition-to-initiative/article_a35843fa-e1ec-11e1-a2bb-001a4bcf887a.html (accessed December 20, 2013).

17. Montana Secretary of State, Initiative No. 166, "Corporations are not entitled to Constitutional Rights," http://electionresults.sos.mt.gov/resultsCTY.aspx?type=BQ&rid=45 0000370&osn=650&map=CTY (accessed December 20, 2013).

18. Colorado Secretary of State, http://results.enr.clarityelections.com/CO/43032/116650/en/md.html?cid=3970 (accessed December 20, 2013).

19. Senator Tom Udall of New Mexico has introduced this amendment as S.J. Res. 19 in the Senate. Representative Jim McGovern of Massachusetts has introduced the Political Equality Amendment in the House as H.J. Res. 20. Both have numerous cosponsors.

20. S.J. Res. 18; H.J. Res. 21.

21. H.J. Res. 29.

22. Free Speech For People, http://www.freespeechforpeople.org/amendments.

23. http://www.freespeechforpeople.org/get-involved; https://movetoamend.org/toolkit/resolutions; http://www.democracyisforpeople.org/page.cfm?id=21.

24. There are other approaches as well, such as the Fair Elections Now Act. Public Campaign is a good source for information on these bills. http://www.publicampaign.org.

25. Commission on Governmental Ethics and Election Practices, *Guidebook for 2010 Gubernatorial Candidates: Running for Office in Maine*, August 20, 2009, http://www.maine.

gov/ethics/pdf/publications/2010_gubernatorial_guide_mcea_final.pdf (accessed June 18, 2011).

26. Details of the Maine system are available from Maine Citizens for Clean Elections, https://www.mainecleanelections.org (accessed January 22, 2014).

27. Edwin Bender, *Evidencing a Republican Form of Government*, 74 *Montana Law Review* 165, 172 (2013), citing data from the National Institute on Money in State Politics, National Institute on Money in State Politics, http://www.followthemoney.org/database/graphs/competitive/index.phtml (accessed December 19, 2012).

28. *American Free Enterprise Club PAC v. Bennett*, 131 S.Ct. 2086 (2011). The decision, the dissent, and all the briefs may be found at SCOTUS Blog, http://www.scotusblog.com/case-files/cases/arizona-free-enterprise-clubs-freedom-club-pac-v-bennett/ (accessed January 22, 2014.)

29. http://anticorruptionact.org.

30. Greenfield, *Failure of Corporate Law*, is very helpful in this regard.

31. Ibid., p. 127.

32. Delaware Code, Title 8, Chapter 1, Section 284, http://delcode.delaware.gov/title8/c001/sc10/index.shtml#284 (accessed July 30, 2011).

33. Regnat Populus, http://rparkansas.org; Kent Greenfield, "A Campaign Funding Mess," *Boston Globe*, January 23, 2010, http://www.boston.com/bostonglobe/editorial_opinion/oped/articles/2010/01/23/a_campaign_funding_mess/ (accessed April 24, 2011).

34. Thomas Byrne, *False Profits: Reviving the Corporation's Public Purpose*, 57 *UCLA Law Review* 25 (2010).

35. Center For Responsive Politics, Top Individual Donors, https://www.opensecrets.org/orgs/indivs.php and 2014 Top Individual Donors, https://www.opensecrets.org/overview/topindivs.php.

36. Daniel J. H. Greenwood, "Democracy and Delaware: The Mysterious Race to the Bottom/Top," *Yale Law and Policy Review*, Spring 2005, pp. 381–454, http://people.hofstra.edu/daniel_j_greenwood/html/Mysterious04.htm (accessed June 18, 2011). See also Daniel J. H. Greenwood, "Democracy and Delaware: The Strange Puzzle of Corporate Law," 2002, http://people.hofstra.edu/Daniel_J_Greenwood/pdf/DemocAndDelGWU.pdf (accessed June 16, 2011).

37. Regarding proposed federal charter revocation see, Note, *The Case for Federal Charter Revocation*, 80 *George Washington Law Review* 602 (2012).

38. SEC Rule 14a-11, "Facilitating Shareholder Director Nominations," August 25, 2010, http://www.sec.gov/rules/final/2010/33-9136.pdf (accessed April 24, 2011).

Chapter 8: Do Something

1. Abraham Lincoln, Second Annual Address, December 1, 1862, proposing constitutional amendment to abolish slavery.

2. *USA Today*, December 5, 2013 (http://www.usatoday.com/story/news/nation-now/2013/12/05/nelson-mandela-quotes/3775255/0

3. Michael McCarthy, "I Served My Country in Uniform. I Won't Stand By," *The Guardian*, January 17, 2014, http://www.theguardian.com/commentisfree/2014/jan/17/new-hampshire-rebellion-government-corruption-lawrence-lessig (accessed January 24, 2014).

4. http://www.freespeechforpeople.com/sites/default/files/MT%20Amicus%20Brief.pdf.

5. https://movetoamend.org/oh-brecksville.

6. Information available at https://represent.us, and you can see a photo of Elizabeth Lindquist and the Illinois chapter at https://www.facebook.com/AntiCorruptionAct.

7. http://www.freespeechforpeople.org/corporatecharterreform.

8. More on Comet Skateboards at http://www.bcorporation.net/community/comet-skateboards.

9. http://www.bcorporation.net.

10. Theda Skocpol, *Building Community Top Down or Bottom Up?*, http://www.brookings.edu/research/articles/1997/09/fall-communitydevelopment-skocpol (accessed January 22, 2014).

11. Thomas Jefferson, letter to Samuel Kercheval, July 12, 1816.

Resources

1. *Dred Scott v. Sandford*, 60 US 393 (1856).
2. *Minor v. Happersett*, 88 US 162 (1874).
3. Handlin and Handlin, *Commonwealth*, p. 92 and n. 18.

Index

About the Author

Twitter: @ClementsJeff
Email: jclements@freespeechforpeople.org
www.freespeechforpeople.org
www.corporationsarenotpeople.com

JEFF CLEMENTS is cofounder and Chair of the Board of Directors of Free Speech For People, a national nonpartisan campaign to overturn *Citizens United v. Federal Election Commission*, challenge excessive corporate power, and strengthen American democracy and republican self-government. He cofounded Free Speech For People in 2010, after representing several public interest organizations with a Supreme Court amicus brief in the *Citizens United* case.

Jeff has served as Assistant Attorney General and Chief of the Public Protection Bureau in the Massachusetts Attorney General's Office. As Bureau Chief, he led a staff of more than a hundred in the enforcement of environmental, health care, financial services, civil rights, antitrust, and consumer protection laws. In private practice, Jeff has been a partner at Mintz Levin in Boston, as well as in his own firm.

Jeff also has served in leadership capacities on numerous boards, including that of the Portland Water District, a public agency responsible for protecting and delivering safe drinking water and ensuring proper treatment of waste water for 160,000 people; Friends of Casco Bay, an environmental organization he cofounded with others to protect and enhance stewardship of Maine's Casco Bay; and The Waldorf School in Lexington, Massachusetts.

In 2012, Jeff cofounded Whaleback Partners LLC, which provides cost-effective capital to farmers and businesses engaged in local, sustainable food and agriculture.

Jeff graduated with distinction in History and Government from Colby College in 1984 and *magna cum laude* from the Cornell Law School in 1988. He lives in Concord, Massachusetts.

Berrett–Koehler
Publishers

Berrett-Koehler is an independent publisher dedicated to an ambitious mission: *Creating a World That Works for All*.

We believe that to truly create a better world, action is needed at all levels—individual, organizational, and societal. At the individual level, our publications help people align their lives with their values and with their aspirations for a better world. At the organizational level, our publications promote progressive leadership and management practices, socially responsible approaches to business, and humane and effective organizations. At the societal level, our publications advance social and economic justice, shared prosperity, sustainability, and new solutions to national and global issues.

A major theme of our publications is "Opening Up New Space." Berrett-Koehler titles challenge conventional thinking, introduce new ideas, and foster positive change. Their common quest is changing the underlying beliefs, mindsets, institutions, and structures that keep generating the same cycles of problems, no matter who our leaders are or what improvement programs we adopt.

We strive to practice what we preach—to operate our publishing company in line with the ideas in our books. At the core of our approach is stewardship, which we define as a deep sense of responsibility to administer the company for the benefit of all of our "stakeholder" groups: authors, customers, employees, investors, service providers, and the communities and environment around us.

We are grateful to the thousands of readers, authors, and other friends of the company who consider themselves to be part of the "BK Community." We hope that you, too, will join us in our mission.

A BK Currents Book

This book is part of our BK Currents series. BK Currents books advance social and economic justice by exploring the critical intersections between business and society. Offering a unique combination of thoughtful analysis and progressive alternatives, BK Currents books promote positive change at the national and global levels. To find out more, visit **www.bkconnection.com**.

Berrett–Koehler
Publishers

A community dedicated to creating
a world that works for all

Dear Reader,

Thank you for picking up this book and joining our worldwide community of Berrett-Koehler readers. We share ideas that bring positive change into people's lives, organizations, and society.

To welcome you, we'd like to offer you a free e-book. You can pick from among twelve of our bestselling books by entering the promotional code **BKP92E** here: http://www.bkconnection.com/welcome.

When you claim your free e-book, we'll also send you a copy of our e-newsletter, the *BK Communiqué*. Although you're free to unsubscribe, there are many benefits to sticking around. In every issue of our newsletter you'll find

• A free e-book
• Tips from famous authors
• Discounts on spotlight titles
• Hilarious insider publishing news
• A chance to win a prize for answering a riddle

Best of all, our readers tell us, "Your newsletter is the only one I actually read." So claim your gift today, and please stay in touch!

Sincerely,

Charlotte Ashlock
Steward of the BK Website

Questions? Comments? Contact me at bkcommunity@bkpub.com.